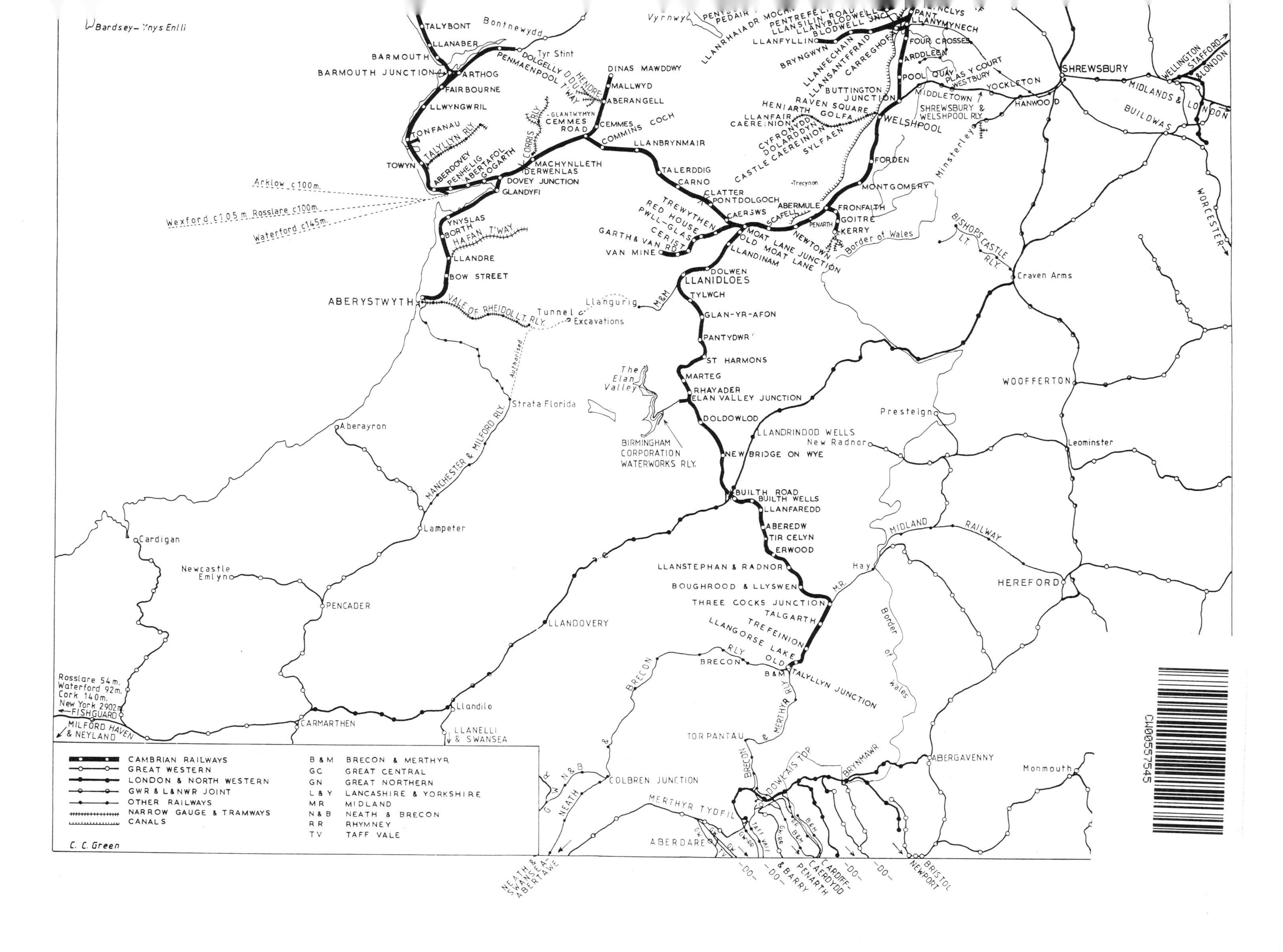
Bardsey-Ynys Enlli
TALYBONT
Bontnewydd
LLANABER
BARMOUTH
BARMOUTH JUNCTION
ARTHOG
Tyr Stint
DOLGELLY
PENMAENPOOL
DDUALL T'WAY
HENDRE
FAIRBOURNE
LLWYNGWRIL
TONFANAU
TALYLLYN RLY.
TOWYN
ABERDOVEY
PENHELIG
ABERTAFOL
GOGARTH
CORRIS RLY.
GLANTWYMYN
CEMMES ROAD
DINAS MAWDDWY
MALLWYD
ABERANGELL
CEMMES
COMMINS COCH
LLANBRYNMAIR
MACHYNLLETH
DERWENLAS
DOVEY JUNCTION
GLANDYFI
Arklow c100m.
Wexford c105m. Rosslare c100m.
Waterford c145m.
YNYSLAS
BORTH
HAFAN T'WAY
LLANDRE
BOW STREET
ABERYSTWYTH
VALE OF RHEIDOL LT. RLY.
Tunnel
Excavations
Llangurig
M&M
Authorised
Strata Florida
Aberayron
MANCHESTER & MILFORD RLY.
Lampeter
Cardigan
Newcastle Emlyn
PENCADER
TALERDDIG
CARNO
CLATTER
PONTDOLGOCH
TREWYTHEN
RED HOUSE
PWLL-GLAS
CERIST
GARTH & VAN RD.
VAN MINE
CAERSWS
MOAT LANE JUNCTION
OLD MOAT LANE
LLANDINAM
DOLWEN
LLANIDLOES
TYLWCH
GLAN-YR-AFON
PANTYDWR
ST HARMONS
MARTEG
RHAYADER
ELAN VALLEY JUNCTION
DOLDOWLOD
The Elan Valley
BIRMINGHAM CORPORATION WATERWORKS RLY.
NEW BRIDGE ON WYE
LLANDRINDOD WELLS
New Radnor
Presteign
BUILTH ROAD
BUILTH WELLS
LLANFAREDD
ABEREDW
TIR CELYN
ERWOOD
LLANSTEPHAN & RADNOR
BOUGHROOD & LLYSWEN
THREE COCKS JUNCTION
TALGARTH
TREFEINION
LLANGORSE LAKE
OLD
BRECON
RLY.
B&M
TALYLLYN JUNCTION
LLANDOVERY
Llandilo
LLANELLI & SWANSEA
CARMARTHEN
Rosslare 54m.
Waterford 92m.
Cork 140m.
New York 2902m.
FISHGUARD
MILFORD HAVEN & NEYLAND
Vyrnwy
PEDAIR
LLANRHAIADR MOCHNANT
PENTREFELIN
LLANSILIN ROAD
LLANYBLODWELL
BLODWELL JNC.
LLANFYLLIN
BRYNGWYN
LLANFECHAIN
LLANSANTFFRAID
CARREGHOFA
PANT
LLYNCLYS
LLANYMYNECH
FOUR CROSSES
ARDDLEEN
POOL QUAY
PLAS Y COURT
WESTBURY
YOCKLETON
BUTTINGTON JUNCTION
MIDDLETOWN
RAVEN SQUARE
HENIARTH
GOLFA
LLANFAIR CAEREINION
CYFRONYDD
DOLARDDYN
SYLFAEN
CASTLE CAEREINION
WELSHPOOL
SHREWSBURY & WELSHPOOL RLY.
Minsterley
HANWOOD
FORDEN
MONTGOMERY
Trecynon
ABERMULE
SCAFELL
FRONFAITH
GOITRE
PENARTH
KERRY
NEWTOWN
Border of Wales
BISHOPS CASTLE LT. RLY.
Craven Arms
SHREWSBURY
WELLINGTON
STAFFORD
MIDLANDS & LONDON
BUILDWAS
WORCESTER
WOOFFERTON
Leominster
MIDLAND RAILWAY
HEREFORD
Hay
M.R.
Border of Wales
BRECON & MERTHYR RLY.
TORPANTAU
DOWLAIS TOP
BRYNMAWR
ABERGAVENNY
Monmouth
COLBREN JUNCTION
NEATH
N&B
G W R
MERTHYR TYDFIL
ABERDARE
GW
TV
GW-RR
TAFF VALE
RR
B&M
NEATH & SWANSEA-ABERTAWE
-DO-
& BARRY
PENARTH
CARDIFF-CAERDYDD
BRISTOL
NEWPORT
CAMBRIAN RAILWAYS
GREAT WESTERN
LONDON & NORTH WESTERN
GWR & L&NWR JOINT
OTHER RAILWAYS
NARROW GAUGE & TRAMWAYS
CANALS
B&M BRECON & MERTHYR
GC GREAT CENTRAL
GN GREAT NORTHERN
L&Y LANCASHIRE & YORKSHIRE
MR MIDLAND
N&B NEATH & BRECON
RR RHYMNEY
TV TAFF VALE
C. C. Green
CW00557545

THE COAST LINES
OF THE
CAMBRIAN RAILWAYS

'Barnum' class 2—4—0 No. 3213 arriving at Machynlleth in September 1928.

Roye England

THE COAST LINES
OF THE
CAMBRIAN RAILWAYS

VOLUME ONE

MACHYNLLETH TO ABERYSTWYTH
including a general history of the
Aberystwyth & Welsh Coast Railway

BY

C. C. GREEN M.B.E.

WILD SWAN PUBLICATIONS LTD.

SYMBOLS USED ON PLANS

ELP	Electric light post
GDS	Goods
HSE	House
OFF	Office
PW	Permanent way
REFR	Refreshment
RM	Room
SP	Signal post
SMR	Station master
TP	Telegraph post
TT	Turntable
WTG	Waiting
WHSE	Warehouse
WM	Weighing machine
	Embankment
	Edge or change of surface
	Hedge
	Wire fence
	Fence
	Wall
	Running lines
	Shunting roads
	Loco service roads
	Standage

PLANS

There was no official policy for holding reference plans for the entire line. Engineer George Owen did not need them because he knew exactly where he had put everything since the earliest days.

His successor A. J. Collin reported this lack to his Board and announced his intention of remedying it, but possibly never succeeded. Some of his 1 chain to 1 inch plans have survived. A similar state of affairs would then have been inherited by his successor G. C. McDonald. However, all three seem to have been able to produce reasonable drawings when they had to convince the Board that some envisaged expenditure was necessary. Usually these plans are to the scale of 40ft to 1 inch, and crosschecking two plans of the same place can throw up inexplicable differences in distances between immovable buildings, etc. For some places the 1 in 2500 land plans are all that have been discovered so far.

ISBN 1 874103 07 0

Designed by Paul Karau
Printed by Amadeus Press Ltd., Huddersfield

Published by
WILD SWAN PUBLICATIONS LTD.
1-3 Hagbourne Road, Didcot, Oxon. OX11 8DP

DEDICATION

To the memory of George Dow, railwayman of considerable eminence, founding President of the Historical Model Railway Society and giver of much sound counsel on the subject of historical railway research.

CYFLWYNIAD

Er cof am George Dow, gweithiwr rheilffordd o gryn enwogrwydd, Llywydd Sylfaenol Cymdeithas Hanesyddol Modelau Rheilffyrdd, a rhoddwr hael ei gyngor dilys mewn gwaith ymchwil y rheilffyrdd.

COSTS

For those interested in relating costs mentioned in the text to present-day money, a table of very approximate multipliers is attached. This has been compiled from the proper tables kindly provided by the Economics Division of the Bank of England, and to which a little guesswork has been added, hopefully, to bring them up to 1993/94. It was considered that to give a present-day equivalent after each cost in the book would both disjoint the flow and date the text unduly.

1855-1857	30	1902-1914	40	1920 & 1921	15
1858-1878	35	1915	30	1922-1926	20
1879-1885	40	1916	25	1927-1939	25
1886-1901	45	1918 & 1919	20	1940-1948	18

Thus that first-class hay stacked at Derwenlas in the 1880s which fetched £2 10s 0d per ton might nowadays be deemed to be worth £100 per ton.

ACKNOWLEDGEMENTS

My thanks and appreciation of much kind help are due to the following: Desmond Abrahams, H. J. Arnold, James and Peggy Barfoot, Denis Bates, Mrs. Lingard Bell, James I. C. Boyd, Larry Bridges, Gwyn Briwnant-Jones, H. W. Burman, John Burman, W. A. Camwell, Roger Carpenter, George Clifford, Pat Dalton, David Wyn Davies, Jack Davies, John A. Davies, Tony Donovan, George Dow, Andrew Dow, John Edgington, A. E. Edwards, Margaret and Tom Evans, Richard Foster, Patrick Garland, L. T. George, Norman Greenwood, Glyn Griffiths, Lewis Hamer, W. E. Hayward, Frank Hemming, Selwyn Higgins, H. R. Hughes, Griffith Humphries, J. Humphries, Colin Jacks, Owen Baul Jenkins, Ben Jones, Frank Jones, K. Jones, R. W. Kidner, Phil Lewis, Peter Matthys, Bob Miller, Barry Morgan, Harold Morgan, Duncan Morris, Colin Mountford, Eric Mountford, Owen H. Owen, G. B. Pearson, Albert Potts, Chris Preston, V. C. Price, Harry Rees, J. P. Richards, Frank Roberts, K. F. Robinson, J. P. Rudman (Archivist, Uppingham School), Dick Squires (Warden, Ynys-hir Nature Reserve), R. E. Thomas, Oliver Veltom, E. A. Wade, Hubert Wheeller, Patrick Whitehouse, John Wildig and M. Williams.

I am particularly indebted to Mike Christensen not only for his expertise on Cambrian Railways signalling but also for casting a very astute eye over the manuscript. Especial thanks are also due to three friends of very long standing, Eric Hannan, Ifor Higgon and Mike Morton Lloyd (Cambrian Steward of the Historical Model Railway Society). For overseeing my halting efforts to put English equivalents to the Welsh place names, and for the dedication and postcript, I would like to thank Mr. Tom Evans, the well-known presenter for BBC Wales. My thanks are also due to the Lewis family for their kind permission to include the A. J. Lewis photographs.

I am most grateful for unfailing kindnesses and help received at Birmingham City Council Reference Libary; the offices of British Rail; Ceredigion Museum at Aberystwyth; Mrs. Margaret Evans's 'Aberystwyth Yesterday' exhibition above the station building at Aberystwyth; The House of Lords Record Office; The National Library of Wales at Aberystwyth; The Public Record Office at Kew; The Powysland Museum at Welshpool; The Royal Commission on Ancient Monuments at Aberystwyth; The Welsh Industrial and Maritime Museum at Cardiff.

The following periodicals have also been consulted: *The Cambrian News; The Times and Express Gazette; The Welsh Gazette; The Great Western Railway Magazine; The Locomotive Magazine; The Railway Magazine; The Engineer* and *Engineering.*

FOREWORD

The great beauty of this land of Wales needs no wordy descriptions from the author; all has been told already and we will let the photographs and historical extracts speak for themselves as we go. 'Go' really is the active word as each item of interest is presented in the order in which it would be seen when going on holiday by train. In railway terms this direction is referred to as 'down' while the return journey to London and to many of the large cities is 'up'.

Place names were frequently given an Anglicised form in timetables, handbills, advertisements, and on the station nameboards to attract and assist the visitors. As a courtesy, both forms are given in all the place histories. Nearly all the Welsh place names are impressive or charming descriptions of the place, or its character or where to find it, and the nearest English equivalent is given where attainable.

Distances are given in miles and chains as all old railway records were so presented, e.g. 78m 32c. Mileposts on station plans are shown as railways show them, e.g. 82.III MP is 82¾ and also 82m 60c.

I hope to cover the remainder of the coast lines and the rest of the Cambrian Railways system in a series of volumes, and perhaps in the future a special volume may have to be considered on operation with details of services, timetables and tickets, and possibly another on Oswestry where the Cambrian Railways Society is still keeping traditions alive with its restorative work on engines and with its extremely interesting museum.

CONTENTS

ROUTE MAP & GRADIENT PROFILE

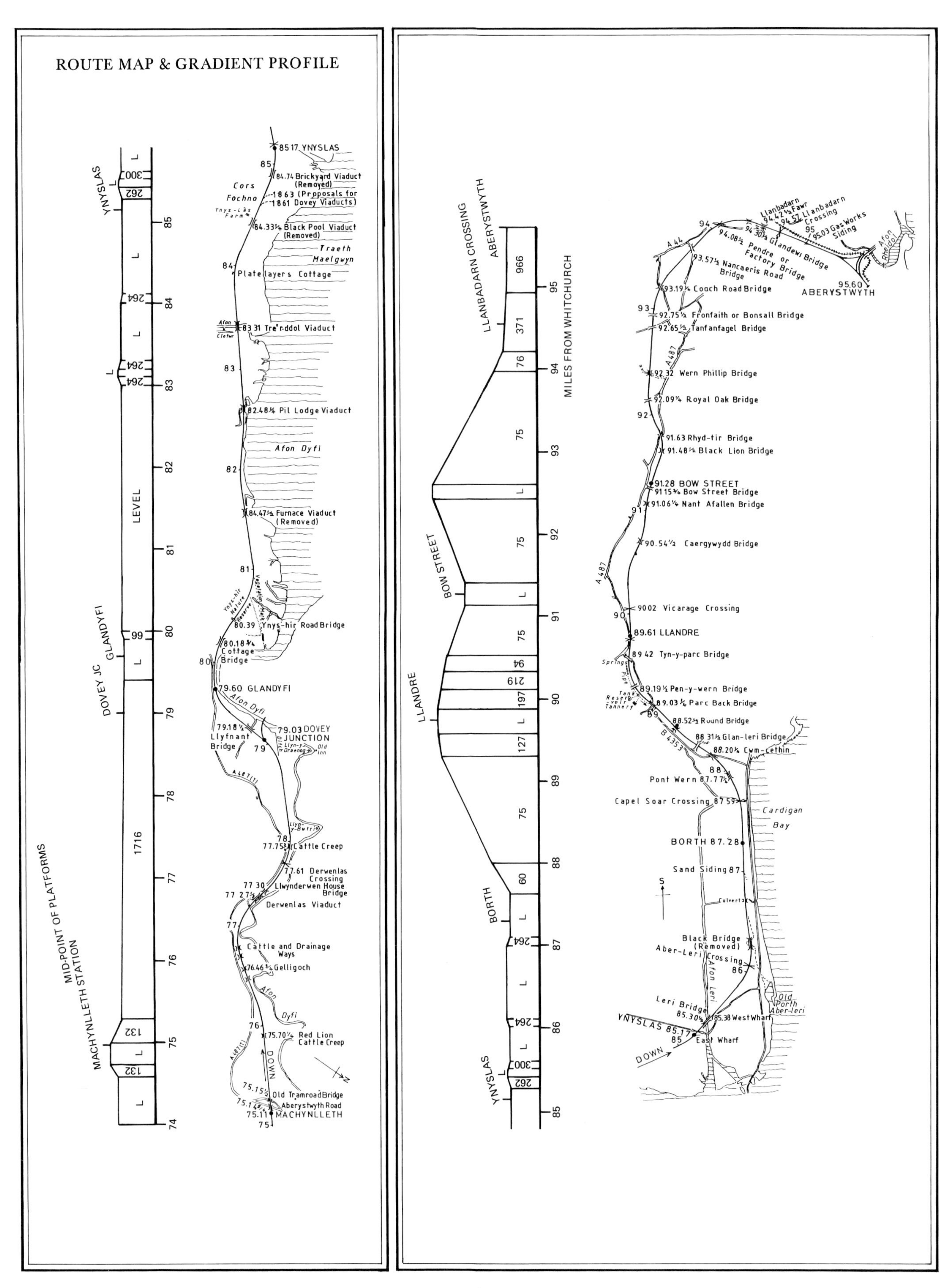

THE ABERYSTWYTH AND WELSH COAST RAILWAY

1860 AND 1861 – THE FORMATIVE YEARS

A study of modern business methods would have taught the Victorian railway promotors absolutely nothing about industrial dirty tricks; they had them polished to a fine art well over a hundred and fifty years ago.

Of the Montgomeryshire railways, the first two, the Llanidloes & Newtown (incorporated in 1853) and the Oswestry & Newtown (incorporated in 1855), were generally friendly towards each other, and had directors common to both boards. While these companies had been establishing themselves, they had been outwitted in their plans to extend their little conjoined empires to Machynlleth and onwards to the coast by a board of a totally different composition. This was the Newtown & Machynlleth, which had got itself onto the statute book on 27th July 1857.

This 'cuckoo-in-the-nest' company had been greatly helped in its promotion by an able Machynlleth solicitor, David Howell (who became its company secretary), while his brother Abraham was company solicitor to the other two concerns. By November 1858, all three companies had their contractors at work, and would eventually be united at Newtown and at Moat Lane. After the Oswestry & Newtown had dismissed its rather unsatisfactory contractors, all three shared the same firm, Davies & Savin, until that pair dissolved their partnership; indeed, the only railway that Davies and Savin actually finished together was the Llanidloes & Newtown, which was opened on 2nd September 1859.

This occurred only a month after another event, which was to have a considerable effect on the working and revenues of the future 'Coast' line and its inland supporters. On 1st August 1859, the Vale of Llangollen Railway Act received Royal Assent; this had been the sixth attempt to promote a Bill for a line probing westwards out of the Ruabon-Wrexham area since 1847. The Vale of Llangollen was to leave the Great Western's Shrewsbury & Chester line just to the south of Ruabon, and, naturally, had the full support of that far-sighted and income-minded organisation. The GWR was to continue with its supportive and fostering role behind the promotion of the Llangollen & Corwen, which was destined to meet the Denbigh, Ruthin & Corwen just to the east of the latter town, possibly an attempt to secure a route which tapped the London & North Western's north coast preserve at Rhyl, and certainly a second step towards obtaining the potential revenues from the Cardigan Bay area. The former intention was to fail, but the latter scheme was to become a success which proved disastrous to the future prosperity of the 'Coast' line and its allies.

Meanwhile, the Newtown & Machynlleth had directed their engineers, the Piercy family, to draw up plans for a line to be called The Machynlleth, Aberystwyth & Towyn Railway. At about the same time, the Llanidloes & Newtown and the Oswestry & Newtown had instructed their engineers (by then the Piercy family in each case!) to draw up a set of plans for a coast scheme extending from Aberystwyth to Pwllheli, with several branches. So far, history is silent about who really moved first and who leaked what to whom, but some such covert activity has to have taken place.

The earliest written evidence found so far proves that the Board of the Newtown & Machynlleth discussed the possibility of obtaining powers to extend to Aberystwyth on 21st August 1860. At that time, the Llanidloes & Newtown had been opened for barely a year, whilst the Oswestry & Newtown needed another ten months of building; the N&Ms own contractor would be battling on for another two and a half years!

Eight days later, the directors' report to the shareholders of the Llanidloes & Newtown followed a reference to the position of the Manchester & Milford Railway with the statement: 'No line has at present been secured to Aberystwith and it is with much satisfaction that your Directors have been informed by their Engineer that he is engaged in preparing plans for such an extension from Machynlleth', followed by 'Another line of greater importance, your Directors have reason to believe, will also be submitted to Parliament next session, namely a Coast line from Aberystwith and Machynlleth to Porthdinllaen'.

From these extracts, it is evident that both sets of interests had been hard at it behind each other's backs for some months at least. It now became imperative that the Newtown & Machynlleth should make its claim publicly, which they did on 1st November 1860 by announcing their proposed Machynlleth, Aberystwyth & Towyn Railway. This was supported in principle by contractor David Davies who, naturally, knew of his partner Thomas Savin's involvement not only with the scheme that was to become The Aberystwith & Welsh Coast Railway, but also with a number of other 'profit on the side' plans (whereby Savin was hoping to make himself a really wealthy man). The rather more moral David Davies naturally disapproved, and started moves towards severing their partnership. Savin countered (behind Davies's back) with an offer on 5th November 1860 to take over and become the sole contractor to the Newtown & Machynlleth. Soon afterwards, the *Aberystwyth Observer* announced that both Coast schemes were to be submitted to the next session of Parliament. The deadline for this was 8 o'clock on 30th November 1860, and while the Aberystwith & Welch Coast [sic] were permitted to lodge their petition and plans (albeit with a few mistakes, and a few hours late), somehow the Machynlleth, Aberystwyth & Towyn's plans had been handed for formal printing to a lithographer who was quite unable to meet that decisive date.

While this progress was being made in the Montgomeryshire boardrooms, Savin had been busying himself in the Clwyd area with plans which, had they succeeded, would have defeated the Great Western's plans to reach Barmouth, but would have been an equal drain on the revenues of the projected Montgomeryshire coastal line. Savin & Davies had the contract for the construction of the Denbigh, Ruthin & Corwen, and Savin was showing interest in the proposed Corwen, Bala & Barmouth, which had popped up before the Great Western had seen to it that any further extension westwards from Corwen would occur only under its own supervision. At the same time, the West Midlands Railway (then hoping for an amalgamation with the Great Western on better terms than that company had in mind) sought to increase its own value by trying to promote a West Midland, Shrewsbury & Coast of Wales Railway. The Great Western promptly aligned itself behind the Corwen, Bala & Barmouth, and Savin switched to an extension of the Denbigh, Ruthin & Corwen to Bala, which would join onto another promotion, the Merionethshire Railway, which was heading for Dolgelley. All these schemes collapsed, withdrew, or were thrown out in the Committee stage in the House of Lords, so leaving the Aberystwith & Welsh Coast triumphant – but only so far.

Although the companies took note of the dissolution of Davies' and Savin's partnership on differing dates, David Davies had formally broken free from Thomas Savin on 30th January 1861. After he had completed his work on the Heads of Agreement, separating their liabilities, assets and work, David Howell withdrew from the associateship he had had with the rival 'Coast' line, and thereafter worked solely for the Newtown & Machynlleth. After this, Savin would go on to complete the Oswestry & Newtown, and work both the eastern companies, while David Davies would complete the Newtown & Machynlleth.

By 2nd May 1861, the 'Coast' promoters felt sure enough that their Bill would be passed, and they held the first meeting of their provisional board of directors; this consisted of George Hammond Whalley (chairman of the Llanidloes & Newtown), Edward Williams (chairman of the Oswestry & Newtown) and Richard Kyrke Penson (director and consultant architect to both companies). All three had been signatories to the petition for obtaining the Act of Parliament under which the 'Coast' line might be built. With them were four other gentlemen, all directors from the same two companies. After deciding that the power given to Mr Loveden of Gogerddan (in consideration of his promised support) to appoint his nominee as a director must be revoked as it would prevent the project from receiving local support, they got down to the real business of the meeting. The solicitors, Bircham & Company, were instructed to prepare a contract for the construction of Railways Nos. 1 and 5 and a separate one for the construction of Railways Nos. 2, 3 and 4, and to provide letters of guarantee as surety of their services (a business practice of those days). Also in attendance were the expectant engineer, Mr Benjamin Piercy, the expectant secretary, Mr William Roberts, and the expectant contractor, Mr Thomas Savin.

Two days later they met again, and heard the reports of Messrs Piercy and Roberts on the public meetings held at Harlech, Dyffryn, Barmouth, Aberdovey and Aberystwyth at which, following their explanations of the new marvel-to-be, 'the project met with unanimous enthusiastic approval' but with a down-to-earth footnote to the effect that they were unable to follow up the canvass for shares. Finally, they added their own personal note by stating that they had no intention of applying to the provisional directors for their expenses (another custom of the time). Soon after this indulgence in arrogance and élan, Savin completed the Oswestry & Newtown, and started operating it on 10th June 1861.

Meanwhile, the Bill itself was having an unusually easy passage through the Committee stages, as there were only two objectors of any importance. The West Midlands Railway (working in the interests of its intended amalgamation with the Great Western) got very little credence, and the interests of the Newtown & Machynlleth were considered to have been sufficiently recognised by the insertion of a clause which required the construction of a link to Ynyslas within three years, and of another clause giving them the power to construct that link if the petitioners had commenced construction but had failed to complete. Potential objections by the Manchester & Milford had already been averted by the voluntary insertion of a clause which required the Aberystwyth to Ynyslas sector to be completed no less expeditiously than the Ynyslas to Aberdovey, Towyn and Barmouth, thus giving them what they hoped would be a profitable connection northwards.

The news was now being spread around that the foster-parent companies would each and all be contributing towards the capital of the 'Coast' line, but this inaccuracy was highlighted by an explosive contradiction in the *Shrewsbury Chronicle* for 6th May 1861 denying that the Newtown & Machynlleth would be doing any such thing. In the event, the Llanidloes & Newtown took powers to subscribe to and take up £25,000 in shares in the 'Coast' line, while the Oswestry & Newtown looked like being much more generous, at £75,000; this was later increased to £100,000, but the amount actually subscribed was £75,000. Including shares and debentures, the total authorised capital was £334,375 for making a railway between Aberystwyth, Machynlleth & Portmadoc, so nearly one third was handed to the infant by its foster-parents. The value of that £100,000 in 1861 was close on three and a half million pounds in current measure, so it really was a substantial backing for its time. Of course, this was for the building of lightly-laid and barely half-ballasted track with few sidings, and only shacks for stations; a modern line built to current weights and safety regulations and under modern Trade Union rates of labour would cost many times more. The figure given included legal costs, locomotives, rolling stock, and all equipment.

The Aberystwith and Welsh Coast Railway Act reached the statute book on 22nd July 1861, and a subsequent report to the shareholders of the Llanidloes & Newtown Railway read: 'the Welsh Coast Railway promoted in the interests of this Company and of the Oswestry & Newtown has succeeded in defeating the attempt to secure for the benefit of another District the traffic of the Welsh Coast from Aberystwith to Portmadoc'. This came after an exposé in a previous paragraph of the machinations of the Great Western and the London & North Western along the Welsh borderland as being 'a matter of common notoriety' – truly an example of the proverbial pot calling the kettle black; but, of course, the two companies thus named were very much better at intrigue than most of the others.

NOTE

In the very earliest references, and on the gilt-lettered covers of the first books, the company title was 'The Aberystwith and Welch Coast Railway'. The solecism 'Welch' was corrected almost immediately, but the promoters went to Parliament for an 'Aberystwith and Welsh Coast Railway' and that is the legally correct name; 'Aberystwith' appears in all Acts of Parliament, in all references in the Board minutes, and on the covers of all the minute books, ledgers and registers. Too many 'Aberystwiths' would look jarring and pedantic, and therefore the form we are familiar with is used, except when quoting the Acts of Parliament and the minutes.

1861 TO 1865 – THE YEARS OF INDEPENDENCE

The Aberystwith and Welsh Coast Railway Act of 22nd July 1861 conferred, in seventy-eight clauses (spread over twenty-two pages) the following items of more particular interest:

1. To raise £400,000 (approximately £14 million in modern values) as share capital, and to borrow one third of this amount after all the capital had been subscribed and after half had been paid up (i.e. another £133,000), making a total of around £533,000.
2. To appoint no fewer than five directors or more than eight.
3. Seven directors were appointed to hold office until the first General Meeting of Shareholders, and all were directors from time to time of the foster-parent companies. Each had to take up and pay for £1,000 in shares, in his own right.

Having this initial controlling body and the expectancy of raising what was hoped would be enough capital, the infant company was to make the railways as follows:

No. 1. From Aberystwith to Penmochno Embankment in the Parish of Llancynfelin (a little to the east of Ynyslas, in a field called Caepenmochno).
No. 2. From Penmochno to Towyn.
No. 3. From Towyn to Barmouth.
No. 4. From Barmouth to Portmadoc.
No. 5. From Penmochno to join the Newtown & Machynlleth Railway at Machynlleth (later called The Machynlleth Branch).

These railways were to be made within the following restrictions:

No. 1 was not to be made more expeditiously than Nos. 2 & 3. Nos. 1, 2, 3, & 5 had to be completed within four years of the passing of the Act and No. 4 within five years. If Nos. 1 and 5 had not been completed within three years, the Newtown & Machynlleth might apply for powers to complete and the 'Coast' company were prohibited from making any objections; and there were other clauses protecting 'The Machynlleth Company'.

Three years were allowed for the completion of the acquisition of land.

There were special clauses protecting the estuaries.

Any deviation waterwards from the centre line of way marked on the plan must have the approval of the Admiralty; and the Admiralty could 'abate every such Deviation or any Part thereof' and could recover the cost from the company as a debt due to the Crown. Further, the working of the line and opening bridges were not to detain unnecessarily 'any Vessel, Barge, or Boat' navigating the estuary of the River Dovey. Also, where any construction work had converted water to land, the company was to have no right over 'Lands Inned, Gained, or Reclaimed from the Water'.

There was one clause typical of those directed towards the propitiation of a wealthy landowner which declared that a first-class station had to be provided at Bow Street or at some other point on the line convenient to the Gogerddan Estate.

Being then a legal entity with a registered address at No. 28 St George Street, Westminster, London, and the will to start (but no money), the newly-born company appealed to the Oswestry & Newtown, whose line had just been completed (on 10th June 1861), and who were therefore in a position of strength. The latter company obliged almost immediately (on 2nd September) by approving the payment of £15,000 to Savin, to recoup the Parliamentary expenses which he had paid out of his own resources, and to enable him to buy land in advance. Meanwhile, Savin had made initial arrangements, and was setting up his first construction yards. Progressively, he was to work from Machynlleth, Derwenlas, Ynyslas and Aberdovey.

On 24th September 1861, the formal appointments of Birch, Dalrymple & Drake as solicitors, of William Roberts as secretary, and of Benjamin and Robert Piercy as engineers, were approved. Savin offered to perform under the terms of a lump sum contract 'to complete the Railway, discharge all liabilities incident thereto and to deliver the Railway to the Company approved by the Board of Trade including Stations, Telegraphs and other usual appliances', and this, too, was approved. Three days later, they set up Finance and Land Committees.

At Machynlleth, the problem of bringing the line down from the ledge (on which the Newtown & Machynlleth's terminus had been built) to the valley floor was the subject of a carefully-argued piece of opportunism by that Railway. Robert Piercy's need for rock with which to make a long, descending embankment provided a gain to the N&M occasioned by his bringing down more of the cliff face, and so widening their yard space. Then there was the natural reluctance of the Newtown & Machynlleth to be seen helping the enemy without due return; to assuage their feelings on this point, they used the opportunity to obtain a concession at Newtown from the Oswestry & Newtown as an extra.

Meanwhile, the Great Western-backed flanking shot at the revenues of the Welsh companies had reached its target, and the Vale of Llangollen Railway opened for goods traffic on 1st December 1861, worked of course by the Great Western.

On 25th October 1861, the Board approved an optimistic Company Seal, with the great Dovey bridge as its principal feature. They also sanctioned:

1. Agreements with the Oswestry & Newtown and with the Corris, Machynlleth & River Dovey Tramway Company.
2. The promotion of a Bill authorising extensions to Pwllheli and Porthdinllaen.
3. Applications to the 'foster-parents' for their subscriptions to the full extent of their powers.

On the same evening at the Hunnemans Hotel (and presumably after a good dinner), they agreed that Savin should have payment of Certificate No. 2 for £16,000 in fully paid-up shares.

The first Ordinary Meeting of Shareholders was held on 21st January 1862, at which Mr Whalley congratulated the assembly (and himself, thereby) on obtaining their Act of Parliament, and described how their engineers were busy setting out the line. He also recounted how the contractor, Mr Savin, had brought large quantities of material onto the ground, ready to commence.

On 24th January, the Board was told that Savin had obtained the release of the £32,000 from Chancery, which had been deposited against the lodging of the petition, and for which he had already been reimbursed. This sum was now available to expend, as well as the directors' first instalments on their qualifying shares, and such other share instalments that had by then come in from the general shareholders. They approved the lodging of the petitions for the extensions to Porthdinllaen and to Dolgelley, and voted to seek Counsel's opinion on a course of action against the impending Nantlle Railway Company's Bill.

On 7th February 1862, the Oswestry & Newtown agreed to bring the 'Coast' line into their agreement with the London & North Western so as to make its capital expenditure rank in calculations for rebates on traffic under the rather complicated accounting structure that had been installed (naturally, in the end, more advantageous to the London & North Western).

On 26th February 1862, the Newtown & Machynlleth Board was viewing these proceedings with some concern, and approved the lodging of various objections to the second 'Coast' Bill.

On 19th April, it was approved that the 'Coast' Board should have two directors permanently appointed by the Oswestry & Newtown, following behind-the-scene negotiations designed to protect that company's £75,000 investment. About that time, Savin opened another construction site at Towyn. Soon afterwards, the Board voted to lodge petitions opposing the construction of railways connecting Corwen, Bala and Portmadoc, the Bala & Dolgelley, the proposed Carnarvonshire Railway and, just to keep themselves informed, even the proposed Dovey reclamation scheme, which could have eased their difficulties around Ynyslas. They also heard a proposal, to be put to the Llanidloes & Newtown and to the Oswestry & Newtown, for Savin to be given up to £20,000 in fully paid-up shares in those companies instead of an equivalent amount in 'Coast' shares; possibly Savin considered such shares to be better security?

On 2nd June 1862, the first service passenger train steamed through to Llangollen, on the Great Western's Vale of Llangollen Railway.

In Parliament, by opposition to various other companies' Bills, the 'Coast' company won the right (of dubious value) to have running powers it already had over the Denbigh, Ruthin & Corwen extended to include Corwen to Dolgelley. The phraseology used was that 'all persons and Companies lawfully using the Denbigh, Ruthin & Corwen Railway' would qualify for such powers.

In 1862, Savin was re-presenting Bills for both his Bala Extension, and that other scheme for which he was providing the preliminary expenses, the Merionethshire Railway, thereby countering the Great Western's promotion of a Corwen, Bala & Portmadoc Railway. However, the Great Western was also backing a cut-down version of the West Midlands scheme of 1860, now called the Corwen & Bala, as well as a Bala & Dolgelley. Engineer Piercy deliberately blundered in the presentation of his evidence, so that the potential menace of allowing Savin sway over his two proposed schemes, to add to his influence over the 'Coast' railway, would become readily perceivable to all. The Savin-presented petitions were rejected, and the Great Western's two short lines entered the Statute Book on 30th June, though without the longed-for power to attain Barmouth or Portmadoc.

Piercy was never forgiven for his part in the rejections.

The 12th July 1862 saw the Board deep in considerations of their own Extension Bill (then before Parliament) as well as the Carnarvonshire Railway's Bill; they viewed the overlapping of powers to make a railway between Afon Wen and Portmadoc with some misgivings. Savin urged acquiescence as, he said, opposition would reduce the Carnarvon company's prospects for raising capital, while he was confident that the Board's railway would be built before that of its rival. Both Bills were passed on the same day.

The Aberystwith and Welsh Coast Railway Act of 29th July 1862 conferred the following extensions of powers:

> To raise additional share capital of £250,000 and, after all had been subscribed and half had been paid up, to borrow around one third of this amount, as before, i.e. £83,300.
>
> To make Railways as follows:
> No. 6. To Dolgelley.
> No. 7. To Pwllheli.
> No. 8. To Porthdinllaen.
> No. 9. 'A Pier upon the Sea Beach near the Rock called Carreg-yr-afr and a Railway from the Harbour thereto' (the existing harbour at Porthdinllaen).

All these railways had to be completed within five years, whilst the powers of compulsory purchase of land expired after three.

Whereas in the 1861 Act the rights of lands inned, gained or re-claimed were strictly reserved 'for the Benefit of the Queen's Majesty, Her Heirs and Successors and might only be entered with the Consent in Writing of the Commissioners for the Time being of Her Majesty's Woods, Forests, and Land Revenues', there was a different approach in the 1862 Act. Now, by agreement with various Crown and local corporations, the company might within ten years enter upon and take such land, and later even sell it. It had to be marked specially with bound-stones or other marks. This may well be evidence of Savin's interest in his own projected diversifications.

On 28th August 1862, the shareholders were informed of the successful procurement of the 1862 Act, and of the excellent progress being made in the acquisition of land between Aberystwyth, Machynlleth and the Afon Dysinni. The Dysinni to Llwyngwril sector had been arranged for, and steps were being taken to obtain the land for 'the Junction opposite Barmouth'. Finally, a rosy picture was presented of the near completion of Railway No. 5 to about two miles from Borth; no mention was made of the problems being experienced in the attempts to change the natural course of the river at Derwenlas or at Garreg (Glandyfi). Nor, at this stage, was there any comment on the frightful difficulties being encountered in reaching Ynyslas across the Cors Fochno, or on the ominous softness of the ground just to the north where the mile and a quarter-long embankment was to be laid across the Traeth Maelgwyn to meet the south end of the great Dovey bridge.

About that time, the Newtown & Machynlleth had completed its negotiations with the Oswestry & Newtown over the extension of its facilities at Newtown, and graciously gave its consent 'for the taking of soil' from the face of the cliff at Machynlleth for the construction of Railway No. 5 (most of which must already have been abstracted!). Although nowhere near to an official opening, some movement of trains was taking place between Aberdovey and the Afon Dysinni.

After these enhanced reports of progress, the Board voted (on 25th September) to authorise the payment of £1,000, to be divided equally between Whalley, Johns, Wilding, Lefeaux and Williams, to recoup their disbursements whilst promoting the company. On 23rd October 1862, Piercy brought matters back down to earth by reporting the necessity for obtaining powers to deviate the line at Garreg, and the promotion of another Bill was approved.

On 3rd January 1863, the grand opening ceremony of the Newtown & Machynlleth took place, albeit without the hoped-for line running onwards to Aberystwyth.

A minute entered on 8th January showed that Savin was accepting fully paid up debentures in payment for his work. The 'Coast' Board then resolved to oppose the Corris Railway Bill for an extension to the Great Western at Bontnewydd and that Bill was duly rejected. Soon after, the Board was informed of an agreement reached with the Manchester & Milford over their proposed Aberystwyth Harbour branch. They also resolved to oppose the Great Western's Bill for amalgamation with the West Midlands Railway.

On 25th February 1863, the shareholders were informed of the stormy weather and floods which had delayed construction, but that the directors were nevertheless 'much pleased' with progress, and expected that a large section of the line would be ready for opening in a few months. It was, of course, quite easy to pull the Welsh wool over the shareholders' eyes at that time; the meetings were held many miles inland, and ready access to the sites could only be gained on horseback. In fact, the rails were down (unballasted) only as far as Derwenlas. They were also told of the intention of applying for powers to build a short branch to the harbour at Aberystwyth, and 'a Branch to the

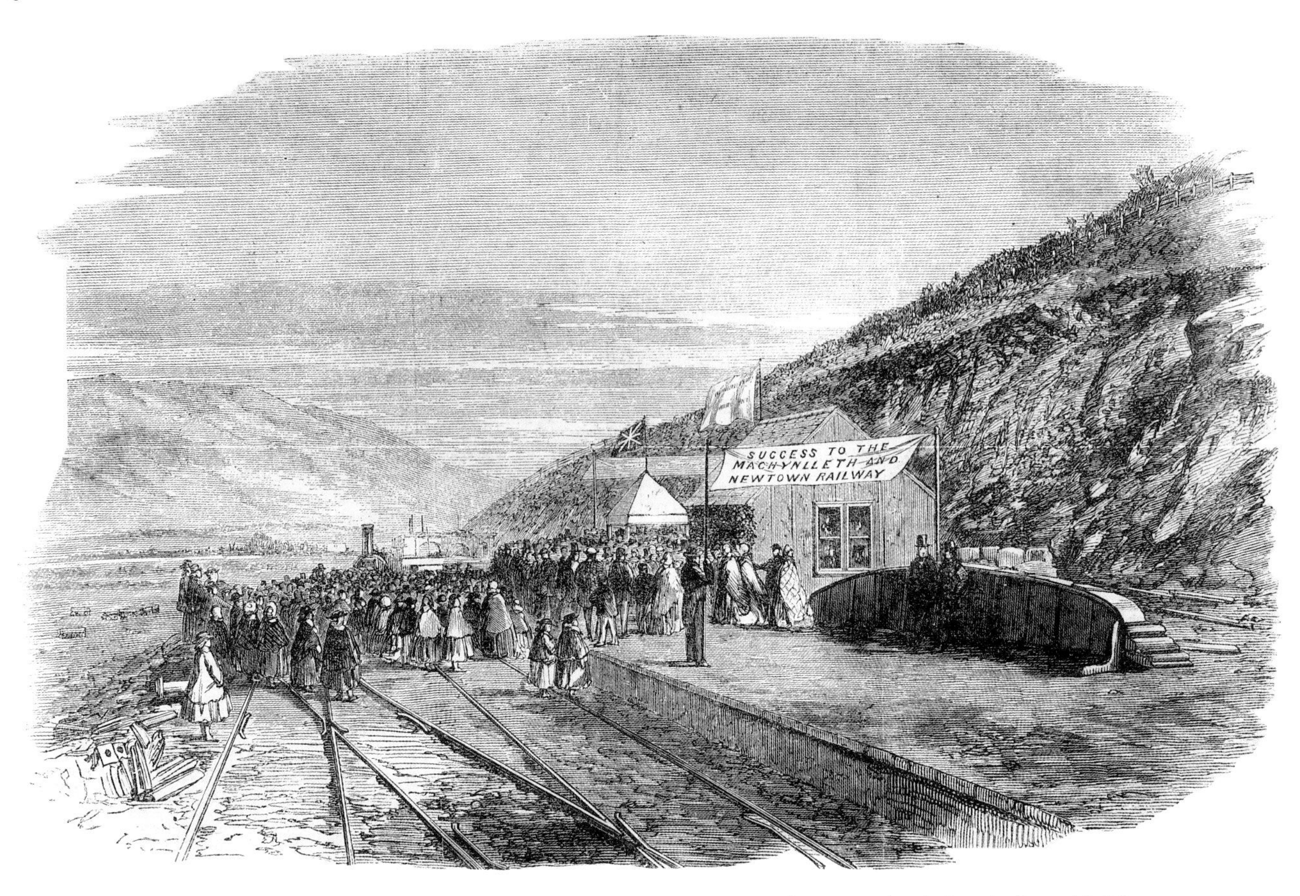

The opening ceremony at Machynlleth, from a contemporary engraving. Note the timber shed provided for a station building, and the girder for the road bridge to be built at the west end of the station, lying on the solitary platform. *London Illustrated News*

great Slate District of Festiniog'. This last item was duly thrown out after determined opposition by the quarry owners, who jointly owned a narrow gauge gravity tramway which ran from the quarries to the harbour at Portmadoc. Thus, the much-loved Festiniog Railway was saved for posterity.

Two days later, the Newtown & Machynlleth were being made to face up to the hard fact that they had been abandoned by the Great Western Railway, whose projected thrust to Dolgelley was becoming secure, and who were expecting the Manchester & Milford to fall into their hands before very long, and who therefore no longer needed such an obstructive little link between Montgomeryshire and the coast. In vain, the owners of the route along the Dovey had pleaded their importance as connecting the Oswestry & Newtown and the Llanidloes & Newtown to 'their ally, The Aberystwyth and Welsh Coast Railway', and they were left to persuade their contractor to run their railway, and go cap in hand to the other companies (already arranging for joint working) for support towards an eventual amalgamation. Of course, David Davies was most happy to step in and run his favourite railway, and the prodigal son was made welcome, but only after agreement had been reached to the effect that he raised another £15,000 of capital to buy the locomotives and rolling stock he did not yet possess.

On 25th March 1863, the Oswestry & Newtown Board resolved:

1. To defer consideration of amalgamation with the 'Coast' company and with the Carnarvonshire Railway.
2. To seek repeal of a clause in the proposed amalgamation Bill which called for the Aberystwyth to Barmouth section to be completed simultaneously with the Aberdovey to Machynlleth (a strange piece of omniscience?).
3. To oppose the Manchester & Milford's opposition to the amalgamation Bill.

The acquisition of land for the Portmadoc to Pwllheli sector was made possible by resolutions in the Boardrooms of the Oswestry & Newtown and the Llanidloes & Newtown, whereby each had resolved to create £25,000 of preference capital stock and to re-invest this money with the 'Coast' company.

The 'Coast' Board approved this start on the acquisition of land on 26th March 1863, and then went on to pass a trivial resolution in which they expressed their regret that their secretary, Mr William Roberts, whom they lauded as 'The Senior Secretary and the Secretary of the greatest extent of Mileage of the Welsh

Railway System', had not been awarded the post of secretary to the Oswestry & Newtown and Llanidloes & Newtown Joint 'Company'. This post had been given to (the later highly respected) George Lewis, then secretary of the Oswestry & Newtown.

On 23rd April 1863, the Oswestry & Newtown resolved to reduce amalgamation plans for 'other Railways' to the Aberystwith & Welsh Coast only. Meanwhile, the 'Coast' Board resolved that steps must be taken to ensure that none of their land could be seized from them by the Bala & Dolgelley Railway under the terms of that company's Bill. Soon after, on 4th May, eight of the little Derwenlas sailing ships landed the remainder of the sleepers needed to complete the track to Borth.

On 25th June, the 'Coast' Board heard that 'the difficulties with the Admiralty as to bridges over the Estuaries at Aberdovey had now been overcome', and that 'the time has arrived to complete the Contract with Mr Savin'. In addition, an agreement with the Oswestry & Newtown for them to operate the service between Machynlleth and Borth was being prepared. Also about this time, there seemed to be some unminuted activity directed towards amalgamation with the Carnarvonshire Railway.

The line was opened as far as Borth on 1st July 1863, being worked by Savin on a semi-official basis. The Board actually met at Borth on that day, although the proceedings consisted only of reading and approving the minutes of the previous meeting, so it was just an excuse for a day out. Later, the shareholders were informed that 'the line has conferred great benefit on the district, a larger number of Tourists having visited than ever before', while the Board heard that 'traffic exceeds anticipations'.

By then, too, Savin's contract was being prepared with quaint provisions which allowed Savin 'to prescribe which form of payment he will take within the Company's powers at the time out of such monies (if any) that may be at the Command of the Company', followed by a list of the alternatives by way of shares and debentures.

The third Bill to be promoted, The Aberystwith & Welsh Coast Act 1863, came into being on 13th July 1863. It conferred the additional power to raise £150,000 by way of additional capital, and to borrow another £50,000. Using this money, the company was empowered to:

Make an Aberystwyth Harbour branch termed 'A Railway or Tramway No.9'.

Make a junction line between Railway No. 1 and the Manchester & Milford line, projected to run along the Vale of Rheidol (Railway No.10).

Make a diversion in Railway No. 5 at Garreg.

Alter the embankment and bridge across the River Dovey 'so as to render the same available for all Purposes of Ordinary Road Traffic as well as for Railway Purposes.

Similarly, to alter the bridge across the River Mawddach, and to make a roadway to connect the roadway across the bridge to 'the Turnpike Road leading from Towyn to Dolgelley' (now the A493).

At the end of the preamble, which described the powers held already, came two interesting provisions. The first concerned the power of the Manchester & Milford 'to enter into and carry into effect joint Traffic, Station and other Arrangements' with the company, whilst the second gave power to the company 'to enter into and carry into effect joint agreements for Working, Traffic and other Arrangements with the Fourteen Companies'. In the order in which they were listed in the Act (obviously in someone's idea of relative importance), these were the Manchester & Milford, Newtown & Machynlleth, London & North Western, Great Western, Carnarvonshire, Bala & Dolgelly, Corwen & Bala, Denbigh, Ruthin & Corwen, Llangollen & Corwen, Vale of Llangollen, Vale of Clwyd, Hereford, Hay & Brecon, Brecon & Merthyr Tydfil Junction, and Bishops Castle Railways.

On 27th August 1863, the shareholders were told that the line from Aberdovey northwards to Llwyngwril had been completed, and that the stations would be finished in two or three weeks. On that same day, they were informed that Parliament had rejected the proposal for the construction of a Festiniog branch. It was noted that the Corris had entertained ideas for an extension northwards to a junction with the Bala & Dolgelley at Tyr Stint (this would have been a costly piece of construction, involving two tunnels and an inclination of 1 in 45).

On 24th October 1863, the first train ran to Llwyngwril; by that time, the Llangollen & Corwen were running trains westwards as far as Berwyn.

The Board determined (on 29th October 1863) that more money was urgently needed, and authorised the secretary to advertise for mortgage loans 'at £5 per cent' interest over periods of 3, 5 or 7 years. Then they directed that a proposal be made to the Oswestry & Newtown for that company to work the line under an agreement for amalgamation.

Elsewhere, on 11th November 1863, the Llanidloes & Newtown authorised their solicitor, Mr Abraham Howell, to promote the amalgamation Bill, and to include the 'Coast' company. On 25th November, the Oswestry & Newtown Board voted that it would 'continue to work the Aberystwyth & Welsh Coast Company's line from Machynlleth to Aberystwyth' for 45% of the gross receipts.

Back in the 'Coast' company's boardroom, the row about Savin's powers (which had been boiling up for a month or so) finally broke out, and resolutions were passed to give the Board a greater measure of control over Savin's future actions. Amongst those resolutions Savin was directed not to put his shares on the open market before the line had been completed, an action which would depress the value of the holdings of the other shareholders. He was to accept restrictions on the voting power conferred by his holdings, in that it would not be used against any director on any question in which he was personally interested; nor was he to sell any shares while reserving their voting rights to himself. Finally, there was to be a penalty on his failure to complete the line to Aberystwyth by 1st August 1864, and so cause the forfeiture of the line to the Newtown & Machynlleth company. The Board then approved the working of their line by the Oswestry & Newtown, the abandonment of any further attempts to promote a Festiniog branch, and granted to the Lords Vane and Powys the power to appoint directors, if restricted to themselves and to their successors.

On 17th December 1863, Henry Gartside, self-appointed spokesman for the shareholders of the Manchester and Liverpool faction (coming himself from Ashton-under-Lyne), was appointed as a director.

The early part of February 1864 was taken up by considerations about future running powers, and the 'Coast' company made inter-related agreements with the Llanidloes & Newtown, the Oswestry & Newtown, the Oswestry, Ellesmere & Whitchurch and the Bishops Castle Railways. It is to be noted that the Newtown & Machynlleth, whose welcome into the family circle was still to be solemnised, was not included in these exchanges. Indeed, while that company's shareholders were being informed as to how their railway was to be worked as a part of the Cambrian or Welsh system, it was still on course with a further 'Precautionary Bill' designed to safeguard their position in case the 'Coast' company failed to complete their line from Machynlleth to Aberystwyth on time.

The 'Coast' company's shareholders' meeting on 25th February 1864 was a most riotous affair, almost leading to violence. It was revealed that 'serious differences have arisen between the Contractor and the Board with reference to the terms of the Contract'; in fact, Savin had already filed a suit against the company in the Lord Mayor's Court Office, and had attached the company's cash, amounting to £39,000. As a result, a cheque for £10,000 issued to the engineer had been dishonoured, and he was requesting the payment in debentures (and possibly voicing a few threats as well). Secretary Roberts did his best to set down what followed, although his first account was struck out; but he still contrived to leave it in that old bound volume, and those turbulent passages are still fairly legible'. 'It appears to the Directors that the real issue is whether a Board representing all the interests in the Company or Mr Savin the contractor and his nominees have the future control of the affairs of the Company'; and 'Mr Savin's efforts are simultaneously directed to influence the election of Directors at those Boards [of the other companies] and should he succeed in those efforts there can be little doubt that the Capital subscribed by those Companies to this undertaking will be in great jeopardy'; and lastly 'The Board feels called upon to state that Mr Henry Gartside and Mr Jasper Wilson Johns, the Directors of the Oswestry & Newtown and of the Llanidloes & Newtown Boards, who there support Mr Savin's views, and are his nominees, represent also at This Board Mr Savin's views and policy'.

In the voting, these warnings were rejected. The ebullient George Whalley, who was trying to avoid being overrun by Savin, was outfaced by the Manchester faction of shareholders led by Henry Gartside, and by the London group led by Jasper Wilson Johns. Despite his appeal for support, he was voted out of office as chairman. And so the Boardroom assassination, which had started in the meetings of the Montgomeryshire companies, had been completed; the man, without whom these little railways might never have been built, was dismissed and discredited, and would be left with little more of his ambition of being the George Hudson of Central Wales than the chairmanships of the tiny Bishops Castle and the extremely shaky Mid-Wales Railways.

The Board then re-elected Henry Gartside and Jasper Johns, set up a committee of enquiry, and thanked Captain Johns for the exertions he had made in preparing the case of 'Gray versus Whalley' – this was probably a trumped-up affair with an awkward bit of truth in it somewhere.

All this furore rather overshadowed a resolution declaring the company's willingness to give the quarry owners of Bryn-yr-eglwys every assistance in the conveyance of slates from their tramway at Towyn, and to transport materials to and from the Anna Maria Mine at three-pence per ton 'exclusive of carriages and motive power; and 'arranged so as not to interfere with the working of the line'.

March went by in an aura of recrimination, protest and high-handed autocracy. Director William Lefeaux's transfer of shares to Savin was ruled to have been invalid and was not to be registered, and so he resigned. The shareholders presented a requisition for an extraordinary meeting in order to reduce the number of directors to six, so as to get Whalley off the Board as well as out of the chair. Whalley, Penson and Wilding all resigned to avoid being thrown off, leaving Gartside and Johns in control; Lawrence Banks, a 'Manchester supporter', was voted on.

The Board then voted for the removal of the company's cash from Barclay, Bevan & Company to the London & South Western Bank, and immediately transferred the sum of £18,000. Following a declaration that the future policy of the present Board was entirely at variance with that of the previous Board, the anti-Savin and pro-Whalley engineer, Mr Benjamin Piercy, was asked to resign. There was to be an immediate investigation by a competent engineer into the state of the account between the company and Mr Savin, and G.B. Bruce was appointed. Later 'Captain Johnes' reported that he could not come to an amicable agreement between the engineers.

In answer to a letter of protest from Whalley, the Board approved 'that Whalley be informed that the

Committee [of Enquiry] was an independent body appointed by the Shareholders over whose proceedings the Board had no control'. In reply to a letter of protest from Piercy that his appointment was 'for the duration of the Construction of the Line', the Board maintained that 'there was no foundation for such a claim, the remuneration arrangement is unusual, the scale of it [5%, agreed on 29th October 1863] is extravagant and unjustifiable', and they then formally rescinded the relative minute approving the 5%. They refused arbitration by two independent engineers or their umpire, and refused to pay for any work carried out by Piercy after the date of their formal letter of reply. The engineers were again instructed to present proper accounts, and Savin's revenge against Piercy for the rejection of his Corwen to Dolgelley schemes of 1862 was complete.

In contrast, the formal decision to withdraw the 'Coast' company from the amalgamation Bill on account of inability to comply with an important provision in standing orders, made dull reading indeed. The condition which had to be attained before a company might be amalgamated with another was that it had to have constructed half of the lines on its deposited plans, and to have expended half of its authorised capital. Neither statutory goal had been attained by 31st March 1864, the date of the Board meeting at which the formal decision had to be taken. So, the other four companies went ahead with the formation of the Cambrian Railways, leaving the 'Coast' company to struggle on in the confusion created by the division of interests between the Manchester and London (coast-oriented) faction and the Montgomeryshire (or inland) faction – the latter being by then the weaker of the two.

Nowhere in this reportage of bother and argument is there any mention of that other cause of dissent, the great Dovey viaduct, the flagship of the line's claim to distinction, which was proving impossible to build as planned. Here, Whalley and Piercy had been dragged down and could be made the scapegoats, while Savin, backed by Gartside, was to be the saviour; a splendid example of unscrupulous opportunism.

A notice was put out for a shareholders' meeting on 26th May 1864, but only a Special General Meeting, chaired by Gartside, was held; the actual shareholders' meeting was not held until 26th August 1864, run by a 'Coast' chairman, David Williams of Castell Deudraeth, with Captain Jasper Wilson Johns as deputy chairman. The three other directors present were William Banks of Brecon, William Gray from Kent, and the inevitable Henry Gartside of Ashton-under-Lyne. The first paragraph of their report was a revolting piece of self-congratulatory smarm:

> 'The Directors are glad to have it in their power to state that the excitement which prevailed at the last half-yearly Meeting has subsided, and that the disagreement and dissatisfaction which then existed amongst some of the Directors and Shareholders have been succeeded by perfect harmony and unity of action.'

The realisation that the Dovey bridge never would be built was crystallized by a report to the Board that Savin had given an undertaking that 'the Deviation shall not cost the Company any more than the Bridge'. Then followed a strangely-worded item: 'If Savin can hand over the Corris Tramway at its par value the Company would withdraw its opposition to the Corris Bill' and 'Savin will transfer his interest in the Corris Tramway to Company's nominees and take payment in Lloyds Bonds.'

The line to Aberystwyth had been declared ready for inspection on 11th June 1864, and was opened for goods traffic on 23rd of that month. It was formally opened for passenger traffic on 1st August, after additional works required by Captain Tyler, the Board of Trade Inspector, had been completed. Casual references appear to confirm that Henry Conybeare had been acting as sole engineer since March, though his contract and first payment were not formalised before 28th August. Compared with its predecessors, the fourth 'Coast' Bill was a meagre little affair of only twenty-five short clauses, aimed mainly at the rectification of the effects of earlier underestimations.

The Aberystwith and Welsh Coast Railway Act of 1864 took effect on 30th June and conferred powers as follows:

> To raise a further £330,000*L* (sic)
> To borrow a further £100,000
> To acquire compulsorily certain additional land near Ynyslas.
> To acquire by agreement up to 100 acres of land 'for the extraordinary purposes specified in the Railway Clauses Act 1845.'
> To be freed from the restriction on making Railway No. 1 not more expeditiously than Railways 2 and 3 (and which the company had already done).

In addition, the Oswestry & Newtown were empowered to subscribe to a further £100,000 in shares of the 'Coast' company's capital, and to raise more capital of their own to pay for them.

Because of objections raised, and existing Parliamentary views on the subject, power to erect and maintain hotel accommodation at the principal stations had been refused. Also, because of the known antipathy of Parliament to railways trying to operate 'Steamboat Communications', that part of the Bill which sought powers to operate steamers between North Wales and Ireland had been withdrawn before presentation.

On 25th July 1864, two other new Acts came into force. Under one, the Corris received power to abandon the tramway to the west of Machynlleth. The more significant was The Cambrian Railways Act 1864, under which the other four companies could amalgamate, with the 'Coast' company being allowed to join them later by deed when they had satisfied the 50% construction and expenditure rules.

Henry Conybeare reported on 12th August 1864 that 'Borth to Aberystwyth had been opened to traffic', that 'the Works and Permanent Way on this portion of your line, as well as those on the two sections previously opened [Machynlleth to Borth and Aberdovey to Llwyngwril] are in perfect order', and 'the section from Llwyngwril to Barmouth (which includes the heaviest works on your line) is now practically completed and will be ready for inspection by the end of next month.

The works on the Dolgelley branch are in a very forward state and are proceeding satisfactorily. I expect that this section will be ready for inspection by the end of the present year'. His last piece of news was 'The working plans of the Aberdovey deviation have been completed, and the tunnel at Aberdovey (the completion of which is the measure of time for the deviation) has been commenced, and is being pushed as rapidly as possible.'

The next paragraph outlined an attempt which was to be made to obtain power to construct the Mindovey Railway, which was to run right along Aberdovey's estuary front. From this, it would seem that the 'pushing' of the tunnel was not really going so well, and that it was considered that a line along the seafront was going to save the day. The Board discussed the possibility of obtaining powers to abandon the Dovey bridge and to construct the deviation instead, and to rectify other vexatious problems. On the next day, they approved that the Cambrian be asked to work the entire line as was then built for 45% of the gross receipts. They also approved a set of rules & regulations (which have not yet come to light).

The Board also discussed Mr Robertson's scheme for a Bala & Festiniog Railway, Mr Le Feuvre's Portmadoc to Beddgelert and Snowdon slate quarries proposal, and Mr Girdlestone's proposition for a Carnarvon to Beddgelert and Portmadoc line.

On 6th October 1864, the Denbigh, Ruthin & Corwen opened a temporary station at Corwen.

During that month, the 'Coast' company prepared the petition for their final Act of Parliament. Captains Vetch and Washington were retained to give evidence in favour of the abandonment of the bridge, while a leading counsel, Mr Elliott Harrison, was retained to present the arguments in favour of constructing the Deviation. In view of what had appeared to be a change of heart on the part of the legislature, they also decided to ask for powers to operate 'Steam-boats'.

In November 1864, the company continued true to form by electing to oppose two forthcoming Bills from the Mid-Wales and the Manchester & Milford, but they were probably doing this to support the wishes of the Cambrian Railways.

In December, it was revealed that Conybeare had still not received any payment, and the Board asked Savin to produce £1,000 for him. They also decided that it would be advantageous to have the same company solicitor as the Cambrian; Mr Drake, the existing 'Coast' line solicitor, 'was most understanding and was thanked for his past services'.

During this period, the Board of the Cambrian Railways was quite attentive to matters which would assist the eventual amalgamation with and the running of 'the Welsh Coast Railways'. Power by Act of Parliament was to be obtained by Savin, acting with the Great Western and the London & North Western, to construct the Aberdovey extension, for the construction of wharfs at Aberdovey, Penrhyn and Ynyslas, for the purchase of tolls at the ferries at Aberdovey and at Barmouth, for the purchase of the Corris Railway, and for the amalgamation with the Aberystwith & Welsh Coast Railway. The Cambrian Railways' agreement with the Electric Telegraph Company was to be extended to Aberystwyth. They were also to cover themselves for future works by obtaining powers to complete the gaps in the coast line, and to establish steam boats between Aberdovey and Waterford. The Cambrian then approved the draft of their agreement for working the 'Coast' company's lines at 45% of gross receipts for fourteen years, or until amalgamation, and adopted a 'Code of Rules and Regulations for the guidance and Instruction of Officers and Men' to include those of 'the Welsh Coast Railways Companies'.

The 'Coast' Board decided, on 27th January 1865, not to oppose the Mid-Wales Bill, but letters were to be sent raising objections to parts of the Manchester & Milford and Talyllyn Railways' Bills. The five directors then decided that it was time they caught up on directors' expenses, and voted themselves a total of over £800.

The Cambrian Board, on the same day, voted to exercise the option in its 1864 Act to contribute (in 1865) the sum of £100,000 to the amount expendable by the 'Coast' company by taking up shares. Four days later, they agreed to withdraw their objections to the Manchester & Milford Bill on the understanding that the 'Coast' company would be allowed full use of the Manchester & Milford's harbour branch at Aberystwyth.

In February 1865, the 'Coast' Board approved a working agreement with the Corris, and decided to oppose the east and west extensions proposed by the Mid-Wales; they also agreed to lodge an opposition petition against the Cambrian amalgamation Bill, to secure the right to appear before the Parliamentary Committee. To this they added another petition, against the Carnarvon & Portmadoc Direct Railway.

On 23rd February, their shareholders were treated to some highly eulogistic reportage of the decision to promote a Bill 'to abandon the Bridge over the Dovey', to build a Portmadoc harbour branch, and for powers to run steamboats from Aberdovey, now that 'a different view of the question has since been adopted by the Legislature' (Parliament had been strongly lobbied by the members supporting the great railways).

The Cambrian had delivered half of the £100,000 it had been empowered to advance under the 1864 Act, and in March, Savin wrote to them for the balance, pleading 'I am going on very rapidly with the works and the money is very much wanted'. Another £25,000 was therefore advanced after the sending of a formal letter by the Cambrian, which asked 'Is your Company in a position to amalgamate?', to which the reply was 'In a day or two this Company will have expended half their Capital and is therefore in a position to amalgamate with your company'. In April 1865, the Cambrian completed the Heads of Arrangement for the amalgamation.

Meanwhile the 'Coast' company had agreed to purchase the Corris for £25,000 and to purchase the new rolling stock placed on the line by Savin directly from him 'at a valuation'. The 'Coast' Board agreed to withdraw the Portmadoc Harbour branch proposal in return for the Portmadoc & Croesor Railway's affording running powers at a royalty of one penny per ton.

On 24th May 1865, the 'Coast' Board was told that their petition in the House of Lords against the Mid-Wales Extension Bill had been thrown out at the last stage. They grumbled about alterations to the amalgamation Bill in the Committee stage made without their authority or agreement, and voted to put in a withdrawal threat (if this could be done as a protest only, without risking the Bill as a whole). Later, this withdrawal proposal was retracted.

At a meeting on the same day, the shareholders duly approved of 'Bills now pending':

1. for the provision and use of steam and other vessels.
2. For amalgamation with the Cambrian Railways.
3. For the transfer of the Cambrian working agreement to Savin.
4. For the lease of the company's undertaking to the London & North Western and Great Western companies and to Thomas Savin, or some, or one of them.
5. For the maintenance of an existing railway from Carreg Hylldrem (the upper Croesor Tramway).
6. The Manchester & Milford Bill, for the abandonment of old routes and for constructing new ones, with the reservation 'approves thereof with such modifications as Parliament may require or permit.'

Alas, the 'Steamboat Bill', which had passed the Committee of the House of Commons, was subject to modification at the hands of the House of Lords; they threw it out, and the 'Coast' Board received the doleful news on 20th June 1865. At that meeting, they were also told that the proposed price in Savin's construction contract would be agreed at £17,500 per mile. They were given one piece of good news – the sections from Llwyngwril to Barmouth Junction and on to Penmaenpool had been passed for traffic on 5th June.

On 5th July 1865, Royal Assent was given to four Acts of Parliament which had varied effects on the 'Coast' line and its future:

1. The Cambrian; Aberystwith & Welsh Coast Railway Act authorised the transfer of the Cambrian agreement to work the 'Coast' lines to Savin, with a lease of the company's undertaking to Thomas Savin.
2. The Aberystwith & Welsh Coast; Cambrian Railways Act authorised the amalgamation.
3. The Talyllyn Railway Act authorised a mixed-gauge spur into the yard at Towyn, but this was not constructed.
4. The Aberystwith & Welsh Coast Railway Act.

The powers conferred were to raise yet more capital, £120,000, and to borrow another £40,000. This additional money was to cover:

- The acquisition of Portmadoc Inner Harbour by compulsion or other means.
- The acquisition of lands needed by compulsion within three years.
- The purchase by agreement of all or any of the ferries or rights of ferries across the rivers or estuaries of the Rivers Dovey and Mawddach.
- The making of the following railways, wharfs, shipping and landing places, bridges, quays, and embankments, harbour and works.

(a) A railway from a point on Railway No. 5 (later known as Glandovey Junction) to a point on Railway No. 2, where it should have been joined by the line across the Dovey Estuary, to be completed by 30th June 1867 (first promoted as the Morben Railway, but renamed The Aberdovey Deviation Railway), and the abandonment of the original Dovey bridge at Aberdovey.
(b) The Aberdovey Harbour branch, limited to a length of one furlong and eight chains. Further promotions were to be restricted to a total length of three furlongs and three chains from the original junction point (This had been promoted as the Mindovey Railway, running all the way along the front to Tunnel No. 3, so eliminating the need for boring out Tunnel No. 4, and attracted so much opposition that the Commons Committee reduced it as promulgated.)
(c & d) Deviations from the original deposited plans.
(e) The Aberdovey Ferry branch, one mile five furlongs and three chains in length.
(f) Wharfs on both sides of the River Leri.
(Note. Savin had already built the eastern branch for his own works; as it seemed to have been regarded as a siding only, it did not need specific mention in the Act.)
(g) A new Inner Harbour at Portmadoc, including the line thereto.
(h) At Portmadoc, a swing or draw bridge in replacement of the existing stone bridge.

Items (b) to (h) were to be completed within five years.

Clause 30 repealed two restrictions upon the Corris Railway, so that henceforth passengers could be carried and trains could be run at more than ten miles per hour (in anticipation of the proposed amalgamation?).

Clause 32 authorized tolls for the crossing of the Traeth Bach bridge.

The 'Coast' company was also accorded running rights over the Bala & Dolgelley, the Corwen & Bala, and the Llangollen & Corwen, with specific mention of the right to use the station at Llangollen.

Similarly, those three companies were given running rights between Dolgelley and Barmouth, and between Dolgelley and Aberystwyth, with specific mention of the right to use the stations at Barmouth and Aberystwyth.

The 'Tolls, Rates and Charges for Passengers and Goods travelling or consigned between Aberdovey and

Borth' were to remain the same as they would have been if the 'Line across the Estuary of the Dovey' had been built.

In all, there were fifty-three clauses filling twenty pages.

The first set of deposited plans for the Morben and Mindovey Railways were used up by lodging them with the Clerk to the County Council. The reduction in the permitted length of the Mindovey Railway was not endorsed on any of the deposited plans, and has to be read from the Act itself.

On 22nd July 1865, the last and Extraordinary Meeting of the 'Coast' shareholders was held. They assented to the directors creating a further £120,000 in 5% preference shares without voting rights, and borrowing another £40,000 by mortgage from the effective date of the amalgamation Act.

The effective date was 5th August 1865, and the future stages in the history of the coast railways were to be approved by Cambrian directors and recorded by Cambrian officers, on whose shoulders had fallen the burden of making half a railway into a whole. Henceforth, Aberystwyth would also be spelt correctly in all references.

The Coast line, although conjoined to the others from 1865, continued to have a separate history because of its unique character, and the intention is to relate this at the commencement of Volume 2.

However, a brief summary is necessary here to clarify the individual station histories in this volume.

The first task awaiting the officers of the newly formed Cambrian Railways was the completion of the line with, in some cases, only temporary huts as stations. How much was accomplished by adding to the existing permanent way gangs and how much by subcontract, is not yet clear. The 'Deviation' line from Dovey Junction was opened through to Aberdovey on 14th August 1867 and the entire line, for passenger and goods, to Pwllheli on 10th October 1867.

As soon as sufficient money became available in 1872, some £17,600 was approved for a massive programme for the building of permanent stations along the entire coast.

The next upheaval occurred in the period 1889–1894, when many station layouts had to be reconstructed to comply with the requirements of the Regulation of Railways Act 1889.

By the 1920s the Government policy of restricting freight charges to help the war effort and maintain manufacturers' profits, had ruined most of the lesser railway companies, and the Government solution was the creation of the 'Big Four', the Great Western, the London, Midland and Scottish, the London and North Eastern, and the Southern Railway companies. By this means the lesser fry were mostly gobbled up by these larger companies, or combinations of them, which earlier on had been their worst enemies in the many petty traffic wars which were such a feature of those times.

As from 1st January 1922, the Cambrian Railways Company was forcibly absorbed into the Great Western system by an unsympathetic cabal of civil servants headed by Sir Eric Geddes who became notorious later for his 'pay cuts for all' policy (nicknamed 'the Geddes Axe'). This occasioned a substantial programme of track and signalling reconstruction designed to overcome the wartime neglect and to bring all up to the mainline standards of the Great Western.

In 1948 came the Labour government's panacea for all evils, nationalisation, and the Cambrian area went with the rest of the Great Western into Western Region; this change did not have much effect by way of disturbance at ground level.

The main changes came after the Beeching report, which had been calculated to show the government how the British railways could be run at a profit by closing most of them. From 1st January 1963 the Cambrian system was swept, along with the rest of the Great Western lines in North Wales, into London Midland Region. The Coast line survived the initial closure proposal, but its goods yards, loops and surplus sidings were lifted or simplified in accordance with a plan which received approval in 1967. The process of closure to goods traffic was hastened by the miners' strike of 1983 which drove many more people to change to oil or liquid gas heating rather than depending on coal, and subsequently by the closure of Barmouth viaduct to locomotive-hauled trains (and to all trains for a short time) because of severe damage to the piles by the teredo worm.

The proposal to close the entire Coast line once again in 1971 was fought successfully by the Cambrian Coast Line Action Group convened originally by John Rogers and this has given it the title 'The Line that Refused to Die'. With modern Sprinter stock and the Radio Electronic Token Block signalling system (installed over the weekend of 1st/2nd October 1988), the Coast line has lived on to celebrate its 125th anniversary marked by British Rail's highly-successful exhibition at Barmouth on 10th October 1992. Now (and with the inland stem commencing at Sutton Bridge Junction and joining the remainder at Machynlleth) the Coast lines are to continue under the historic name of Cambrian Lines.

MACHYNLLETH 75m 11ch

Loop 74m 68c to 75m 21c
East Signal Box 74m 77c
West Signal Box 75m 14c
New Box 75m 4c
Opened 3rd January 1863

An unidentified Sharp Stewart 2–4–0 on a down (westbound) local train. The leading coach is one of the rather cramped 'austerity' 5-compartment 3rd class vehicles built at Oswestry, the second is a 1st/2nd saloon with luggage compartment, the third a 4-compartment 3rd and the last a 6-wheeled brake van. The photographer, John Thomas, is noteworthy for the quality of his work, and the sympathy and understanding displayed in his carefully-composed portrayal of the working people of Wales. ***Cty. National Library of Wales***

Machynlleth is the westernmost market town in Montgomeryshire (Sir Drefaldwyn), with a charter dating back to 1291. Before the coming of the railway the road to the west linking it to the Port of Derwenlas was busy with packhorses and carts. Its traffic inland, despite the restrictions of the surrounding mountains, extended over the whole of Merioneth, Cardiganshire and Radnor. The name is believed to have derived from two words 'ma' and 'cynllaeth' describing 'The Place of Grass'. One can well imagine the thankfulness of the drovers when descending from the inhospitable mountain tracks down to the valley floor where grazing was more plentiful.

Machynlleth appeared for the first time in the minutes of the Board of the Newtown & Machynlleth Railway Company on 22nd November 1858 when it was recorded that the ceremony of cutting the first sod by the Chairman's lady, Countess Vane, would be held at Machynlleth on 27th November 1858.

On 9th August 1859 it was optimistically reported that 'Arrangements are under consideration for the speedy completion and opening of the Railway to the Hotel at Llanbrynmair' (a distance of twelve miles, which would at once place Machynlleth within an easy stage of eleven miles from the station). In reality it was not until 26th February 1862 that the engineer was able to report that one of the disconnected lengths of rail had been laid to within one mile of Machynlleth.

The journey of the first train to get there was marred by Driver Henry Clough who took David Davies's 0–6–0 Class I Manning Wardle saddle tank *Llandinam* too rapidly over Glantwymyn bridge with a trainload of sleepers, and caused it to collapse. The engine was dragged out of the river next day and arrived at

Machynlleth on 1st May 1862. For this account, and for those of three unofficial trains, we are indebted to Mr Gwyn Briwnant-Jones in *Railway Through Talerddig*. The first delivery of goods was made to a monumental mason at Llandinam on 22nd June 1862. A trip was run from Llandinam on 15th August 1862, and another (a Temperance outing) was run from Oswestry on 25th September 1862.

On 13th October 1862 the Board was informed that under the agreement whereby the Great Western Railway Company was to work the line 'The Goods Station was to be built in two months from the opening of the station; and the Engine Shed within five weeks'.

The line through to Machynlleth was inspected and passed by Captain Tyler on 30th December 1862 and the inaugural train arrived on 3rd January 1863. The first public service trains ran on 5th January 1863 and for some time thereafter passengers had to put up with a station which was just a timber shed on a bleak wind-and-rain-exposed platform. This situation was unchanged when the A & WC Railway opened its line from Machynlleth to Borth on 1st July 1863.

An agreement with the Corris Railway Company whereby slate was to be transhipped and forwarded was approved on 2nd July 1863.

The plans for the permanent station, as drawn up by T.M. Penson, were submitted to the Board on 16th September 1863 and it was left for the Chairman Earl Vane to settle the details and finally to approve the design. In fact this task took nearly six months. On 10th March 1864 it was reported that 'Permanent Station Buildings were nearly finished except at Machynlleth' but it became evident that His Lordship meant to permit only the best at his own home station and T.M. Penson's plans as redrawn to meet with His Lordship's approval were produced to the Board once more. They were passed with the following stipulations:

'1. The Platform to be covered and a Weatherboard be placed at the Welsh Coast end of it.
'2. A Cellar to be provided.
'3. Talerddig Stone to be substituted for Bricks in erecting the outer walls with a dressing of free stone. Outer walls to be similar in Style of Workmanship to those at other Stations on the Line. The Woodwork on the outside walls as now shown on the plan to be dispensed with.' [From this it appears that His Lordship had really wanted imitation half-timber styling for the upper storey and that his co-directors thought that this was really going a bit too far.]

So, whilst Machynlleth did not have its proper station by the time that the Newtown & Machynlleth Railway Company amalgamated with the others to form The Cambrian Railways on 25th July 1864, at least it was being built. The work was under the supervision of Engineer George Owen who also became the Cambrian's engineer. The station had a proper engine shed and goods warehouse, as required under the agreement with the perfidious Great Western, though that company had backed out of its offer to run the Newtown & Machynlleth line as soon as it had secured its own rival line to the Coast via Llangollen, Bala and Dolgelley.

By this time the slate wharf would have been about half its ultimate length, with sheds and facilities for the Ratgoed and Aberllefenni Slate Quarry Companies. It appears that the Aberllefenni wharf had been constructed first and that the Ratgoed had to be content with a backshunt crossing over the siding to the Aberllefenni Company's wharf space.

The architect, Thomas Penson, did not live to see his work completed. He was the unqualified younger brother of architect Richard Kyrke Penson who was a director of both the Llanidloes & Newtown and (after the amalgamation) of the Cambrian. Had Thomas lived to see his three masterpieces (he was also the architect of Welshpool and of Moat Lane), they would undoubtedly have brought him an associateship of The Royal Institute of British Architects.

The expansion of Machynlleth's freight-handling facilities began when, on 24th May 1866, an additional wharf for the Braich Goch Slate Company was authorised at a cost of £85. To gain access to the new extension, the Corris had to arrange a reverse-curved line which climbed onto the wharf about halfway along its length and provided a second reverse curve at the west end to release empty wagons. Who built or paid for the 2ft 3in gauge lines on the Cambrian Company's wharf is not known. The situation at Machynlleth was quite different from that at Towyn where the entire wharf had been sold to the narrow gauge company. Locomotives were not permitted on the slate wharf at Machynlleth and each quarry appears to have owned and kept its own shunting horses. The 'blind' turntables along the edge of the wharf were used for turning end-door wagons to face the receiving standard gauge wagons.

It was noted in the 1867 staff report that ten station staff and one signalman were employed. As befitted this substantial station, the Committee approved, on 10th December 1868, the installation of gas lighting.

In 1869 the old stabling for the shunting horses was reported as being 'quite dilapidated' and renewal was authorised for £16 11s 6d. On 7th June 1869 the engineer reported that the siding in the lower yard had been extended with wharfage for the Braich Goch and other quarries, and on 23rd June that the lead ore sheds had been erected and put to good use. He reported again on 2nd September 1869 that a new siding was needed in the lower yard at a cost of £99 3s 4d.

In his report on refreshment rooms, the Traffic Manager described Machynlleth as having 'First and Second Class Dining Rooms, a Kitchen, a Cellar and two Bedrooms', being let at £45 per annum.

On 10th December 1869 the Board ruled that, despite the receipt of local memorials, the station agent (station master), probably a Mr Burke who had been dismissed for his unsatisfactory misconduct, was not to be reinstated.

On 12th May 1870 the engineer reported that a carriage shed was needed because of damage to carriage stock exposed to the weather. 'This could be made to include a private compartment for Lord Vane's private saloon. His Lordship would be prepared to pay a rent on a proportionate amount of the cost which would be about £350.' At the same time the Traffic Manager reported 'The Horse has broken down'. As far as is known, the carriage shed with 'His Lordship's private compartment' was not authorised, but another horse was obtained from Oswestry immediately.

Because of 'crowding in the lower yard', a new siding in the upper yard was recommended on 21st December 1871 'for the ready despatch of marshalled trains'. Machynlleth was now growing fast and by 19th December 1872 there was a need for an additional shed and coaling facilities for four engines costed at £599 6s 0d, though this addition to the engine shed does not seem to have been made. A coal wharf was being set up in the lower yard for use by any merchants prepared to give 'A Guarantee for the payment of at least a specified tonnage conveyed over the Cambrian Railways'.

About the same time the Traffic Committee heard that 'Richard Jones has put a stock of Hay on Company Land and has written to Earl Vane'. He was allowed to keep it there on payment of a nominal acknowledgement of ten shillings provided that he removed the stack by Christmas 1872.

On 22nd May 1873 the engineer reported on the fitting of a 'Jennings Patent Pillar Lavatory in the First Class Waiting Room' at a cost of £4 5s 0d including drainage. In October 1874 the Machynlleth porters made history by presenting a petition for the supply of overcoats and leggings for wearing on the exposed station during the winter months. The Traffic Manager warned his Committee 'If we grant the privilege at Machynlleth we shall have to do so at many other places where the men have an equal claim to it'.

On 21st October 1874 a porter named Richard Jones was trapped between buffers. 'His injuries did not appear serious', reported Mr Henry Cattle, the Traffic Manager, 'he however never overcame them and died on Friday last.'

It was approved on 23rd October 1874 that accommodation should be given to the Corris Railway for the erection of a warehouse which 'was to occupy as little land as was necessary', with the rider that they 'ought to use land South of the Railway'.

In February 1875 a fire broke out 'in the Ladies' Waiting Room and the Stationmaster's Sitting Room'. It was discovered that the cause had been the burning through of an exposed timber beam in the chimney, a common cause of fires in those days.

The facilities at Machynlleth must have been used to the limit by April 1875, for when Messrs Turner, Lamphier & Co of Manchester asked for a slate wharf to be provided, they were told that no space was available either at Minffordd or Machynlleth and they were offered a site at Moat Lane instead. The Engineer was instructed on 14th April 1875 'to look at the boundaries and land purchased from the Corris Company when the Coast Section was built as we are ready to deal with them as to Rent etc.'

It was reported on 24th November 1875 that 'The Goods Office is in a very dilapidated condition. The draught is so serious that the Clerks are often ill; at present there is one off from the effects of a cold received in the place'.

Jane Willington, an old woman over eighty years of age, while collecting coal with a donkey cart on 1st May 1876, 'wandered off from the safe place in which her carter had left her' and had her arm crushed between two wagons, and died later. The company was absolved from any charge of negligence.

On 16th October 1876 the Committee was called upon to consider the application of Mr William Bright, Managing Director of the Abercwmeiddawr Slate Company, for a large space of wharfage. Henry Cattle reported 'there is no room, it would be expensive and I would recommend a smaller provision to begin with as Mr Bright indulges in large expectations with regard to the Quarry'. He went on to inform the Committee that the station was 'dangerously insufficient for the proper accommodation of Passenger Traffic. Both platforms need extending to take two trains each. The Aberystwyth trains have Twelve Vehicles with each Engine and the Coast eight with the Engine'. The cost was estimated at £742 15s 10d and on 26th January 1877 the work was ruled out on the grounds of 'Balance of Capital being so small'.

On 22nd March 1877 the construction of a standard gauge siding for the Abercwmeidaw (sic) Slate Company was reported and they were to 'bring the Narrow Gauge Line round to the Wharf'. In fact the proper name of the quarry company was Abercwmeiddew and this is an unusual example of a private quarry company laying down its own 2ft 3in gauge horse-drawn line in the standard gauge company's goods yard.

Another accident occurred on 12th April 1877, when William Cleaton, 'a labourer working with the Ballast Trains', was crushed between two wagons.

On February 20th 1878 the Traffic Manager asked for 'the extension of the short siding running parallel to the one now used for removing the Stone from the Rock so that the large piece of ground can be used for loading Round Timber', and this was approved. On 5th September, after another summer of traffic overload, he reported again 'the Platforms are insufficient for Passenger Accommodation and I ask for extensions before next summer'.

On 18th June 1879 it was reported that the Abercwmeidawr Slate Company had still not commenced to pay their agreed rent of £20 per annum for their wharf.

In January 1881 the station master was dismissed 'for irregularities' and Mr Hammond was appointed. Memorials on the behalf of the dismissed man were received from the townsfolk but the Board refused to consider the popular Mr Dix's reinstatement.

On 15th July 1881 'Griffith Griffiths was knocked down by a shunting engine while unloading Coal and helping to push a waggon. He took no notice of the whistle and Death supervened in about three hours from injuries and shock to the System.'

The Engineer's report of 21st August 1882 on the state of water supplies to the cattle pens showed that, at Machynlleth, it had to be carried a considerable distance in buckets and that a piped supply to a tap would cost £5 2s 0d. The report had been undertaken after the Cambrian had been prosecuted under the Contagious Diseases of Animals Act. The works recommended at all stations were approved.

In May 1882 an appeal was launched. 'A Boy Number Taker Macaffrey has lost a leg through his own want of caution', the committee were informed. 'An effort is being made supported by the Marchioness of Londonderry to procure him a Cork-leg and thus enable him to obtain a livelihood. Could the Company assist?' Seemingly they could not. At that time few railway companies had any sort of official fund from which they could legitimately make such a payment, but for directors to assist privately was not unknown.

In 1883 there was a general move towards increasing siding accommodation to avoid the use of station loops as sidings, and Machynlleth was recommended for an additional down siding, 147 yards long and costing £179 5s 0d.

On 12th November 1883 'The Ballast engine *Alexandra* came off the rails at the Turntable. Either the Turntable had not been properly set or the Catch flew up.' *Alexandra* was Cambrian No 4, an 0–6–0 Sharp Stewart goods engine.

While the breakdown crane stationed at Machynlleth was being shunted on 26th February 1884, the balance box slid and broke its fastenings 'Due to washer breaking through wear and tear'.

On 30th July 1884 the Committee approved the construction of steps leading down to the Corris station for £20, half the cost to be borne by each company.

On 4th May 1885 the Traffic Manager asked for the down platform to be lengthened for £230 3s 8d and this time it was approved. On 20th May 1885 Shunter Venables 'a very promising servant of the Company was knocked down in the dark by an engine and lost his left leg'. The number of accidents in the yards suggests that they were very busy and dangerous places. Towards the end of 1885 the station building was fenced round so that the Machynlleth staff could examine and collect tickets and relieve the staff at adjacent stations of this work and the associated delay to trains.

On 3rd December 1885 'Number Taker Joseph Thomas slipped and fell into the four foot [between the rails] and the Mail Engine and two wagons passed over him, but he was caught by the ashpan and dragged along the ground for a short distance. His injuries were however very slight and he is progressing rapidly towards recovery.'

There was so much demand for water that the piping system was not coping very well. The water tank was so far away that the Traffic Manager recommended that the platform arrangements should be improved by having 'new water columns with tanks on top' so that there was a reserve on site of nearly 1500 gallons. The installation of 'Two Water Cranes' for £174 10s 0d was approved on 26th January 1887. The need for this had been reported on 11th October 1886 by John Conacher, the forceful secretary who had been Acting General Manager and Acting Traffic Manager as well; but the directors had referred the matter back for a report from Engineer George Owen which they should have been given in the first instance.

During the serious flooding of October 1886, 'Mr Thomas Jarman, Gamekeeper in the employ of the Marchioness of Londonderry, has removed a tree which had been floated onto the line at Machynlleth Station shortly before the passage of an excursion train.' In December the Board resolved that 'The thanks of the Directors of the Cambrian Railway Company be forwarded to him'.

On 12th December 1886 approval was given for the introduction of a tablet system between Machynlleth and Glan Dovey (sic) – actually Glandovey Junction.

On 2nd March 1888 John Lewis, a wagon greaser, 'stepped out of the way of the Ballast Engine and was trapped between the Shunting Engine and the Coal Stage. He sustained severe injuries around the groin and waist and died five days later.'

On 1st May 1888 it was reported that the tablet system between Machynlleth and Glandovey Junction was working well and that the cost had been reduced from £140 to £100 per pair of instruments. John Conacher recommended the transfer of the old block telegraph instruments to the section between Llanidloes and Tylwch.

In January 1889 a portion of the cliff collapsed across the upper yard but nobody was injured.

On 27th January 1890 the Engineer reported on the re-signalling and interlocking required under the Regulation of Railways Act 1889. The work was completed on 20th July 1890 at a cost of £2,113 2s 3d.

Accidents to children continued to be all too common. On 24th July 1890 Fanny Owen, daughter of Goods Guard T. Owen, was standing by the line at a

A train for Corris and Aberllefenni in the narrow gauge station at Machynlleth. This station was rebuilt c.1906 with a new building which stood clear of the running line, and a run-round loop in the platform area. The short slate fencing was typical of that used on the Corris line – large pieces of slate stood on end, retained in line by two lengths of wire along the top, twisted together between each of the upright slabs. The photographer appears to have set up his camera atop a loaded slate train waiting to be shunted into the exchange wharf. The Corris district (and that served by the Talyllyn Railway which served the wharf at Towyn) produced slab slate largely from underground workings, unlike those in North Wales which produced roofing slate. *John Thomas, cty. National Library of Wales*

footpath crossing and 'as the up goods was seven to ten yards away she stepped onto the line in front of the engine and was knocked down and severely cut about the head. Medical assistance was at once obtained and the child is said to be progressing favourably.' Only five days later 'John Hughes, a youth employed by W.H.Smith and Sons' Bookstall, crossed the line while the 4am Down Goods Train ex Whitchurch was shunting and one of the wheels passed across his body after he appeared to have fallen. He was last seen at the end of the platform and when discovered under the wagon it was found that life was extinct.'

On 26th October the Engineer reported that it would cost £1,056 to extend the present engine shed stabling only four engines, to enable six more to be stabled, and this was approved.

In 1892 there was a dispute over Sunday work, about which John Conacher (now the General Manager) reported that he had explained to the men that 'it had not been the practice to pay for Sunday work except at specific stations where the men are on duty for half a day' and 'I have not seen my way to agree to the application'. Thus, besides a six-day week, the company expected the men to give Sunday overtime for no extra pay if less than half a day was worked.

On 27th March 1893 the Engineer quoted two prices for an iron lattice footbridge. For £135 the company could have one with a pier on the up platform but for £220 they could have one clearing the up platform by crossing over it to a foundation built upon the embankment. So, of course, the one which obstructed the up platform was chosen.

Two accidents in early 1894 were typical of the frequent incidents occuring in the yards. On 19th January 'Pointsman Edward Jones received a broken and lacerated arm when he stood on a brake lever and slipped and fell against the wheel of a moving wagon.' On 3rd May 1894 'Fireman H. Harding and Cleaner H. Evans were turning one of the new bogie engines which, when at right angles, projected over the adjoining siding. Hanwood wagon No 62 with a defective brake was shunted off the Down Goods and ran down the siding and hit the buffer of the engine and injured Harding and Evans'.

On 24th March 1896 the Board of Guardians were reported to have requested that members called to a meeting at Machynlleth should be conveyed in the guard's van of the goods train which arrived at about 9 am. This application was refused. (Boards of Guardians were the locally elected bodies responsible for the overseeing of the working of the Poor Laws, and so of the workhouses).

On 31st March 1896 the Board instructed the Secretary to inform the vestry council that 'The Company has no power to contribute towards the restoration of the Parish Church'.

On 23rd August 1898 the General Manager reported that 'The Privilege given to Night Foreman Wakefield and six cleaners to come on at 9 pm on Sundays instead of at 6 pm to allow them to attend places of worship also required that their work did not suffer.' The underlying problem was that the engine cleaning was not being done properly and the drivers had complained. The men on the shift had been ordered to come on at 6 pm as before. When they failed to do so, the men were suspended, pending instructions from the Locomotive Superintendent, Mr Aston. Following this, certain Nonconformist Ministers in Machynlleth asked that Wakefield be given a hearing. One Minister went further and penned a similar request signed by all six of the cleaners. The final outcome was that Wakefield was 'demoted to Extra Fireman at Aberystwyth' for committing 'a most serious breach of discipline aggravated by his inciting the cleaners to join him in resisting the authority of Mr Sanger'. Sanger was the Locomotive Foreman.

There was more trouble with the turntable on 6th July 1898 when a passenger van on the adjacent siding was shunted into the overhanging buffers of an engine. The force caused the handles on the turntable to knock the two operating drivers (Evans and Jones) down into the well, and both were off duty for three days with bruising. It was stated that there was not any room for adjustment and tenders were to be invited for a new turntable.

On 22nd November approval was given for the erection of thirteen gas lights in the upper and lower yards and one in a ground disc, all for £70. 'Mr Harris, Agent' had become incapacitated from duty by failure of health, and it was approved that he be allowed to continue on half pay for another six months in consideration of his length of service and general good conduct.

On 24th April 1899 Thomas Williams, the Lion Hotel's bus driver, fell or walked under a train just outside the station limits. He was probably suffering from the regular occupation disease of horse-drivers as they all appear to have taken to strong spirits to keep warm in the winter.

On 30th June 1899 it was approved that cattle pens should be put up at the extended siding 'under the Rock' to avoid the confusion caused on market days

A scene on the down platform c.1920, with the Cambrian green paint much in evidence. Note the prominence given to the name of the Corris Railway. *Cty. M. E. M. Lloyd*

Looking east through Machynlleth station on 2nd July 1909. This is the only photo so far discovered showing the Cambrian Railways waiting shelter on the up platform, just beyond the sign beckoning to the Corris Railway. The substantial nature of the buildings on the down side, erected under Earl Vane's guidance, is instantly evident. The change of gradient from the level section in the middle of the 'hump' at Machynlleth was near the centre of the station. *H. L. Hopwood/LCGB*

by driving cattle through the coal yard. The cost was £275.

The foundations for the new fifty-foot turntable had been completed by 25th September 1899 and installation was reported as complete and connected on 12th December 1899. (The old forty-foot turntable had been sited on the shed neck, well past the water tower.)

An accident which, because of the personality involved, had to be dealt with 'with the utmost severity', happened on 23rd December 1899. 'While a London and North Western saloon containing the Earl of Winchelsea and party was being shunted for transfer to the Coast train, Signalman Jenkins moved the point lever and derailed the saloon. Lord Winchelsea had to move to another carriage and was greatly inconvenienced.' Jenkins, aged 61, was moved to the lighter duties of extra Platform Porter but was allowed to remain at Machynlleth. His wages were reduced from twenty three shillings per week down to fifteen shillings per week.

The General Manager requested some minor improvements on 10th May 1900. These were: 'Foreman's Office near the Shed £60', 'Alterations to Loco Stores £10', 'Loco Office to be removed to Cloak Room £5', and 'Removal of Lamp Room £1–10s-0d'.

Fireman John Graham had claimed that on 2nd March 1901 he had been knocked down while holding over 'a pair of points'. The truth of it was that a gust of wind had blown his cap off, he had run after it and had been struck by a wagon. He sustained an injured back and right leg and a laceration over his left eye.

On 25th June 1903 the Committee heard of a letter from the Board of Trade concerning an allegation by a Mrs Turner that she had fallen down when getting out of a carriage because the platform was too low. They resolved 'that the Board of Trade be informed that the Company cannot see their way clear to raise the platform at Machynlleth'.

On 9th June 1904 the Board agreed to an exchange of lands bordering the goods yards with the Corris Company. This was to enable the Corris to enlarge its passenger facilities by doubling the line at the terminus and building a new station. The exchange deed was signed on 22nd October 1904. From the exchange the Cambrian gained the east to west portion of the old tramroad as an access lane from the main road to the end of their own private trackway leading to the line, opposite the old coal wharf, much used by permanent way men.

Here a note on the topography at the northern edge of the yard will not come amiss. When David Davies

2–4–0 No. 43, built by Sharp Stewart, on the Cambrian's 50ft turntable at Machynlleth on 2nd July 1909. *H. L. Hopwood/LCGB*

2–4–0 Sharp Stewart No. 28 beside the east end of the goods warehouse. The heavy lifting jack beside the smokebox was carried by all Cambrian locomotives after the Welshampton accident of 11th June 1897 in which eleven children on a school outing were killed.
H. L. Hopwood/LCGB

laid out the yard for the Newtown and Machynlleth, he had built an 8ft high wall of rough stone and had filled in the whole area nearly to the top of the wall. The tipped area had settled unevenly which explains the unlevel state of the slate wharf. When the Corris had first asked the Cambrian for a site for their passenger station, they were offered a piece of land next to the abandoned portion of the tramroad, roughly opposite the end of Pens Siding, which was possible as the Corris still owned the tramroad land and it might well have been preferable to the passengers; but the Corris pressed for the cheaper site needing little extension of track.

On 2nd February 1905 instructions were given for negotiations for an additional strip of land at the top of the quarry (or cliff?) as all the ballast that could be safely taken was exhausted. Also concerned with land

4–4–0 Large Sharp Stewart No. 66 drawing into the station with a down train made up of GWR and LNWR coaches, watched closely by the wheeltapper. c.1920.
H. W. Burman

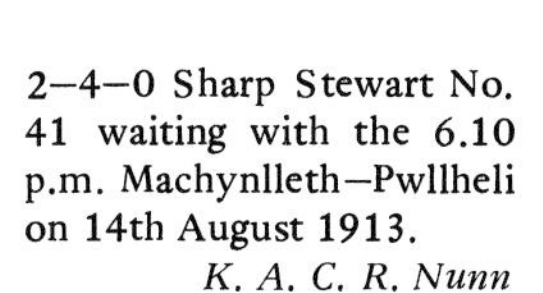

2–4–0 Sharp Stewart No. 41 waiting with the 6.10 p.m. Machynlleth–Pwllheli on 14th August 1913.
K. A. C. R. Nunn

Cambrian Railways No. 1, purchased from the GWR where it had carried the number 212. It later became GWR 1329. *Cty. R. E. Thomas*

4–4–0 Large Sharp Stewart, formerly CR No. 62, later GWR 1090, standing under 'The Rock' at the west end of Machynlleth shed on 9th June 1925. *A. W. Croughton*

The Cambrian acquired 0–6–0 Manning Wardle No. 30 from the ailing Mawddy Railway. *Photographer unknown*

4–4–0 Large Sharp Stewart, formerly Cambrian No. 67, then GWR 1100, being prepared for duty at the west end of Machynlleth shed c.1925. The mean proportions of the Cambrian's three-ridge shed, and the narrow doorways behind the outward-hung doors are apparent here. At least one man was severely injured through being caught between a doorway and a moving locomotive. *H. W. Burman*

Aston Goods GWR 880 (Cambrian No. 77) outside the east end of the 1963 engine shed. The point indicator disc is a design very different from that shown on page 34. *H. W. Burman*

Jones Goods No. 894, formerly Cambrian No. 100, at the east end of the shed. *Photographer unknown*

Former Metropolitan Railway 4–4–0 tank No. 13, running (with condensing gear removed) as Cambrian No. 34 at the west end of Machynlleth shed. Limited coal and water capacity led the two ex-Metropolitan tanks (31 and 2) to be confined to use on banking duties from Machynlleth but they were not successful even on these relatively short runs. *Locomotive Publishing Co.*

Stephenson 4–4–0 GWR 1043 (Cambrian Railways No. 98) standing on Machynlleth shed on 25th August 1931. Note the arrangement of the two spare headlamps. *D. S. M. Barrie*

0–6–0 Sharp Stewart goods engine No. 14 on a down goods train with an assisting engine in rear on its over-long train in 1919. This picture shows the original layout of the station end of the 'Aberystwyth Road' siding beside the goods shed – a double trap point with one indicator disc – compare with the later arrangement shown on pages 34 and 36. *H. W. Burman*

was a proposal made in May 1906 for a 30,000 gallon water tank on top of the cliff. It is not known whether this foundered because of cost or because Sir Watkyn Wynn refused to sell the land.

A new slate wharf was put up in September 1908 for a Mr W.J. Lewis who intended to erect a shed for the production of printed and enamelled slate slabs for chimney pieces. On 21st December 1908 the Committee approved an annual subscription to the Londonderry Cottage Hospital. Whilst not really having the powers to do this, they stretched a point as the hospital would be of assistance in caring for injured railwaymen and passengers.

On 26th July 1910 'A young woman who has not yet been identified travelled by train from Dolgelley and threw herself under a train in Machynlleth'. Later she was found to be a Miss Reitlinger from London who was suffering from religious depression and had been missing from her home for three days.

On 3rd October 1910 'Cleaner David Lloyd Jones was knocked down and killed by a shunting engine he had requested for moving a dead engine and he stumbled just as the two engines were being buffered and he was to connect them'.

In February 1914 the Clerk to the Machynlleth Urban District Council wrote 'My Council's attention has been drawn by the travelling public to the urgent need for a covered bridge over the line of railway at Machynlleth station owing to the exposed position of the bridge and the want of protection from the storm and the rain to which the public are subjected.' The Engineer's reply was: 'I could not agree to covering this footbridge; it is a very light structure and the weight of the covering would render it unsafe. As there is no covering on the up platform I cannot see that the mere fact of crossing the bridge in the dry would have any useful effect.' The Board agreed with him and declined to order the covering of the footbridge. It should be noted that almost all of Earl Vane's journeys were made in his own saloon or by Cambrian saloon, drawn up against the awning on the down side, and he would then be gently shunted into place on whichever train he was going to use; so he never needed to exercise his 'clout' to get covers over the footbridge or the up platform as the Earl of Powys had caused to be built at Welshpool over the footbridge and the down platform there.

In 1917 the refreshment rooms were noted as being still open despite the war, and a new fitting shop was erected for £120 as 'the old one afforded such poor working conditions'. In 1919 a charge was instituted for admission on Sundays, presumably for access to the refreshment rooms.

The report on signalling and the location of tablet instruments made after the Abermule accident in 1921 recorded that Machynlleth East Box had a full-time signalman and the tablet instruments were in the box. West Box had a part-time signalman.

On 20th February 1922 the Great Western management experienced its first mishap at Machynlleth. In the dark at 8.30pm Driver T. Lloyd was walking from the coal siding to the shed between coal road and middle road, and he slipped off the rails, fell into the ashpit and injured his leg. £180 was voted immediately for additional lighting.

Plans dated 8th November 1923, drawn up for the Traffic Committee, involved doubling the line to Dovey Junction with alterations to the loop points at the down end and a neck siding there (for additional locomotives) beyond the bridges. The entire pointwork at the east (up) end of the station would be renewed to a new layout. The two 'column' water tanks were to be replaced by standard crane arms and the two signal boxes by one central box with fifty-four levers. East Box was to have been converted into a shunters' cabin. The whole idea was scrapped as unnecessary and the sweeping replacements of signalling found at other large Cambrian stations at that time was not done, but the old Cambrian bar point rodding was renewed in Great Western pattern inverted channel on travelling rollers which needed much less effort to move.

So the Great Western's alterations, in addition to the additional lighting by the shed, amounted only to detaching loose rock from the cliff face (it was feared

A view of the eastern end of Machynlleth yard, from beside the shunters cabin. On the left is the Lower Yard shunt neck, and beside that the single main line. The Standard tank loco is on Tank Siding No. 1 with empty carriages on Tank Siding No. 2. 1965. *Author*

This graceful culvert is at the end of the up sidings. It is made of stone brought down from the great cutting at Talerddig. 1965. *Author*

The throat at the eastern end of the shed yard, with the line ascending from the lower goods yard on the left. The wagons on the right are alongside the former Cambrian Railways loco coal bank. The wide gap between this siding and the adjacent one (which splits beyond to form the two Tank Sidings) betrays the one-time presence at the end of the loco coal siding of the Cambrian's 40ft turntable. The clearance between the turntable and the adjacent siding must have been very tight, hence the accidents caused by collisions between wagons being shunted on the siding and locos on the turntable and the men pushing them round. 1965. *Author*

The River Dovey in flood c.1903. The embankment of the Corris Railway can be seen striking diagonally across to the far bank – small wonder that river erosion was the final cause of that line's demise. The Cambrian's loco coal bank and the water tank, with a trace of smoke from the boilerhouse chimney, can be seen. *Author's collection*

A view of the water tank from the hillside above. The collection of boarding, which may once have formed a roof to the tank, lay in a confused heap by the time this 1965 view was taken. *Author*

Looking towards the station from beside the shunters' cabin with, on the right, the shunting neck falling away down to the Lower Yard. The track in the foreground was laid (in GWR style) on concrete blocks connected at intervals by stretcher bars, rather than on conventional sleepers. The two lines adjacent to the neck are the up and down running lines, and to the left of them are the Tank and old loco coal stage roads. 1965. *Author*

that there might be a fall of rock), enlarging the down platform across the road underbridge at the west end of the station, and the entire renewal of the gas service for £840. 1924 ended with some repair work on the engine shed roof. A study of the plans of 1923 and 1925 has revealed that neither the engineers nor the solicitors of the Great Western had any idea of what 2ft 3in gauge trackage lay on and to the north of their slate wharf. All their track plans were adrift and had to be redrawn from other sources.

1925 commenced with a small road diversion and the transfer of a large timber shed from Aberdovey to become the Permanent Way Depot at a cost of £245 (see photo on page 43). In July the drainage from the cattle pens was overhauled for £130.

On 28th June 1928 the Traffic Committee authorised £337 for bringing in a replacement second-hand weighbridge.

On 13th February 1930 the Civil Engineer had the entire station roof reslated for £220.

Looking eastwards, with the photographer standing in the 'four foot' of the down line, and the shunters' cabin on the left. All locos leaving the shed at its eastern end had to run past the hand point on the sidings on the right – the parked wagons had not left much space! 1954.
Author

By 1965 the decline of steam was well advanced and the water tank was slipping into disrepair. The pump was housed in the building below the tank – the well was some yards away to the left.
Author

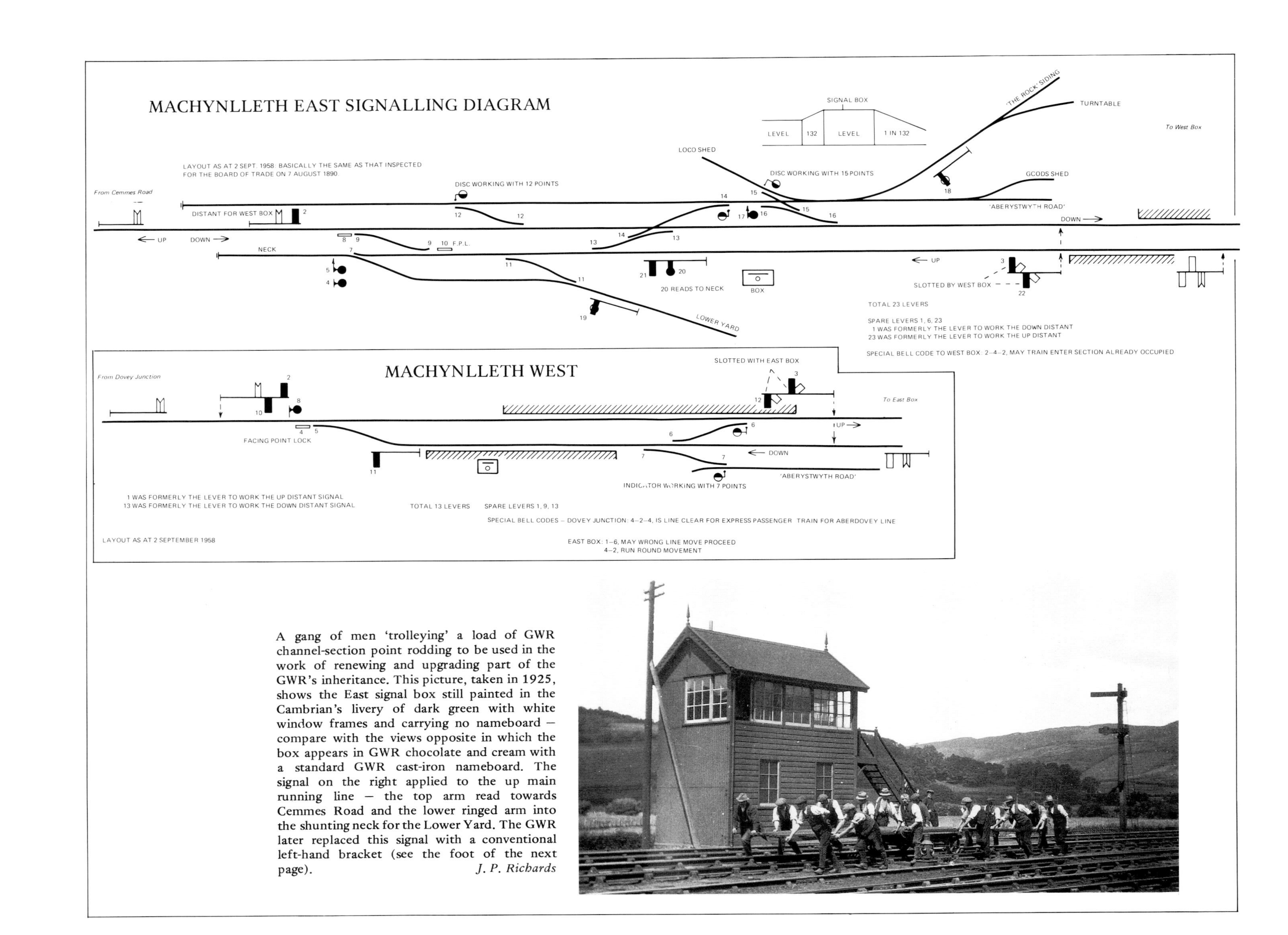

A gang of men 'trolleying' a load of GWR channel-section point rodding to be used in the work of renewing and upgrading part of the GWR's inheritance. This picture, taken in 1925, shows the East signal box still painted in the Cambrian's livery of dark green with white window frames and carrying no nameboard – compare with the views opposite in which the box appears in GWR chocolate and cream with a standard GWR cast-iron nameboard. The signal on the right applied to the up main running line – the top arm read towards Cemmes Road and the lower ringed arm into the shunting neck for the Lower Yard. The GWR later replaced this signal with a conventional left-hand bracket (see the foot of the next page).
J. P. Richards

On 3rd August 1930 the Great Western acquired the Corris Railway as an unwelcome extra to their takeover of the Corris Company's attractive and effective little bus service. The Corris Company had run horse-bus services from 1879 onwards. A steam-hauled passenger service to Corris began on 4th July 1883 and extended to Aberllefenni on 25th August 1887, most of the time with horse buses acting as feeders. To match the lengthening of the passenger stock, a carriage shed was erected in 1908 at Machynlleth behind Braich Goch's portion of the wharf. An undated drawing shows that the narrow shed end-on to the new station was intended to be a loco shed, but after it was put up c. 1906 it was only used as a warehouse.

In May 1908 hired motor buses were used for the first time and the company did extremely well right through the 1920s. The GWR made a successful bid to acquire the railway and bus undertaking as from 3rd August 1930. On the following day the Great Western transferred its bus services in the area to Western Transport Ltd, in which it had the majority shareholding, and the Corris station became the local office

The East Box c.1950, showing the neat porch at the top of the steps. *Photomatic*

The other end of the East Box was much less attractive, the original cladding having been covered with corrugated iron, making it much less easy for the painters to carry the brown and cream livery round the end of the box. The open window and stain down the front of the box betray where the signalman kept the all-important teapot. 1954. *Author*

1965. Two views showing the roof of the engine shed, as rebuilt by the GWR (the Cambrian shed originally had separate ridges over each track). The vans in the left background are in the Lower Yard, and the eastern end of the narrow gauge slate transhipment wharf can be seen behind them. *Author*

Top right: This view was taken a few yards further east than the two on the left, to show the pointwork in the main lines at the east end of the shed. Latterly the grounded van body on the left served as the shunters' messroom, and the cabin further up the neck was the messroom for the carriage cleaners (carriages were often stabled in the Tank Sidings). 1965. *Author*

Of the original shed, only the outer walls remained after the GWR rebuilding – and these had to be demolished when collapse was imminent. *Author*

Left: The scene looking into the station from atop the bracket signal visible in the photo above, and showing the 'step' in the side of the two loco sheds (that of 1863 is the nearer, with the 1873 shed beyond). In addition to re-roofing the sheds, the GWR also provided new doors and frames. The flat-roofed building was to have been the fitters' cabin but was actually used by the boilersmith and the carriage & wagon examiner. The gabled building butting on to the shed was the sand drying room. When the new signal box (in the right background) was put in, the track layout was simplified and the connection from the line beside the shed on to the down main line was removed. The DMU stabled on the 'Aberystwyth Road' was ready to form a connecting service. 1965. *Author*

A photo taken beside the west end of the shed, looking towards the passenger station and past the shed to the 'new' coal stage, turntable road and the Rock siding. *Author*

The extent of the reconstruction of the engine shed by the GWR can be gauged by comparing these two views with those on page 22. The locos are Collett 0–6–0 No. 2286 and 'Dukedog' No. 9003 which is coaled and ready for duty. The ironwork in the left foreground is part of the column water tank at the east end of the up platform. 3rd August 1955. *Cyril Mountford*

Even in 1965 steam locos were still to be found 'on shed', and here 46521 stands over one of the outside pits at the west end of the shed. The building on the right, with a north-light roof, was the fitters' cabin and workshop. *Author*

Above: Machynlleth shed on 20th July 1951. *Below right:* The east end of the 'new' coaling stage, with wagons of loco coal standing on the 'Hoist Road' in the foreground, and railborne fuel tank wagons in the distance. *Photos: B. M. Barber and Author*

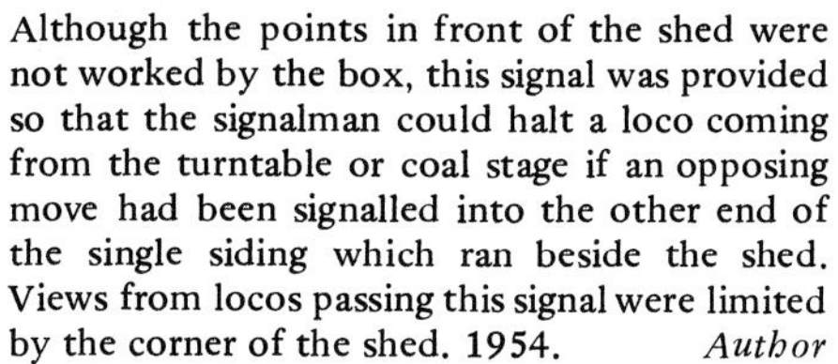

Although the points in front of the shed were not worked by the box, this signal was provided so that the signalman could halt a loco coming from the turntable or coal stage if an opposing move had been signalled into the other end of the single siding which ran beside the shed. Views from locos passing this signal were limited by the corner of the shed. 1954. *Author*

Locos took coal on the Back Road of the coal stage – a rather inconvenient arrangement because one loco could not follow another through. 1965. *Author*

A view from 'The Rock' down into the Upper Yard, showing the old Newtown & Machynlleth Railway goods shed. Latterly a dock (with awning above) had been added to the shed to allow the loading of road vehicles. The line of the hedge at the top marks the route towards Derwenlas of the former Corris, Machynlleth and River Dovey tram road. The old slate wharves can be seen at the top right, with the girders recovered from the old Corris Railway bridge across the River Dovey lying on the former Aberllefenni slate wharf. April 1953.

Gwyn Briwnant-Jones

The catchpoint at the station end of the 'Aberystwyth Road' (which lay between the down running line and the goods warehouse) and its associated point indicator, which was replaced by a ground signal worked from the box when the new signal box was commissioned. This picture was taken in 1954.

Author

of Western Transport. A scheme was drawn up at Swindon for a 15ft wide brick and corrugated-iron garage to be built end-on to the station on the demolished warehouse and for a similar garage and workshop on the site of the carriage shed. The garage was built entirely in corrugated iron and the garage and workshop building seems to have been made by demolishing the carriage shed and re-using the materials from this and the dismantled loco shed to produce a building with a three-centred roof. Both had pits.

The Great Western's next action was to close the Corris Railway to passenger traffic from 1st January 1931.

On 12th February 1931 the Civil Engineer received his committee's vote of £125 for repairing the verandah roof. This could not be completed within the twelve months' currency of the vote and he had to report back on 15th December 1932, both for the renewal of the original vote and for an additional £20 overspent. Meanwhile he had had to obtain authority to reconstruct the roof of the shed at a cost of £2,200 on 28th July 1932.

On 1st May 1933 some legislation, designed to rationalise bus services generally, resulted in Machynlleth yard becoming Machynlleth Sub Depot of Crosville, in which the LMS had considerable shareholding. So the much sought after bus service was left sharing the yard with the unwanted and declining Great Western goods service to the slate quarries and farmers of the Corris, but in alien hands and for only one year. In 1934

This photo, taken mainly for the detail on the rear of the loco tender, shows the southern face of the original N & M goods shed. *Author*

This grounded carriage body in the Upper Yard was taken by some to be a 6-compartment, 6-wheeled, third class, but was in fact 6 compartments of a former 8-compartment bogie third (as witnessed by the marks where there was the luggage rack). 1954. *Author*

The Upper Yard, viewed from 'The Rock' in 1965. The carriage body shown on the previous page had survived, but the goods warehouse (and beyond it the signal box) had been renewed. In the foreground was the breakdown train. To the right of the grounded coach body (used for locomen's mutual improvement classes) was the bicycle shed and then the messroom for loco and shed staff. The row of huts across the driveway from the coach body were (from left to right) the PW mess cabin, a tiny bill-poster's hut, the S & T office (with the old Corris Railway signal box behind acting as the locking fitter's hut) and then a larger pair of huts for the S & T plant and machinery workshops. *Author*

Looking east from the footbridge c.1960, with the goods warehouses standing out as conspicuously new. By this time there was no connection from the Warehouse Road on to the adjacent Aberystwyth Road – the crossover which had been roughly where the van is standing had been removed. On the right is the carriage dock. The height difference between the Upper and Lower Yards is evident here. Note the GWR pattern 6-ton crane in the Lower Yard. *K. G. Draper*

Looking north-west across the whole station site, with, on the right, the Lower Yard and the former Corris Railway station buildings visible just above the (flat-roofed) new signal box. The buildings near the end of the new goods warehouse included the timekeeper's office (where the men signed on), the shedmaster and shed foreman's offices and the loco stores. 1965. *Author*

A view of the Upper Yard in 1965, showing the steps to the new goods warehouse on the right and the breakdown train on the 'C & W Road' in the centre, with the turntable road to its right. *Author*

A view along the Warehouse Road to the carriage dock at the end, with a DMU stabled on the Aberystwyth Road on the right. The nearest huts were those of the S & T Department – beyond was the former Corris Railway signal box, and the bill poster's and PW huts. The round-topped shed at the far end served as a lamp room. 1965. *Author*

No. 7819 *Hinton Manor* barely fitted on the GWR-installed 55ft turntable – there was certainly no more than 9 inches to spare. A Class 4 4–6–0 could be turned if there was enough weight in the tender to balance the weight of the loco. (August 1953). By comparison, a 4–4–0 GWR 'Dukedog' No. 9020 fitted on the table with ease. (3rd August 1955.) These pictures remind us of an art which disappeared with steam – the careful inching of the loco until its weight was exactly balanced on the greased central pivot so that the runner wheels at both ends were just clear of the ring rail.
Photos: Cyril Mountford

A nice view of the 55ft turntable and its shallow pit, with 0–6–0 Collett Goods No. 2244 balanced for turning. 'Dukedog' No. 9000 stands on the C & W siding. The snowploughs stored between the two sidings had to be bolted on to the front of an engine if needed (no mean task in itself!).
Photographer unknown

Crosville moved its operations to a new sub-depot elsewhere in the town.

In 1934 a simple roof over the loco coal wagon siding was devised to keep some of the rain off the unfortunate firemen and yard men who had to fill the tenders by hand.

In 1936 a proper house for a resident Permanent Way Inspector was considered to be an essential and a detached house was built by William Humphries for £654 12s 6d in 1937. Other work in 1937 included raising the very low up platform to normal level (at a cost of £340) and a new waiting shed was provided on that platform at a cost of a further £130.

On 30th October 1942 the Great Western Board authorised the expenditure of £1,765 on additional siding accommodation, all most meticulously allocated between 'Civil Engineer £1,455, Signals Engineer £69 and Chief Mechanical Engineer £250'.

In 1943 F.W. Hughes & Sons gave notice terminating their tenancies of all the former Cambrian station

This picture shows the 55ft turntable in the Upper Yard, and the fuel oil storage tanks standing on an isolated siding under 'The Rock'. One of these was built on the frame of an old tender. The petrol pump in the foreground was for servicing the road motor lorries using the goods warehouse. *Author*

A typical line-up on Machynlleth shed on 2nd August 1953, with 'Dukedogs' 9028 and 9024, with 0–6–0 former Jones Goods No. 844 (Cambrian No. 15) and No. 849 (Cambrian No. 29) on the Ballast Siding. *Ifor Higgon*

refreshment rooms, and new terms were negotiated for them to continue at Machynlleth on payment of only 3% of the gross receipts.

On 28th May 1943 the Board authorised the raising of the level of the coal wharf (cost £175) and on 1st October had to authorise an additional £110 for surfacing it in concrete. In 1944 a PW hut was burnt down, costing £120 to replace, and in October 1944 the cattle pens had to be entirely renewed for £325. In September 1945 it was approved that £117 should be spent on improved office accommodation for the yard foreman.

The Great Western's last contribution towards Machynlleth's facilities was the new coaling stage authorised by the Board on 18th July 1947. A 55ft turntable was also installed to accommodate the larger 4–6–0 'Manor' class engines which had first appeared in 1943. One account suggests that this turntable had been

A view from 'The Rock', showing the west end of the Lower Yard (with the old Corris Railway building prominent in the centre) and the footbridge between the platforms. The 'pagoda' waiting shelter on the up platform was a GWR addition. 1965. *Author*

This slightly different view, taken a few feet from the photo above, reveals the 55ft turntable and the back of the station buildings. The hut next to the footbridge was for the yard foreman, and the light coloured building almost touching the foot of the stairway was the PW salt and weedkiller store. *Author*

Another view of the Upper Yard from 'The Rock', looking east towards the coal stage in 1965. *Author*

The Loco C & W van on the C & W Road, and a snow plough. *Author*

Looking across the turntable, to the former C & W shops, latterly used as the PW department offices. *Author*

A view from 'The Rock' above the station in 1965, looking westwards across the cattle pens and the Esso petrol unloading facilities later built at the end of the Pens Siding.
Author

Left & right above: The cattle pens were established in the upper yard in 1899 (see pages 18/19) so that cattle could be driven more easily from the market up the wide station approach road rather than under the road bridge and through the coal wharves in the Lower Yard. The concrete posts and iron railings shown were a more modern replacement. The oil depot behind the pens belonged to Bates & Hunt, the local distributors of Esso fuels. The three warehouses to the right of that were leased by BOCM.
Author

The facilities for unloading the Esso oils were limited but adequate. 1965.
Author

transferred from Aberystwyth but there had never been any necessity for a turntable there larger than 50ft.

By 1948 the Dovey River had damaged the Corris bridge (and in particular the approach embankment and abutment on the Machynlleth side) so badly that the narrow gauge line had to be closed. The last train ran on 20th August 1948 though happily the GWR put the locomotives into store from which they were subsequently resurrected for service on the Talyllyn Railway.

During the withdrawal of steam between 1964 and 1967 the original coal siding became the dumping ground for the unwanted locomotives, minus their number plates, awaiting removal to the breaker's yard.

Machynlleth is now the administrative, operational and servicing centre for Cambrian Lines which extend from Aberystwyth to Pwllheli and inland right up to

A photograph taken from the same location as that on the facing page, but looking in a north-west direction into the station approach road and yard. The square yard in the centre was used by the Permanent Way Department. The large building was the PW office, with a carpenter's shop behind. To the right of this was the PW Sub-Inspector's office. The structure with a flattish roof was the oil and grease store, with a small timber store alongside. The black shed beside the fence housed 'PW odds and ends' and the shed adjacent to it, and next to the BOCM warehouse, housed the PW Department's motor van. *Author*

The PW Department office and carpenters' shop. This is the 'large timber shed' brought from Aberdovey in 1925 (see page 27). The photographer was standing beside the pillars supporting the footbridge. 1965. *Author*

The station at Machynlleth was indeed an impressive one, as befitted Earl Vane's involvement in its construction. This 1949 view manages to cut out much of the clutter in the Upper Yard, which somewhat detracted from the elegance of the station building.
L & GRP, cty David & Charles

Sutton Bridge Junction outside Shrewsbury. The large stores and the offices of the foremen and their staffs occupy the warehouse and some smaller buildings house other components of the engineering, permanent way, and signals and telegraph organisations.

Running repairs and train servicing are carried out at the sheds which now consist of three pits in the open (where the Cambrian three-road shed has recently had to be demolished because of structural failure) but with a new concrete surface, and inside the original Newtown & Machynlleth two-road shed, again refloored in new concrete. All the coach interiors are cleaned and serviced and the driving ends are also cleaned externally. The work of Signals & Telegraphs includes the servicing of all radio electronic token block equipment in the cabs and of all the external radio installations.

Fuel oil is delivered by road tankers and a concrete apron has been laid down over the site of the turntable to facilitate turning round and discharging. The waste oil storage tank once standing on a wagon chassis on Pens Siding, is now inside a brick-walled container apron nearby.

The passenger station at Machynlleth is reached by a wide roadway leading up from the road which passes under the line at the west end of the platforms, by the bridge seen at the left of this photo. 1965. *Author*

The offices of the Line Manager and Station Manager and the booking office are housed in new brick buildings at the up end of the old station building. The scheme for converting the old station into a museum and art gallery was rejected by the planning authority and at the time of writing a fresh use for T. M. Penson's masterpiece is being actively sought.

The station building stands on the down platform and is seen here from the vantage point of the footbridge, with the solid Cambrian Railways awning covering just the area immediately in front of the building. As it was an exposed walk in the rain to reach the footbridge, it was hardly surprising that the Engineer was not impressed by pleas that the footbridge itself should be covered over! 1965. *Author*

Above left: The centre part of the building contained the entrance hall and booking offices. The wooden Victorian station letterbox on the left survived long after this 1965 photo was taken. *Above right:* The structure supporting the Cambrian Railways' station awning. 1965. *Author*

The west end of the building housed the refreshment room, with its bay around the doorway – very convenient for looking to see whether your train was approaching without going out into a storm! 1965. *Author*

The station on 17th July 1955, showing the full length of the building and the end of the West signal box, on the down platform just beyond.
T. J. Edgington

At the bottom of the footbridge steps was the tiny office of the District Inspector. Latterly he resided in the former station master's office at the other end of the station. 1965. *Author*

A roadside view of the eastern end station buildings in 1965. *Author*

Looking westwards from the station footbridge in April 1948, with the West signal box all but hidden behind the awning over the down platform. The slightly higher level of the down platform where it was extended across the road bridge can be seen. The waiting shelter on the up platform replaced the earlier one seen on page 19. *L & GRP, cty. David & Charles*

The tank was based upon a substantial six-ribbed casting. *Author*

The water tank at the end of the down platform and its 'fire devil' – a long-necked stove to try to keep the water in the tank and pipework from freezing. 1955. *Author*

A 1955 view showing clearly the extent to which the up platform (on the left) and the down platform were 'staggered'. The girders of the road underbridge can be seen in the 'six-foot' between the two tracks. *Author*

The up platform was 'staggered' way beyond that on the down line as shown in this photograph. The 'Aberystwyth Road' on the right was often used to hold connecting trains so that they could move quickly into the down platform when the main train had departed. The East signal box is in the distance. Note the post with arms for both up and down trains – there was not room for a post for a down line signal between the running line and the 'Aberystwyth Road'. c.1948. *P. J. Garland*

The up and down platforms were linked by this somewhat insubstantial footbridge, a structure which the Engineer decided could not support the weight of a roof over the bridge even if one were desirable. The West signal box can be seen beyond the station building. 1954. *Author*

Despite its use for many of the journeys starting from Machynlleth, the up platform was poorly provided with passenger shelter. The 'pagoda' shed was provided by the GWR to afford some cover which could quickly be reached from the footbridge in wet weather – of which Machynlleth enjoys its full measure. 1954. *Author*

A detailed view of the footbridge, and the clutter which inevitably seemed to accumulate beneath it. 1965. *Author*

Detail of the valve lever on the tank at the end of the up platform. *Author*

The waiting room – little more than a shed really, which the GWR erected on the up platform to replace an even smaller Cambrian building. 1965. *Author*

An up train taking water. The signal which is 'off' applies to the down line – not such an inconvenient arrangement since GWR engines were driven from the right-hand side. This view, taken in 1955, shows the Lower Yard full of wagons – what a change the next ten years were to bring! *Author*

The waiting room for the up platform was built on a foundation reaching back from the embankment. The footway down to the Lower Yard once bore notices beckoning passengers to the Corris Railway terminus, which was off to the right of this view. 1965. *Author*

The foundations for the waiting rooms were substantial. No danger of subsidence here! 1965. *Author*

The cart weighbridge in the Lower Yard, with the walkway to the up platform behind. The two Iron Mink wagons to the left were filled with stone and treated as buffer stops! 1965. *Author*

The entrance to the lower yard, with the abutment for the bridge over the road just visible on the right. The two tiny offices were for coal merchants – slate was handled at the wharves to their left. The building on the left was a store for the County Council. It is easy to see why the cattle merchants preferred not to try driving beasts to loading pens through such an extensive (and dusty!) yard. 1965. *Author*

Looking towards the entrance of the Lower Yard, showing the access roadway past the buffer stops at the end of the sidings. 1965. *Author*

The coal wharf in the Lower Yard, with the coal merchants' huts beyond and an Esso petrol tanker being unloaded to a road lorry. 1965. *Author*

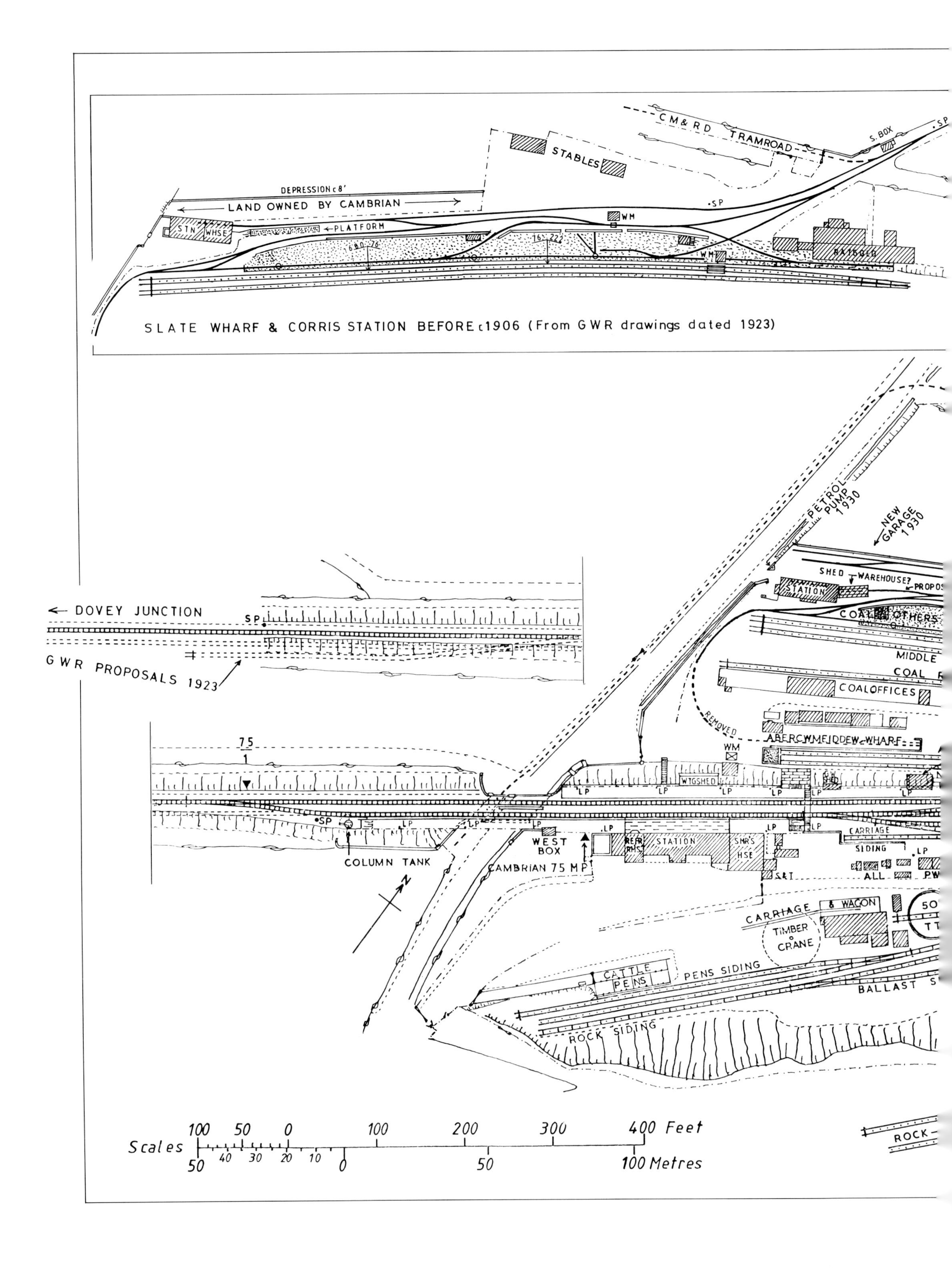
CM&RD TRAMROAD
S. BOX
STABLES
DEPRESSION c 8'
LAND OWNED BY CAMBRIAN
STN
WHSE
PLATFORM
WM
SP
SLATE WHARF & CORRIS STATION BEFORE c1906 (From GWR drawings dated 1923)
PETROL PUMP 1930
NEW GARAGE 1930
SHED
WAREHOUSE?
STATION
COAL & OTHERS
MIDDLE
COAL OFFICES
REMOVED
ABERCWMEIDDEW WHARF
WM
WTGSHED
LP
DOVEY JUNCTION
SP
GWR PROPOSALS 1923
75
1
SP
COLUMN TANK
WEST BOX
CAMBRIAN 75 MP
REFR RMS
STATION
SMRS HSE
S&T
CARRIAGE SIDING
ALL
PW
CARRIAGE & WAGON
TIMBER CRANE
CATTLE PENS
PENS SIDING
BALLAST
ROCK SIDING
ROCK
N
Scales
100 50 0 100 200 300 400 Feet
50 40 30 20 10 0 50 100 Metres

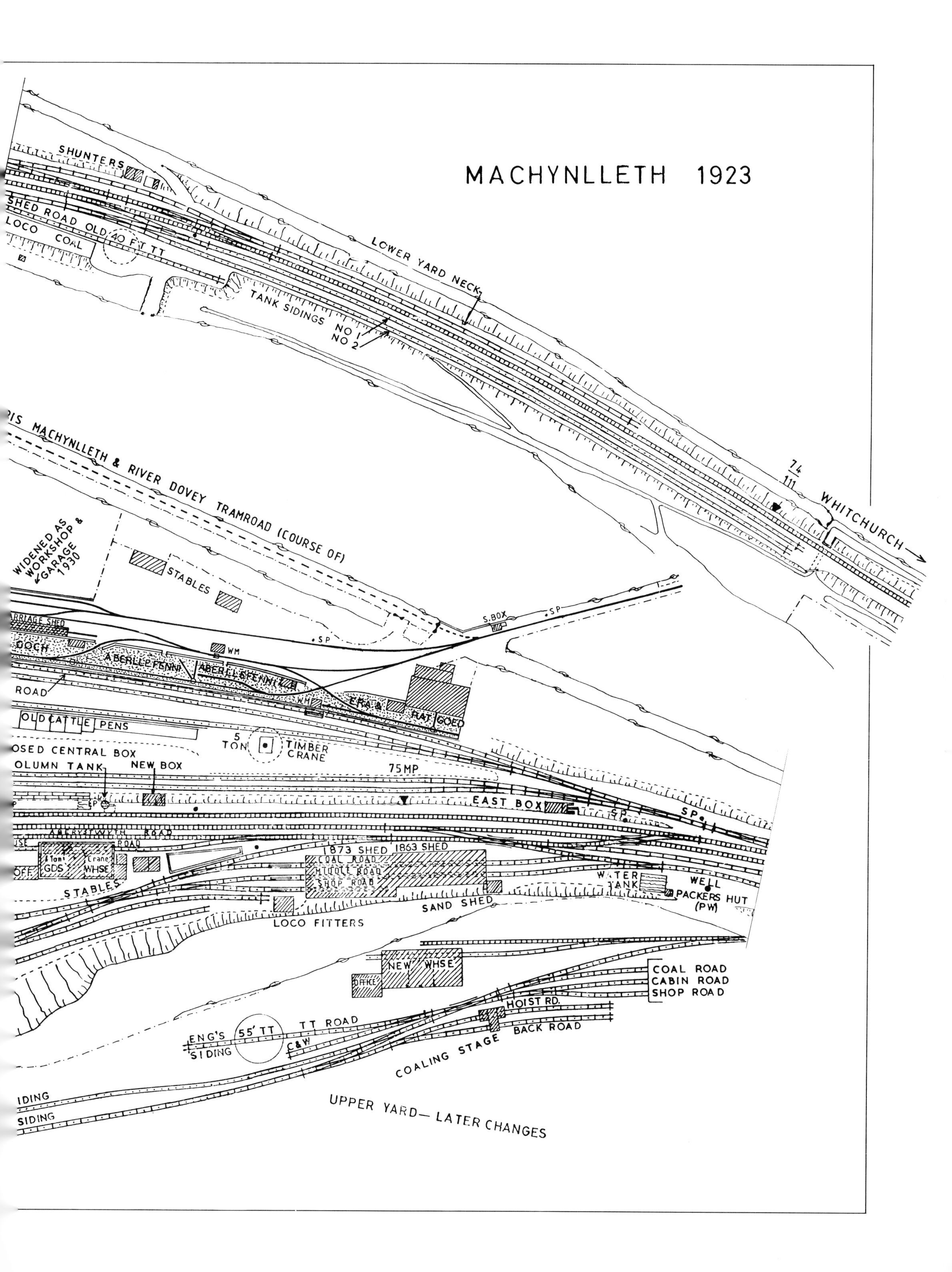
MACHYNLLETH 1923
SHUNTERS
SHED ROAD
OLD 40 FT TT
LOCO COAL
LOWER YARD NECK
TANK SIDINGS
NO 1
NO 2
74
111
WHITCHURCH
MACHYNLLETH & RIVER DOVEY TRAMROAD (COURSE OF)
WIDENED AS WORKSHOP & GARAGE 1930
STABLES
S.BOX
SP
WM
ABERLLEFENNI
ERA & FFAT GOED
ROAD
OLD CATTLE PENS
5 TON
TIMBER CRANE
OSED CENTRAL BOX
OLUMN TANK
NEW BOX
75MP
EAST BOX
ABERYSTWYTH ROAD
1873 SHED
1863 SHED
COAL ROAD
MIDDLE ROAD
SHOP ROAD
GDS
WHSE
STABLES
WATER TANK
WELL
PACKERS HUT (PW)
SAND SHED
LOCO FITTERS
NEW WHSE
OFFICE
COAL ROAD
CABIN ROAD
SHOP ROAD
HOIST RD.
TT ROAD
ENG'S SIDING
55' TT
C&W
BACK ROAD
COALING STAGE
IDING
SIDING
UPPER YARD— LATER CHANGES

This was the first glimpse that intending passengers crossing the footbridge from the down platform of the Cambrian/GWR station got of their connecting train on the Corris Railway – it seemed quite a long way off across the whole of the Lower Yard. Passengers had to descend from the footbridge (from which this photo was taken) to the up platform and then down a long sloping ramp to reach the Lower Yard. This view, taken c.1930, shows a bus standing at the entrance of the garage. In the foreground is the top of the GWR's 'pagoda' waiting shed on the up platform, and beyond are the two lines of the coal sidings, and the slate wharf road and slate wharf.

J. E. Kite

Corris Railway No. 4, built by Kerr Stuart (works No. 4047) and delivered on 10th June 1921, was purchased because of the poor condition of some of the company's other locos (Nos. 1 and 2 were withdrawn from service when the GWR took over in 1930). She is seen here on the run-round loop in Machynlleth station. As with most narrow gauge lines, the 'platform' was just a patch of level ground with a surface of rolled gravel and ash. c.1930.

H. G. W. Household

The rebuilt Corris Railway station c.1906, with a typical passenger train of two coaches and a brake van waiting to depart behind one of the company's 0–4–2 tank locos built by Hughes Locomotive and Tramway Engine Works Ltd. of Loughborough in 1878. The platforms of all the Corris Railway stations were on the same side of the line, so both the passenger coaches and the van had doors on one side only. The embankment by which the station area was raised above the level of the flood plain of the River Dovey is evident from the height of the slab slate retaining wall, originally constructed by the Newtown & Machynlleth Railway to protect its goods yard. The corrugated iron shed, which never served as a loco shed and may only have been used as a goods warehouse, is on the left. *Cty. J. I. C. Boyd*

29th June 1932, a year and a half after the withdrawal of railway passenger services and their replacement by buses. The former station buildings, into which the Corris Railway had moved its official headquarters, was now the offices of the bus organisation. Beyond is the new bus garage. *S. W. Baker*

Goods trains continued to run into BR days, and this photo taken on 29th June 1932 shows a typical short train of dumb-buffered wagons standing on what had been the passenger platform line at Machynlleth, awaiting the photographer's pleasure before departing. *S. W. Baker*

An 'after closure' view of the station on 9th June 1936 with rubbish beginning to accumulate on the single track in the station. Crosville no longer used the former carriage shed (with its unusual 'triple-curved' roof) as a bus garage. The buildings on the left were the stables of the Corris Railway.
D. W. K. Jones, cty. R. Humm

Over the years the GWR duly repainted the wagons of the Corris Railway and gave them its own numbering series. These metal-bodied wagons were amongst the largest (and heaviest to manhandle!) on the line. This rake of wagons is standing on the 'Goods Line' which ran behind (on the south side) of the garage and station buildings. In the foreground a siding rose from the level of the Goods Line on to the west end of the slate transfer wharf – note the old bridge rail still in use here.
J. I. C. Boyd

Looking westwards from the mid-point of the Corris Railway yard, with, in the left foreground, a siding ascending on a sharp curve to the Braich Goch Company's part of the slate transfer wharf. The building beyond was the former carriage shed erected as part of the company's remodelling of the station in the first decade of the 20th century, to provide covered protection for its new bogie coaches. This had been rebuilt to serve as a bus garage, the necessary widening (for Corris coaches were really quite narrow – only 5ft wide!) showing in the extra two curved roof panels either side of the original roof. To the immediate right of the carriage shed is the Goods Line, with a crossover on to the main running line. Beyond that is the run-round loop for the passenger station, with a trap point (and associated disc signal) worked by a ground frame out of view to the right. Prior to the 1905/6 reconstruction work, as part of which the running line and loop were added, the Goods Line seen here had been the line to the passenger station. *Hugh B. Tours*

No. 2, in a rather sorry state, stands on the short neck siding outside the carriage shed on 16th April 1927. This view shows the roof before it was altered to the form of that shown in the previous photo. The hut behind was the office of the Braich Goch Quarry Company.
Ifor Higgon

This photo, taken to show the East signal box and the eastern end of the loco shed, shows the line leading up to the Ratgoed Company's part of the slate wharf, and the siding on the wharf face.
Ifor Higgon

Transferring the heavy slab – these probably went for mantelpieces or engraving for tombstones – to a standard gauge wagon was no easy task. The Aberllefenni Company provided a crude fixed jib crane which required that the slate, once hoisted, be pushed over the standard gauge wagon, but plain manhandling was often preferred. Since the wagons had a fixed trestle at the centre, the wagon turntables were essential in allowing the wagon to be turned so that both sides could be unloaded. The clear division between the two parts of the standard gauge loco shed can be seen in the background, the 1863 shed on the left and the 1873 addition on the right. This photo was taken on 30th July 1948, less than a month before the flood damage closed the Corris line. *S. W. Baker*

Typical of the product of the Corris area is this slab slate, shipped ready for paving or cladding on buildings (Corris slate is not fine enough for use on billiard tables). This photo shows the manner of securing the slabs on a narrow gauge wagon — two poles (with suitable packing) tensioned together at the top. Aberllefenni wharf c.1948. *J. I. C. Boyd*

A nicely posed photo on the Aberllefenni wharf c.1930 (the date evidenced by the conversion of the former carriage shed). The gentleman on the left is David Owen, the manager, and third from the left is John Rowland Jones. The slate from the Corris area did not split easily into the roofing slate like that found in North Wales, and the cut slab stacked in these wagons was notably thicker. Note that the stub of the line to Ratgoed wharf, cut off by the addition of the standard gauge weighing machine, has been lifted. *Cty. David Wyn Davies*

The line up to the Aberllefenni part of the wharf crossed the siding to the part used by the Ratgoed Company, and then curved on to the edge of the wharf, past the hut which served as the company's offices. Note the 'stub' points leading to a short siding — no locomotives worked up to here! The derrick crane in the standard gauge yard was used primarily for loading timber. The extension to the office building was for a 'bucket and chuckit' lavatory required by Public Health Regulations. *Hugh B. Tours*

Looking eastwards from beside the ground frame controlling the loop line points, showing the main line on the left. Of the two arms on the signal post, the one facing the photographer protected the points round the corner forming the junction with the slate wharf line, and was worked from a signal box which is just out of sight. The other arm, viewed from the back, protected the points between the running line and the run-round loop and the goods line, and is believed to have been worked from the ground frame. The building in the foreground is the weighbridge office for the narrow gauge siding on the right. Beyond is the works of the Ratgoed Slate Company – the extension on the back may have been Lewis's dressing shed. The ornate signboard on the right stood on the part of the wharf used by the Aberllefenni Company and advertised its product. Behind that can just be seen the office for the standard gauge weighbridge situated on the slate wharf.
H. F. Wheeller

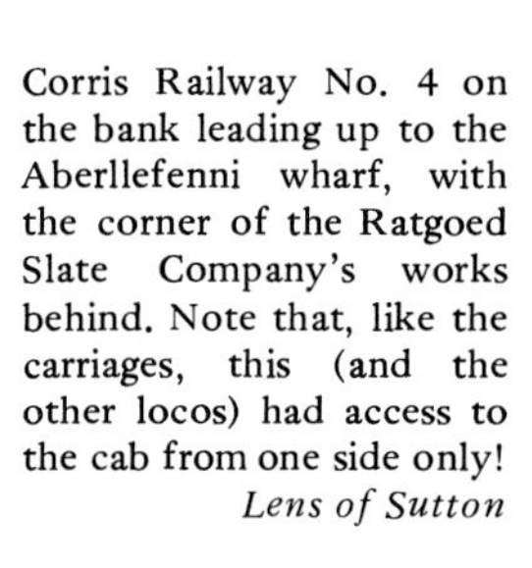

Corris Railway No. 4 on the bank leading up to the Aberllefenni wharf, with the corner of the Ratgoed Slate Company's works behind. Note that, like the carriages, this (and the other locos) had access to the cab from one side only!
Lens of Sutton

A view back towards the Lower Yard, with the Corris 'main line' on the right and the 'Goods Line' diverging to its left to run parallel around the corner. The connection adjacent to the trap point (and associated disc signal) at the end of the Goods Line led up to the Aberllefenni Company's part of the slate wharf, and disappears between the standard gauge weighing office (on the left) and the Aberllefenni Company's hut (on the right). The narrow gauge weigh office is behind the signal post on the right. The demolished building on the left was the former Ratgoed slab slate works. In the foreground, slate slabs and the check rails denote the occupation crossing at the end of the tramroad lane, which continued up to the shunters' cabin. Note the derrick loading cranes in the standard gauge yard. *Hugh B. Tours*

Looking north-eastwards from the Lower Yard, with the Corris line disappearing towards the bridge over the River Dovey. The signal box on the left was later moved to serve as a hut in the upper yard. The point disc is the same as that shown in the previous photo, and helps to link the two views.
Lens of Sutton

The Corris Railway 'signal box', on its slab slate base, was little more than a shed erected to provide some protection from the rain for the lever frame.

Looking eastwards from the footbridge c.1933, with 'The Rock' prominent behind the goods yard. The siding beside the goods shed, Aberystwyth Road, was used for the short-term holding of portions of Aberystwyth-bound trains detached from trains going on to Pwllheli, and for the overnight storage of empty passenger stock. The crossover to Warehouse Road was used for placing or removing wagons from the building. Locomotives were not permitted inside warehouses and the detailed shunting required for unloading and loading inside was done by horse or by shunter's pole levered between trunnions and spokes. Any driver 'puffing' through a goods warehouse instead of using a rake of stock to reach required vehicles (or at least stopping short outside) could find himself in trouble. This picture shows the much lower level of the main goods yard, and the extensive traffic in 'round timber'. *L & GRP, cty. David & Charles*

MACHYNLLETH TO DERWENLAS CROSSING 75m 09c to 77m 60c

NOTE *All mileages are from Whitchurch Junction and given as miles and chains.*

The end-on connection to the Newtown & Machynlleth Railway's terminus was about 130 yards to the east of the eastern buttress of the road bridge. Having established a small yard there, Savin would then have had to erect a temporary trestle bridge across the road (now the A487), and across a tram road before he could bridge the road permanently. In the artist's impression of the opening ceremony of the Newtown & Machynlleth can be seen, standing on the platform on the right-hand side, a bridge girder of Piercy's underhung deck design. The girders would have been jacked or levered up onto rollers and pushed into place across the trestle bridge. To the two bridges, the girder bridge across the road and a stone arch over the extension of the Corris tram road to Derwenlas, the Great Western added the two-span structure carrying the down platform extension across both, at the time when the loop was extended.

To account for the progress reported, Savin must have anticipated the official date for permission to take stone from the cliff face, and have got on with the construction of the embankment by using the tem-

2–6–2T No. 4599 at Machynlleth with the Pwllheli portion of the down Cambrian Coast Express in July 1956. *V. R. Webster*

porary trestle bridge. The terrain for the nearly-straight run to Derwenlas was not too soft, but has needed deep side drains and flood relief openings (which also serve as farmers' occupational ways).

Near to the 76 mile post (and to its south-east), a knoll projects towards the line; here, a ledge round the base can be seen, and this carried the tram road. The line then squeezes between the river and the hillside and, just at the point where the foreground opens out again, is the location at which a Mr W. Boynton asked for a siding to be built in 1916 for the carriage of a stand of oaks; he was willing to pay the £356 that the Cambrian asked for but, in the end, they were taken by road instead.

Machynlleth, looking towards Dovey Junction from the end of the up platform. The girder supporting the down platform is longer than that between the tracks because the bridge supporting the platform (provided when the GWR lengthened the loop) spanned both the road and the route of the erstwhile tramroad in one span.
Author

The venue for Savin's first two bridges. The old tramroad bridge on the right is much as he left it but Aberystwyth road bridge has been widened by cutting back the buttress on the left and replacing the bridge girders. The narrow gauge lines in the foreground were all that remained of the former curve of the Goods Line round to the wharf of the Aber-cwmeiddaw Slate Company.
J. I. C. Boyd

The first quarter of a mile of the Aberystwyth & Welsh Coast Railway looking north-west. The level of the flood waters shows how rapidly the line descended to the valley floor (actually more steeply than shown on Piercy's diagrams).
Cty. J. Scott Morgan

Waterlogged land around 75m 60c. September 1967. *Author*

The stretch to Derwenlas had to be flanked on both sides by deep drainage ditches with cross connections. In this view looking westwards, the signal is the up fixed distant for Machynlleth. *Author*

Red Lion cattle creep. The dual function as a drainage relief is clearly evident! September 1967. *Author*

Below: Nearer to Derwenlas. *Author*

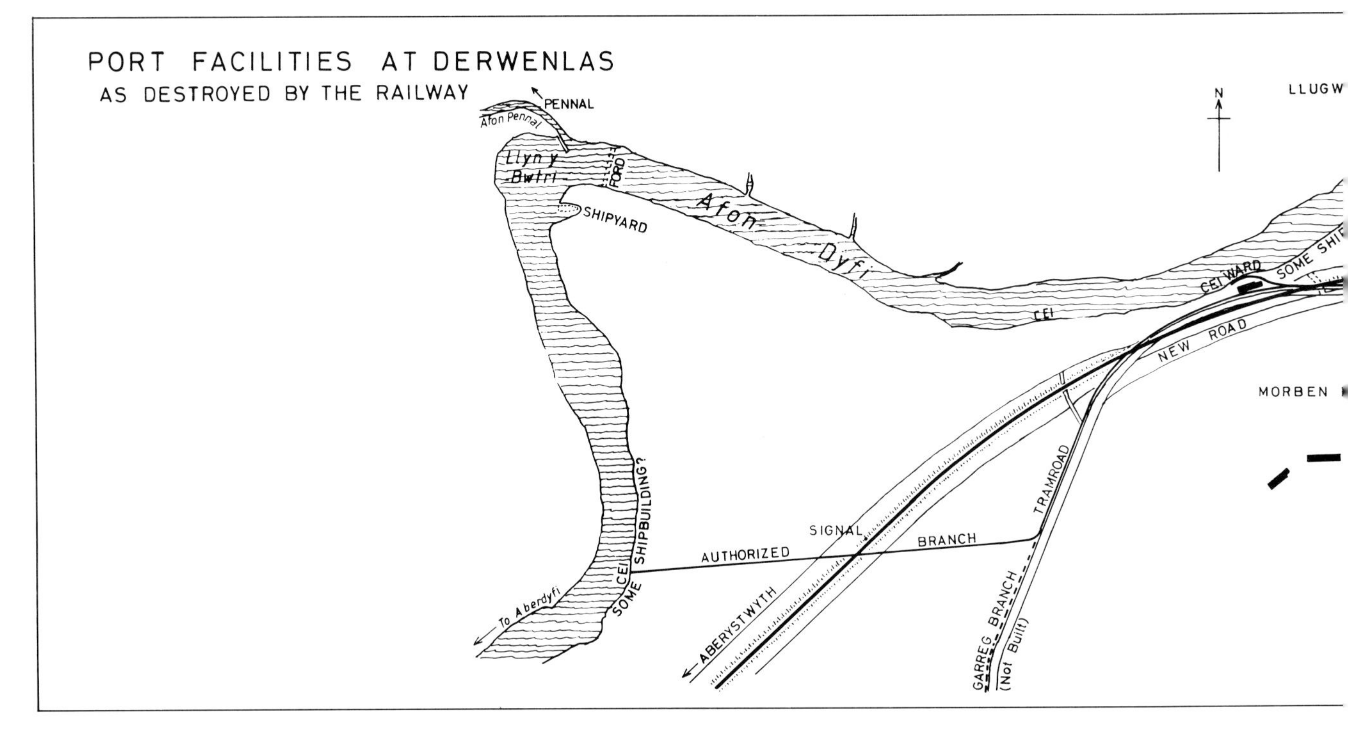

DERWENLAS

(Greenoak) – c.77 miles

Here, the railway curves gently across an open area, from which the village may be seen against the hillside, until the line crosses what appears to be a dried-up, semi-marsh area, which is in fact the old course of the River Dovey. Formerly, there was a full three-span timber pile bridge across the old exit from the artificial ox-bow lake formed by the diversion of the river by the railway builders. This cost the Great Western £325 to rebuild in 1926, but when it needed further work in 1962, the Western Region replaced it with three Armco pipes, as all major flow had long ceased. It was while working on diverting this section of river that the engineers convinced themselves that the great diversion planned at Glandyfi should no longer be attempted. In forming loops, rivers are reacting naturally into patterns dictated by width, depth, rate of flow, and by the viscosity of the water. No sooner had the engineer constructed the embankment than the restricted river took its revenge by carving three quarters of an acre off the opposite bank, land forming part of the Llugwy Estate belonging to a Cambrian director, Mr R. C. Anwyl. He plugged one of the erosion holes with one of the last two boats to ply from Derwenlas, and donated stone so that the Cambrian could make a good job of it. He had offered to give land as well, but somehow he seems to have received a nominal sum due to the legal situation relating to the transfer of ownership of land. Then, to counter the effects on the opposite bank of the reflex flow off Mr Anwyl's new groynes, the contractors had to make a long revetment, at a cost of £180.

THE PORT OF DERWENLAS

Derwenlas was a small but extremely busy harbour that was utterly destroyed by the coming of the railway. It had developed at the tidal limit of the river, as the inland port for Maldwyn (or Montgomeryshire). The merchants and traders had for centuries looked west to the sea for the movement of most of their goods,

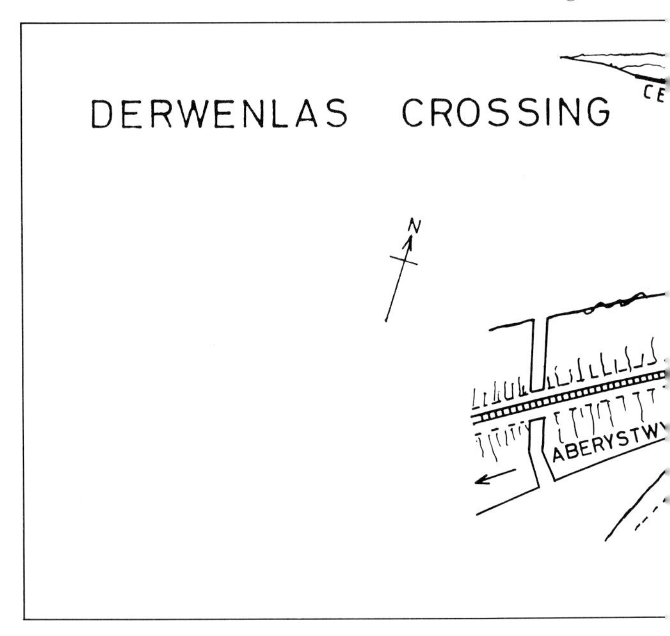

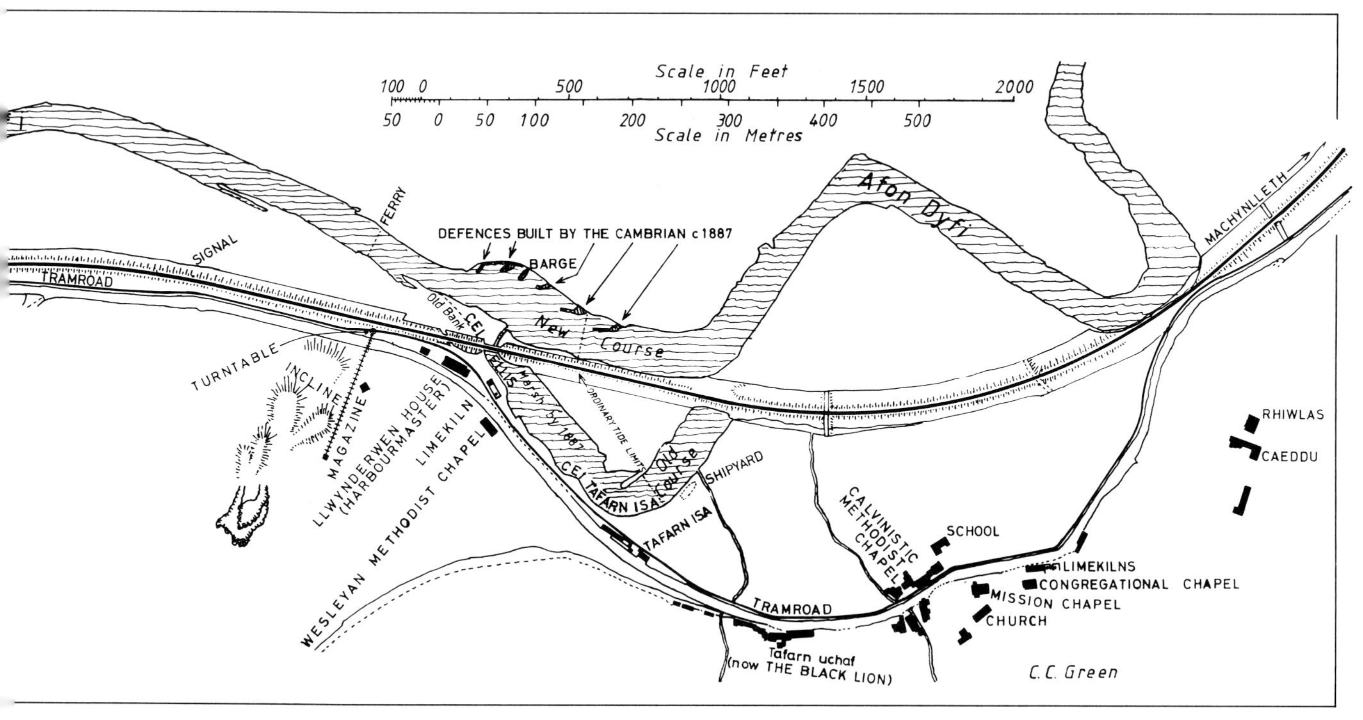

which were carried in small strangely-named craft – barges, dandies, flats, pinks and scows, few of which (if any) were rated at more than fifty tons. At the seaward end of their wind and tide-borne voyages lay the port of Aberdovey, which did a fair trade in transhipping cargoes between sea-going sailing ships and the little estuary boats.

The layout of the port can best be understood from a map. The village was effectively divided into three portions: at the north-east end stood Pentre Cilyn, housing most of the limekilns; the main centre, about the brook, was Pentre Nant, while Pentre Efail was located at the west end, where there was a smithy. The entrance to the port was by Tafarn Isa, which also gave its name to the first quay, Cei Tafarn Isa. Isa was short for isaf (lower), and the quay was so named because it was further downriver than Tafarn Uchaf (or upper tavern, which is now the Black Lion). Then came Cei Ellis, which may be the oldest of them all, and probably took its name from a quarry owner. Further round was the harbourmaster's house and office, of which part has survived as Llwynderwen

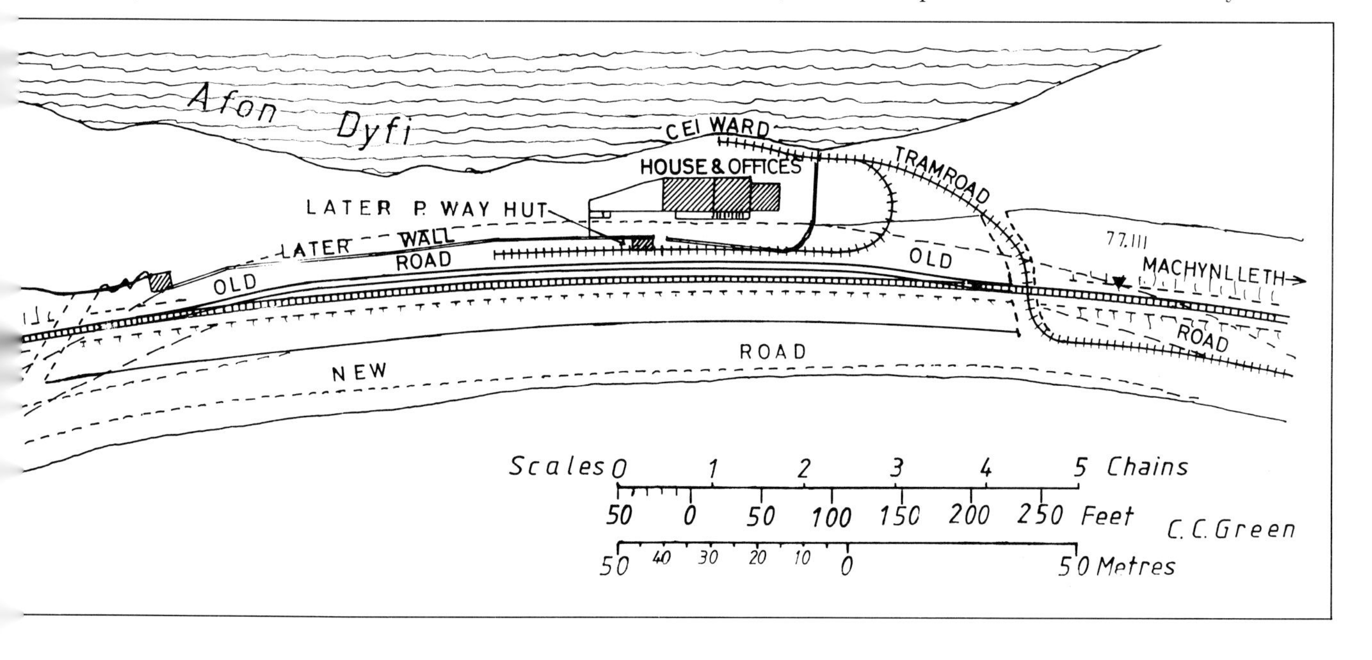

House. Just above Tafarn Isa there was a boatbuilder's yard, right on the tide limit. The later developments were sited further downriver.

Annually, up to 500 tons of bark (a by-product of shipbuilding and pit-props), 40,000 ft of timber, 150,000 oak poles for the mining industry, 1,500 tons of hard silurian slab slate, and around 1,500 tons of lead ore were despatched from these little mooring places. Inwards came 5,000 qtrs of rye or wheat, 1,000 tons of coal, 11,000 hides (English or imported), miscellaneous goods to the value of up to £14,000 and, for the limekilns, some 2,000 tons of limestone. These figures are as for 1847, and the limestone and consumer items would have grown by 1864.

When they saw the benefits that the railway would bring to them, those same merchants and traders abandoned the port in favour of the new technology; none worked to save it from being stamped over and cut off by the embankment, and the only argument was over the proposal to re-route the road between the railway and the river. Just one partly-completed boat was floated away to below Cei Ellis to be completed elsewhere, possibly near Morben Yard.

DERWENLAS CROSSING c77m 60c

Opened as Contractor's Yard in 1862.
Opened for Traffic 1st July 1863.
Out of use by 9th November 1886.

At Cei Ward was the terminus of the tram road down from Corris, and the railway had to cross the tramway on the same level. The railway company was required by its Act to avoid obstructing the use of the tram road by the horse-drawn waggons. Initially, the 'Coast' line promotors had tried to minimize the importance of the tram road by leaving it off the deposited plans west of Tafarn Isa but they were not allowed to succeed with so blatant a deception. To the west of the crossing, Savin put in a loop siding, on a down grade, with his second works yard.

A ground frame controlled signals and gates, and the line had to be closed every time a tramway driver turned up with his horse and waggon – a landborne equivalent of steam propulsion being obliged to give way to sail. The trackage drawn for the tramway is conjectural, but it could have worked as drawn. Other boats were built at the nearby Morben Yard, and larger ocean-going schooners were launched from the yard at Llyn-y Bwtri (Buttery Lake) – 'Llyn' was much used to describe the larger pools and reaches on Welsh rivers. There is local opinion to the effect that the tramway was laid to the Llyn y Bwtri yard, and it might have been extended to run along an embankment to another quay below Llyn-y-Bwtri.

The contractor's yard was in use by 1862, and there must have been more anticipation of the permission to remove cliff face at Machynlleth to make the embankments, for ballasting was in hand during February 1862. The shareholders left their meeting on 28th August 1862 thinking that the rails had nearly reached Borth!

After the opening of the line, the loop was used for crossing the short trains of the period. In a report of 19th January 1871, it was stated 'Already there is a signal box with all the requisites, signals etc. in which a man is constantly kept by the Company for the purpose of protecting the roads leading to the wharfs and shipbuilding yard'.

At that time, the gentry were considering the provision of a horse, carriage and cart ferry, and were asking for a station to be built (with platforms and an additional siding), which would have cost about £160. The engineer reported: 'If the Station were built no additional traffic would be placed on the line [it would have been in competition with Machynlleth] and it would be most objectionable being on a curve where trains follow frequently'.

As traffic increased, so did the use of the loop for crossing trains (instead of being used as a siding); accordingly, a block telegraph was installed in 1874, followed by a larger signal box in 1875, costing £111 15s 0d in all.

On 18th September 1876, the 0–4–2 Sharp Stewart Engine *Volunteer* on the 4.40 a.m. ex-Welshpool Down Mail broke a tyre and 56 cast iron chairs. The latter items cost £3 10s 0d to replace, and 'trains were thrown into confusion all day'.

In 1878, the tramway was formally abandoned. The crossing and gates had to be left for the use of the farmers, and on 11th January 1884 one of them left a gate open, and a horse strayed onto the line and was killed.

In the same year, the Board refused to erect a Flag Station, and in 1886 (a slump year) the traffic manager reported that he could save £60 a year if he could close the signal box. The loop seems to have remained for a short time, until a runaway at the downhill end of a loop siding elsewhere served as a warning, and the down (and downhill) end points were taken up.

On 28th November 1900 Doctor C. W. Jones claimed he was violently thrown against the side of the carriage on the bend at Derwenlas, and painfully injured his hand. After due legal argument, he was offered compensation of one hundred guineas (£105) to accept 'or to take what course he wishes'. Being a doctor, he was stated to be 'a man of good position whose evidence would have weight with any Jury', or so that other professional gentleman involved, the company's solicitor, stated.

Various repeated requests for a road, a footbridge over the river, and for stations or halts continued to be received. All would have been mainly at the company's expense, but nothing came of any of them, and Cei Ward settled down to being a private home with its own accommodation crossing.

There was one prominent feature not yet mentioned – the ganger's haystack. In a good year, by the end of the summer's mowing of the lineside there could be between six and seven tons of hay. Being of good composition, with a high proportion of wildflower admix (which would be more valued today than it was then), it brought the company £2 10s 0d per ton in the 1880s.

DERWENLAS CROSSING TO DOVEY JUNCTION 77m 60c to 78m 32c

The line leaves Derwenlas in a gentle curve to the south-west, running onto an embankment which traverses fairly solid ground. Almost immediately, it crosses a low causeway which was an authorised branch of the tram road, running below Llyn-y-Bwtri. Level with Morben-isaf, the line bends south to Dovey Junction, crossing ground which needed supportive brushwood rafting (as was used to cross the better-known Chat Moss). The only feature of note is a neat little occupational bridge at 77m 75c, although there are also three minor cattle underpasses which double as flood relief openings. Also level with Morben-isaf is a reach of the river with the delightful name Llyn-y-Draenog (Hedgehog Pool). There was a small landing stage at this location, and a small riverside tavern, too – crews of tide or wind-bound Derwenlas ships could leave them moored, row ashore in their tiny boats (which were always towed astern), and pass the wearisome hours until conditions mended.

Derwenlas Crossing and Cei Ward House, looking in the down (westwards) direction. The loop siding used in the era 1862-1886 commenced just beyond the occupation crossing (the site of the former tramway crossing) and ran through the location where the PW hut seen here was later built.
Author

Dovey Junction was typical of stations which serve as interchange points – short bursts of activity with long gaps between. In this scene, looking towards Machynlleth, a Coast line train (in the platform to the left) is connecting with one on the main line. Note the 'finger-sign' destination board and the fact that the interchange traffic was concentrated on the narrowest part of the platform. This was the place where, if the passengers were not extremely watchful, it would become a case of 'bed & breakfast in Aberystwyth and baggage in Barmouth'!

G. H. W. Clifford

DOVEY JUNCTION

78m 72c to 79m 8c (Coast loop to 79m 9c)
formerly Glandovey (Doveybank) Junction

An up short passenger train leaving Dovey Junction for Machynlleth. It was common to couple 'light engines' to trains to save on line capacity – always a problem on the largely single-track routes of the Cambrian Railways system. *Photographer unknown*

Junction at 78m 74c
Station at 79m 3c
Signal Box at 78m 78c
Opened 14th August 1867.

Glandovey Junction was always more of a passenger exchange point than a normal station, and has never provided a proper public road or footpath. It came into being when the Aberdovey deviation was opened on 14th August 1867. Frequently, secretarial staff were confused as to whether they were referring to Glandovey Junction or Glandovey station, barely a mile onwards.

The ground was extremely soft, and all structures had to be built on piles sixty feet deep to penetrate the peat. Even the platforms had originally to be of timber so as not to sink under their own weight.

Glandovey Junction was located on the western border of Montgomeryshire (Drefaldwyn), whilst a (later) up distant signal was in Cardiganshire (Ceredigion), with the bridge-keeper's house in Merioneth (Meirionydd). A modern map would show these points to be in Powys, Dyfed and Gwynedd respectively.

The first station had an inadequate shed, and so in 1868, the platforms were lengthened and a waiting shed brought up from Ynyslas. There was no accommodation for staff, who consequently had to travel to their place of work. On 25th January 1870, Pointsman (Signalman) E. Finchett, on his way home, signalled the train to start and while trying to jump into the van, fell under it, and was killed.

This accident brought about changes. The platforms were still considered to be dangerous, and were lengthened again. There was to be a signalman's house (on piles) as near to the signal box as possible [work never done!], and the old station was to become a waiting room with a ladies' W.C. and 'a small place for the Ticket Collector'.

In September 1871, the engineer was still reporting that the signalman had a mile to walk to work, and that 'no good Man will stay'. After a derailment of an engine and three carriages because the signalman was 'not sober' and had not lit the distant signal or the facing point indicator, the committee did approve the expenditure of £250 for the house.

A month later, the committee also agreed to the provision of 'a clock from a good maker, either from Mr Walker of Cornhill or from Mr Joyce at Whitchurch'.

NOTE

Glandovey should have been spelt 'Glandyfi' from the outset ('Afon Dyfi' is 'The Dark River').

In 1872, a wooden building (with verandah) to provide station and office accommodation was erected at a cost of £500; and the station master was sacked for poaching. After all, it was Sir Pryse Pryse's land; the site was extremely tight to the boundary, and someone was having to persuade him to sell the company a narrow strip for £1 so that the verandah at the west end would not have to be made narrower than the rest. There was also a strangely-worded piece of information 'that Mr John Edge Jones cannot have access from his proposed Refreshment Rooms onto the Station and when the line has been doubled from Machynlleth the trains will not stop at the Junction.'

In 1874, the engineer reported that the tides were getting higher, and that additional flood openings were needed in the embankment (which was sinking). The sum of £92 1s 9d was so spent, and was seen to be justified on 22nd February 1877 when a wind from west of south-west veered to a full Atlantic gale from north-west by north. This brought one of the highest

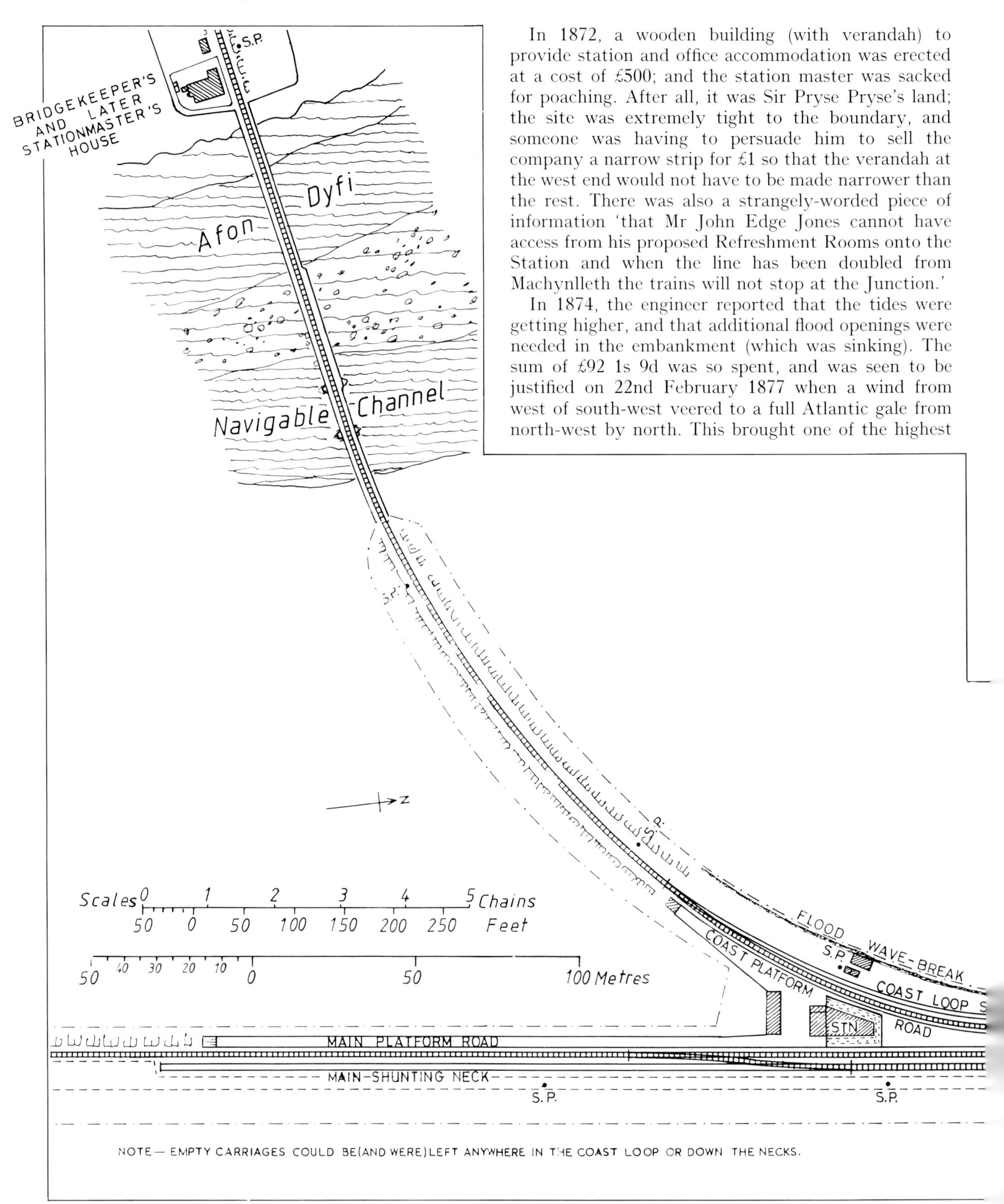

tides (if not *the* highest) then on record. The whole area was under water, lead sheeting was stripped from the roof, 'Signals were twisted like pieces of wire', and traffic was halted while debris was cleared off the line. Two hundred men were brought in for the task, and traffic could not be resumed for several days. The fences had been out of sight in places.

On 18th January 1878, a down train had forced an incorrectly-set pair of trailing points, and had broken the connection to the Stevens facing point indicator. The 0–6–0 engine on the subsequent 6.0 p.m. ex-Aberystwyth Up Mail jumped those points, and ran along the sleepers for nearly 50 yards, although the tender and carriages stayed on the rails. The station-master was reprimanded for leaving to attend his mother's funeral before his relief had arrived, and the latter was also blamed for not making himself familiar with the working of the points.

In 1881, the company spent nearly £100 to move the 'gents' into a separate building, and to 'throw out a Ladies W.C. into the General Booking Office', so as to make room for a refreshment room. The station then looked as it was to remain until the mid-1950s, with the rear verandah cut off, and several odd buildings tacked on. The refreshment room was let to one Charles Mytton, and opened on 12th October 1881.

Dovey Junction c.1900, showing the twin load gauges across the Coast loop siding and the Coast platform road, necessary because the tunnel clearances on the Deviation line to Aberdovey were more restrictive than normal. In re-touching this photo, the postcard makers placed a non-existent post right beside a rail on the Coast loop siding. The elaborate station nameboard was illuminated.
Author's collection

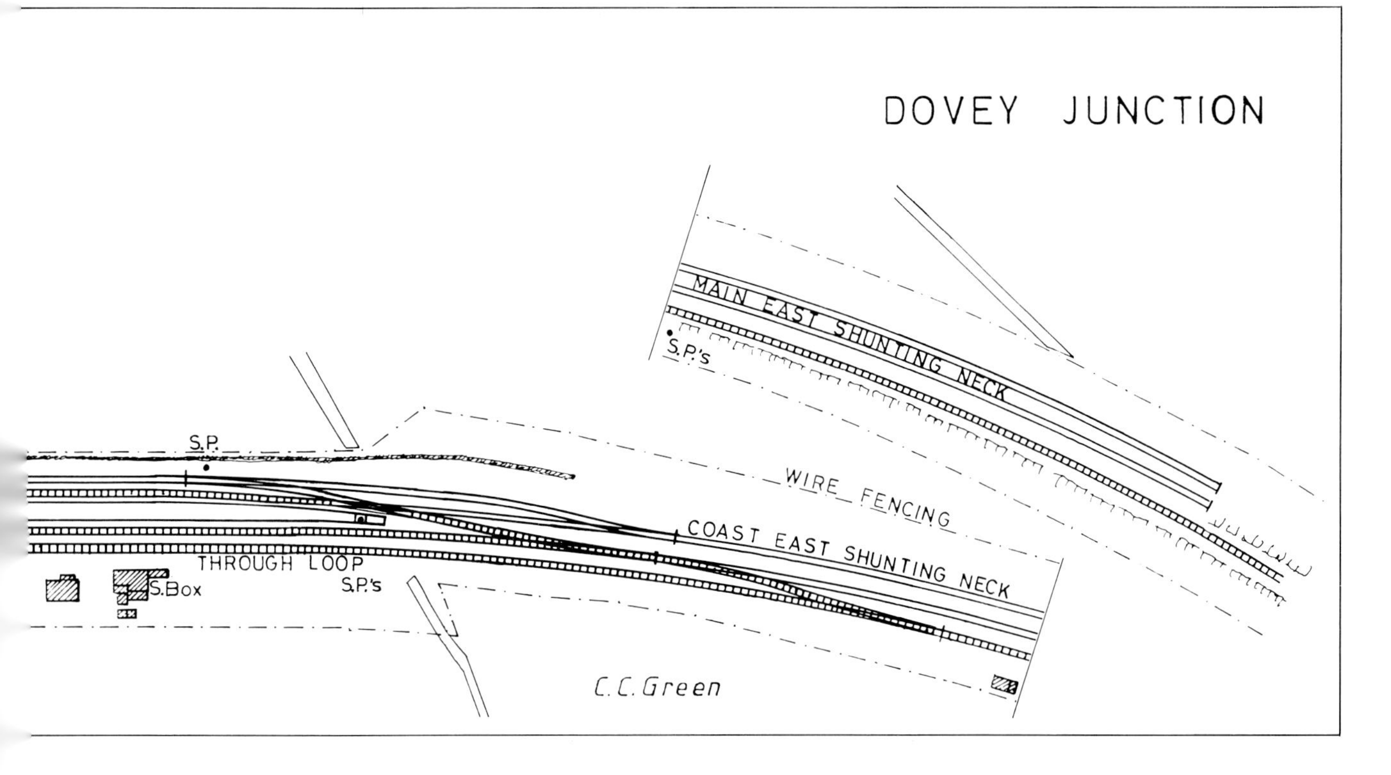

'Dukedog' No. 9016 running into the main platform at Dovey Junction with a down train bound for Aberystwyth on 25th August 1948. The branch platform line passed to the left of the Cambrian Railway trespass notice (the GWR painted out the Cambrian Railways name) and merged into the main line just beyond. Just to the right of the smokebox of the loco, barely discernible through the smoke, is the down home signal gantry. The 4—4—0 has not got '16 on'! The apparent length of the train reflects the fact that the branch sidings were often used for storing carriages, and, to avoid moving them every time another shunt had to be made, it was the practice to stable stored coaches hard on to the buffer stops. This photo thus reveals the great length of these sidings. The wave-break wall running right to the end of the sidings is clearly shown on the left. *H. C. Casserley*

The four-doll Cambrian gantry carrying the down home signals. By the time this view was taken (c.1936), the arms and balance weights had been renewed with GWR standard apparatus. The arms are (from left to right) 51, 50, 49, 48. No. 49 is 'off' for the train to run into the Coast (branch) platform line.
G. H. Platt

In 1883, a goods engine derailed 'for no ascertainable reason', and another high tide brought a foot of water over the rails. In July 1883, the committee approved the making of an approach road, but when information was given to them in February 1884 that it was going to cost £1,576 10s 0d, they went off the idea, despite reports that passengers were trespassing on private property and along the line to reach the station.

By the end of 1886, Messrs Spiers and Pond had the refreshment rooms and a spirit licence, and were asking for more room. It was also reported that there was a need to rebuild the (unsafe) platform, so that 'near the sea' the ends of the ramps 'came at the same place'. A luggage crossing and a gangway on the island platform could also be constructed, all for the sum of £528 19s 9d, which was approved. On 8th/9th December, another severe storm put the platform under water and took out miles of fencing. The Up Mail was stopped at Borth, and a down ordinary train was stopped at Machynlleth, the latter being sent back to Whitchurch with the carriages loaded with mail from Machynlleth onwards.

Around this time, the committee were being advised to approve the purchase of the new tablet instruments. These cost £70 each or £140 a set to have installed. There were already four 'Block Telegraphs' between Machynlleth and Glandovey Junction (which had cost £18 each), and 'which might be bought back by the Contractor'. On 27th October 1886, the adoption of a tablet system generally was approved and the use of tablet instruments between Dovey Junction and Machynlleth was authorised on 12th December 1886. The cost of the instruments came down to £100 per pair, and on 1st May 1888 John Conacher (the Secretary and Traffic Manager) reported that the tablet instru-

A view from the end of the platform at Dovey Junction in 1935, looking towards Machynlleth with the Coast/branch platform and loop line to the left. The bracket signal prominently in the foreground is the up platform starters 31/33/29/32/30. Note the very large spectacle glasses on No. 30 signal (a feature of only a few Dutton signals on the Cambrian Railways), the signpost beckoning to a rather uninviting footpath across the marshland as a 'Way Out' and the loading gauge atop the branch loop siding. *G. H. W. Clifford*

Dovey Junction station in 1956, a few months before the old Cambrian wooden station was demolished. The Coast line curves away to the right. The GWR signal with 3-way mechanical route indicator replaced the Cambrian multi-arm signal (26/27/28). *C. L. Mowat*

The signal cabin viewed from the main line platform in 1955. This box was provided in place of an earlier one which stood to the north (left in this photo) when the station layout was enlarged and resignalled as from 28th June 1890. By 1955 the failing foundations caused the box to sag in the centre. *J. J. Davis*

A detail view of the steps of the box in 1955. Deterioration resulting from 65 years service in this very damp location and with the failing foundations is clearly evident. The right-hand view shows the north (Machynlleth) end of the box. The bargeboard and finials characteristic of a Dutton-built signal box are clearly shown. The lamp illuminated ground-level token exchanges made after dark on the main through loop line. *Author*

A rear view of the box c.1955, showing a state of disrepair and lack of paint. Beyond can be seen the WR bracket signal (with route indicator applying to the Coast branch platform line, which had replaced the elegant Cambrian signal shown on the opposite page. *Author*

ments were working well, so he recommended that the old block instruments be transferred to the section from Llanidloes to Tylwch.

On 22nd October 1889, the general manager put in a report on the possible closure of the less remunerative stations, and mentioned the Junction, along with Glandovey. This did not, however, come to pass and in 1890 the engineer was advising further extensions to the platforms (required by the longer trains with six-wheeled carriages). In that year the platforms were extended at both ends, in connection with layout remodelling and signalling work needed to comply with the Regulation of Railways Act 1889. The signalling work was completed on 29th June 1890 at the (then quite substantial) cost of £3,651 0s 2d.

The general manager also requested authority to spend £341 on extending the shunting necks, but as money was short that year, it brought a visit from on high. Both the chairman and Mr Bailey Hawkins (who knew much better than the general manager) decided that it could wait, and it took until 9th May 1894 to get the needed approval. The Board of Trade inspection of the relocated points at the Aberystwyth end of the extended main through platform took place on 20th July 1894, so the work was done quickly, in time for the summer season.

On 10th September 1890, the engine, tender and brake coach of the 6.0 a.m. ex-Pwllheli up passenger derailed at the up coast facing points because Signalman G. Hamer got confused, and moved the points when the train was closely upon them. The new interlocking was not totally proof against such errors. He was suspended, and moved to less exacting duties.

The signal box, viewed from the Aberystwyth end. Most, but not all, of the woodwork absent in the photo above had been patched up. 1955. *Author*

On, 23rd March 1891, Foreman Edward Evans became the Cambrian's first casualty with the new-fangled tablet apparatus. He 'sustained a badly-wrenched arm when trying to take a Tablet from the Driver (sic) at an incorrect place when the Engine was going too fast'.

On 5th October 1892, the engine of the 4.0 p.m. ex-Pwllheli Up Mail derailed on facing points. Major Yorke suggested that the signalman had copied his predecessor and had moved the points, but the case was not clearly proven.

The Junction's first reported accident to a child happened on 14th October 1893. Seven-year-old John C. R. Williamson fell out of a carriage because of a broken doorlock spring, and was found unconscious by the side of the line. He was taken to the Londonderry Cottage Hospital at Machynlleth, and was out and about again three weeks later.

On 1st October 1894, the engineer reported that as business had so much increased, it was necessary to spend £35 on shelter work so that a door put in on the coast side could be left unlocked. It had to be kept

The up platform starting signals, seen 16th August 1935, with an up train leaving. Afterwards the train from which the photo was taken completed its run through the main loop to set back along main platform road. It was a complicated and time-consuming process to pass two stopping passenger trains at this junction! *H. F. Wheeller*

Dovey Junction station, Aberystwyth platform, looking towards Machynlleth on 15th January 1955, from a series of views taken shortly before demolition of the old buildings began. Inside there were watermarks up the wall, a legacy from, and record of, the many floods which had swept through this place.
BR Civil Engineer

Detail of Aberystwyth platform, looking from Machynlleth. *BR Civil Engineer*

The buildings seen from the 'Coast' platform edge, with a goodly collection of luggage trolleys to assist with the frequent transfer of luggage and parcels traffic at this busy exchange junction. *BR Civil Engineer*

A view looking towards Machynlleth along the Coast platform. Beyond the rather elegant (if now dilapidated) buildings shown above were this collection of ramshackle extension buildings. *BR Civil Engineer*

The down main starting signals seen in 1955. The top arms are 22 (on the left), reading from the main loop to main line, and 21, reading from the main platform to main line and Aberystwyth. The lower arms is 23, reading loop to shunt neck. In work done by Dutton & Co. for the Cambrian, much use was made of short cast-iron brackets to support arms for subsidiary moves (see the lower photo on page 79). *Author*

closed so that passengers could shelter in the passageway, out of the draughts. He also reported that 'the existing urinals which are now under the same roof as the Refreshment Rooms are quite unequal to the present requirements. Sir Henry Wiggin will sell 260 yds of land for £16 to enable alterations to be carried out.'

Power was obtained in the Cambrian Railways Act 1896 to buy the land for the missing access road, but when the engineer asked for the serving of Notices to Treat, they all had second thoughts and the powers were allowed to lapse. Local requests for the road were again passed over in 1898 so, in 1901, the locals made a request for a station at Gogarth instead.

In 1901, C. S. Denniss, the recently-appointed general manager, recommended closure of the station, or at least the cessation of the issue of tickets. He could save £236 per annum, and would need only two extra porters at Machynlleth. In his 'new broom' capacity he had a thing about trespassers, and was determined to eradicate them; but still they came flocking to the Junction over the bridge. Certain 'gentlemen' were grudgingly given passes, but ladies were declared 'not suitable to be walking along the line'; as for children and commoners, his attitude was 'under no circumstances'.

On 5th October 1901, notice was to be served on Pennal Parish Council that the station would be closed on 1st January 1902 unless the council would make a road from the west of the river to the company's boundary, and consent to the making of the Dovey River bridge into a fixed one. The company would then continue the roadway across the bridge to the station. The council would not make the road, so the booking office was closed, but the refreshment rooms stayed open for those passengers changing trains.

On 5th July 1904, approval was given for the station's name to be changed to Dovey Junction; thus, the long-standing confusion with Glandovey, just down the line, was ended. The latter station, too, was changed, to Glandyfi. After one fatal accident to a

A view of the rear of the same signal, seen from a train departing for Aberystwyth, with the signal box in the middle distance and beyond that coaches parked in the branch sidings. *Author*

An up train from Aberystwyth arriving at Dovey Junction. The platform had been extended beyond the loop points (No. 17) in the foreground, a significant improvement undertaken by the GWR (compare with the signalling plan on page 88 for an idea of the pre-extension length of the platform). Before coming to a stand, the arriving train pulled past signal 14 (seen 'off') into the platform beside the station buildings, for the convenience of the passengers. The extended platform meant that if necessary a short train could draw in to the platform up to 14 signal, do all its 'station work' and then be signalled into the loop line to cross a down train. 15th January 1955.
R. C. Riley

signalman porter, the Junction remained quiet until the permanent way gangs moved in during April 1911 to use up £139 4s 0d by extending sidings.

In 1914, the inhabitants asked for the Junction to be reopened as a passenger booking station. On 31st January 1916, an awestruck station master reported sighting an airship, but it must have been 'one of ours' from the aerodrome at Anglesey.

The long extension of the platform towards Aberystwyth had been virtually unused for some time, so in 1919 the Engineer was authorised to dismantle it and re-use the timber in repairs to the remaining platforms, and elsewhere. In 1921, the tablet instruments were moved into the signal box (a recommendation of the report into the tragic accident on the Cambrian, at Abermule on 16th January of that year), and a full time signalman was appointed.

As soon as the Great Western took over, they started putting the station into better shape; on 5th July 1923 their civil and signal engineers were authorised to lengthen and raise all the platforms, (including the reinstatement of the long platform on the Aberystwyth side), and to improve the layout and signalling. In all, they spent £17,800.

After that, Dovey Junction was as well maintained as was needed, but with two innovations. The rough stone wave-break wall was laid down for £120 in 1926, and a reasonable footpath from Glandyfi was surfaced for £177 in 1929. Another job read 'repair lavatory and

A rear view of the up main inner home signal, seen again and more fully described overleaf. *Author*

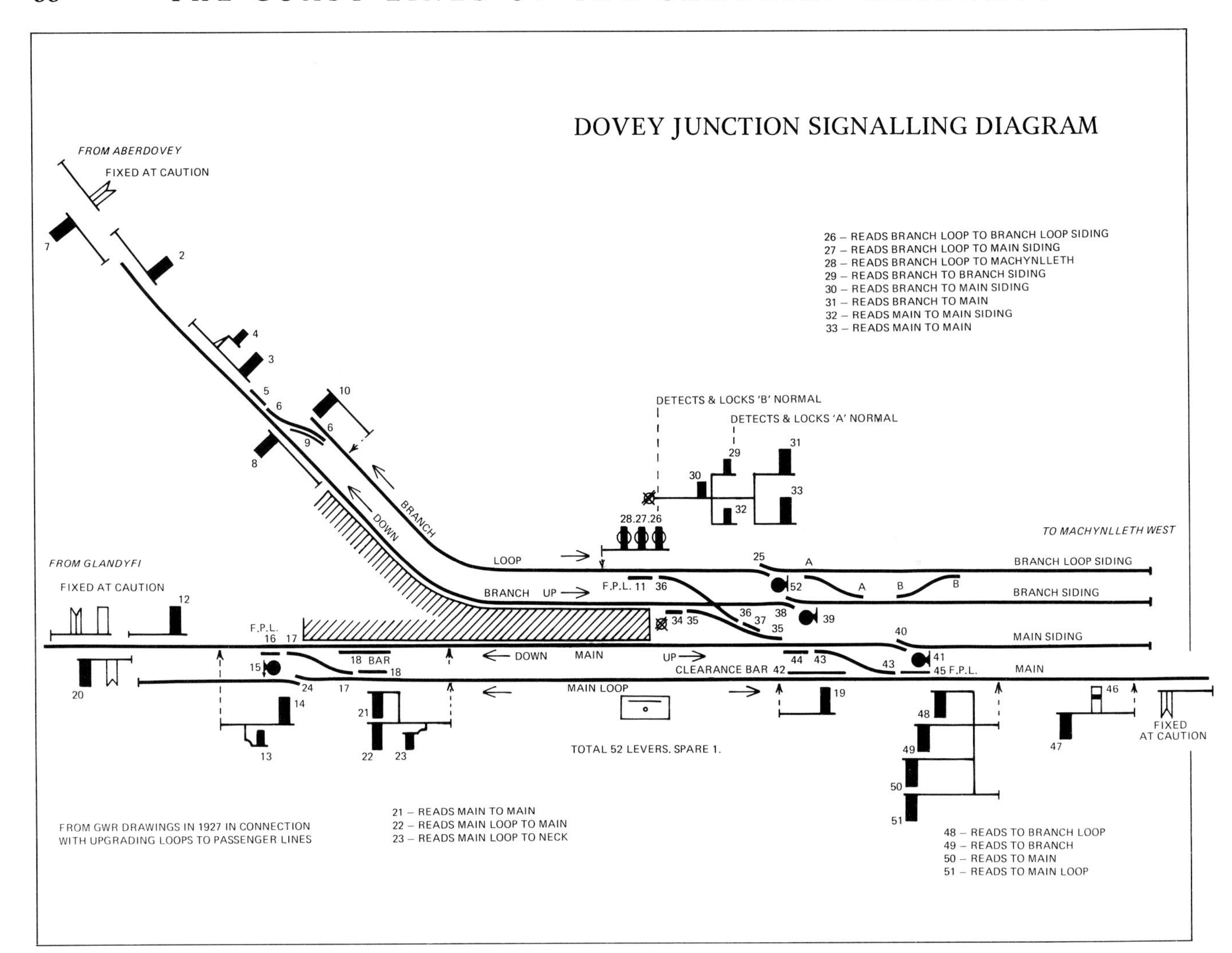

reduce in size'. In 1943, F. W. Hughes, who had succeeded Spiers & Pond in the refreshment rooms, surrendered the lease; it was taken on by George Meehan (who was also a coal merchant).

During 1955 and 1956, the Western Region demolished the old, decaying wooden buildings (which had served for more than eighty years). The platform was completely rebuilt in the form of a box 'floating' upon the bog, and on this was erected a Western Region pattern signal cabin and the triple set of less decorative, but more comfortable, modern flat-roofed 'shacks' for passenger accommodation.

Dovey Junction survived the 'Beeching closures' of 14th June 1965, and carried on with little or no change until May 1986, when the coast loop and the sidings disappeared. The final simplification took place over the four days following 29th April 1988, after which only the two lines against the faces of the platforms remained, and these diverged from one set of points sited nearer to Machynlleth on slightly higher land where the electric point mechanism is less likely to be damaged by flood water. In effect, the points were installed at the Machynlleth end of the main siding shunting neck. The signal box was closed on 21st October 1988, and control of the signalling at Dovey Junction transferred to Machynlleth signal box. The way was clear for the 'Sprinters'. Certain trains still stop for the transfer of passengers between the Aberystwyth and Pwllheli lines, and more use of Dovey Junction instead of Machynlleth for this purpose is planned.

Working Notes

To ease work and to speed the handling of passengers at Machynlleth, the staff of Dovey Junction inspected tickets on at least five up trains and six down trains, and collected tickets for Machynlleth.

Down trains were ordered to go cautiously under the load gauges across coast main and coast loop lines, which were set to detect loads out of gauge for the Aberdovey tunnels.

A Rule Book of 1871 stated that engines from Aberystwyth should give one whistle when approaching, and carry one white light on the

The up main inner home signal arms 14 (upper) and 13. 14 read from the main line to the platform, and 13 into the loop. The post has the slender taper and neat unostentatious cap associated with Dutton signals on the Cambrian, and a conventional arm for 14 signal. 13 signal, however, has the massive (nearly square) spectacle glasses also used on signal 30 (see page 79) and was mounted on one of the short cast-iron brackets.

G. H. W. Clifford and Author

No. 7822 *Foxcote Manor* on the down Cambrian Coast Express minus its headboard, as so often happened during British Rail's 'spoil the image of steam' campaign. Note the Great Western style three-arm and indicator bracket which replaced the old Cambrian signal. April 1959. *Author*

buffer beam. Up trains on the coast line were ordered to give two whistles, and to carry a green light on the buffer beam.

Following the large-scale revision caused by the enforcement of the Regulation of Railways Act 1889, as shown on the signalling diagram dated 1st July 1890, a full scale whistle code was introduced. So far, the following codes and variations are known, and there would no doubt have been more.

WHISTLE CODES

1903

MAIN LINE.	
To and from Aberystwyth on through Platform Road	1 Long
To Western half of Platform through Loop ...	1 & 1 Crow
To West Shunting Neck from Loop	3 Short
From West Shunting Neck to Loop	4 Short
From Main Line Platform to Main East Shunting Neck and *vice versa*	1 Crow
From Down Main Line to Coast Loop Siding ...	3 Long
COAST.	
To and from Aberdovey on through Platform Road ...	2 Long
From Coast Platform Road to Main East Shunting Neck	2 Crows
From Coast Platform to Coast East Shunting Neck	1 Short and 1 Crow
From Loop Siding to Up Main Line	5 Short
From Loop Siding to Coast Shunting Neck ...	6 Short
From Loop Siding to Main Shunting Neck ...	4 Long
From East Shunting Neck to Coast Platform	2 Long and 1 Crow
From Coast Shunting Neck to Coast Platform	3 Long and 2 Crows
From Main Shunting Neck to Loop Siding	2 Long and 2 Short
From Coast Shunting Neck to Loop Siding	3 Long and 3 Short
From Up Coast Main Line to Coast Loop Siding ...	2 Short 1 Crow

1943

MAIN LINE	
West Shunting Neck to Loop and vice versa	2 and 2 short
Main Line Platform to Main East Shunting Neck and vice versa	1 crow
Down Main Line to Coast Loop Siding	1 and 1 crow
COAST.	
Coast Platform Road to Main East Shunting Neck and vice versa ..	2 crows
Loop Siding to Up Main Line	4
Loop Siding to Coast Shunting Neck and vice versa	2 and 1 crow
Loop Siding to Main Shunting Neck and vice versa	3 and 1 crow
East Shunting Neck to Coast Platform and vice versa	5
Coast Shunting Neck to Coast Platform	1 short, 1 long

The BR (Western Region) signal box seen during construction in August 1958. It was brought into use on 21st February 1959. *Author*

There was electric bell communication between the signal box and the station, the bell being under the verandah on the coast side.

1903

"Be Ready"	1 Beat
Down Train from Machynlleth put on Section ...	2 Beats
Up Train from Aberdovey put on Section ...	3 ,,
Up Train from Glandovey put on Section ...	4 ,,

1943

Down Passenger Trains when leaving Machynlleth ..	2 rings.
Up ,, ,, ,, ,, Aberdovey ..	3 rings.
Up ,, ,, ,, ,, Glandyfi ..	4 rings.

A rule of 1943 allowed the setting back of one train towards another stationary train under the personal supervision of the station master or person in charge, with hand signalling in fog or falling snow by 'a competent man who knows where the rear of the stationary train is'.

Whilst the coast loop was nominally reserved for goods trains, coast passenger trains might pass along under supervision.

DOVEY JUNCTION TO GLANDYFI

79m 08c to 79m 43c

The up approach to Dovey Junction from the Aberystwyth direction, looking across the Llyfnant bridge in 1963. The standard WR tubular post signals were installed in connection with the new signal box in 1959, replacing the elegant (and unusual) Dutton arms. *Author*

After crossing the Llyfnant (Calm Stream), the line continues southwards on the straight course which started at the Junction's main line, though over some quite shaky ground. Standing on the path made by the Great Western, one could feel the whole formation dip and rise again as the 108 tons of a 4–6–0 'Manor' class engine and tender pounded by, followed by the minor tremors from the carriage bogies. Level with the village of Garreg, the line curves westwards to run between the river and an outlier of Craig Caerhedyn, which is named Y Garreg (the rock). Some hold that Garreg took its name from a rock in the river.

The dashed line on the map on page *vi* , which cuts straight across from the approach curve to Dovey

Llyfnant bridge, west elevation, showing detail of a typical low timber trestle bridge, and cattle fence in the stream bed. 1963. *Author*

Dovey Junction, viewed from the roadway which runs above Glandyfi station. The nearest signal is the down home for Glandyfi whilst the junction lies in the middle distance with the bridge over the River Dovey visible. The floods get a lot worse than this! *G. H. W. Clifford*

Junction to the continuation from Ynys Edwin, shows the route as it was intended under the original 1861 Act. Any attempt at making formation was abandoned after only the topsoil had been stripped, and not a vestige of this work is now visible at ground level. However, it is clearly revealed on aerial surveys as a long band of different vegetation. By the time the engineers were considering the problems of diverting a massive flow of water, and of keeping it to a straight course, with a long, high and heavy embankment laid on top of spongey ground, they were experiencing other difficulties in containing the less scouring, flailing flood they had diverted at Derwenlas. When one looks at the enormous catchment areas drained by Llyfnant, by the Einion, and by the Alice, now added to the main flow of the Afon Dyfi, it is not surprising that they had to give in and go for a deviation.

By 1896, the Llyfnant pile bridge was in a bad way, and £19 4s 0d was spent in rebuilding it. In the Cambrian bridge survey of 1915, its condition was set down as 'poor' and, despite the need for economies in

4–4–0 'Duke' No. 3255 *Excalibur* piloting an up train out of Glandyfi c.1933/36. *G. H. W. Clifford*

wartime, £100 had to be spent on a full rebuild. The Great Western left an interesting note: 'Cantilevers from the original Railway Bridge 1930'. These timber bridges are extremely strong in small units and, unlike girder bridges, are repairable by replacing single beams or even by splicing a new piece into an older one.

GLANDYFI

(79m 43c to 79m 68c) formerly GLANDOVEY (meaning Doveybank)

Station and signal box, looking towards Dovey Junction from the up platform in 1963. *Author*

Station at 79m 60c Signal Box at 79m 57c Opened 1st July 1863 Closed 14th June 1965

While first appearing in records as Glan Dovey, this station was to have been named Garreg, and appears so on Crutchley's anticipatory Railway and Telegraphic Map of South Wales (1862). Traffic was never very great – a little slate, some timber, not much lead ore (if any), and the farming requirements of the Gogerddan and Ynys-hir Estates.

The first constructional item to be noted in the company records was of £15 being spent on 'an additional platform' (probably the first piece of timber staging on the up side), and in 1871, £50 was spent in lengthening (probably the down side). A reference to £729 related to an additional waiting room, a platform, two porters' cottages and an embankment. The structural work was completed by April 1873.

During August 1876, in the 9.10 a.m. ex-Aberystwyth up goods, an L & NWR wagon dropped its side door, tipped over, and was dragged for half-a-mile to the detriment of 90 chairs and 12 fishbolts costing £6 15s 6d. The driver and guard were out of favour for not having noticed the problem sooner.

On 12th August 1878, John Davies and Robert Jones were journeying from Dinas Mawddwy to Towyn to visit an agricultural show. They missed the change of train at Glandovey Junction and jumped out of the 4.40 a.m. ex-Welshpool Down Mail. One was recorded as having been rendered 'insensible', and the other as 'cut about the face'; both were taken on a light engine to Machynlleth.

In May 1877, there was a reported irregularity in staff working. Thomas Williams, driving an up train, stopped outside the loop before shunting, and walked to speak to Driver Plumb of the down train halted in the loop. Williams forgot to give his staff to the station master, the station master forgot to ask for it, and he let Plumb drive away to Ynyslas without it. Plumb and the station master were both censured and suspended pending the decision of the Board, and were severely reprimanded.

In 1883, the traffic manager reported the need for 'more room', and in 1885 the engineer gave his estimate as £45 14s 0d for 'bringing out the front', whilst cattle

Looking up from the yard in 1963. The loop had originally ended adjacent to the occupation crossing over which the lady is strolling, which gives a measure of the extent by which the GWR extended the loop in 1923/4. *Author*

The rear of the station, taken from the adjacent road in 1963. The wooden-built shed with a sloping roof to the left of the station was the former signal box re-used as a store hut. The 'running-in' board was intended to tempt walkers to alight for the Llyfnant Valley. *Author*

pens, a slate wharf and an extension of the siding accommodation were added for £157 19s 2d. This work left the station building and yard pretty well as it was until closure. In that same year, there was a minor derailment on the curve of a timber truck which had been 'too lightly bound'.

In 1887, the old wooden station in use as a lamproom was set on fire 'through the carelessness of Porter S. J. Pearce'. He had dropped a lighted match onto the floor with the intention of putting it out, but had forgotten, and went away to light the down distant signal instead. A disused shed was brought down from Glandovey Junction to replace it.

In 1888, the engineer reported on the advisability of installing interlocking (by a wire system) on the ground frame and the signals, but the committee deferred the suggestion. On 28th August, a flash flood from a summer storm blocked a culvert and the water came over the rails, causing traffic to be suspended.

The traffic manager reported on 22nd October 1889 on the possibility of closing the station; and this after giving approval to a resignalling and interlocking scheme between Glandovey Junction and Bow Street to meet the requirements of the Regulation of Railways Act 1889. However, his report saved the station:

> 'Glandovey Junction and Glandovey are only 59ch. apart but the business could not be concentrated at the former unless a road 1089 yards in length were constructed from the highway, and sidings were laid out on the boggy land at Glandovey Junction. Besides it would be necessary to raise the Line at Glandovey Junction above the highest flood level. The interest on the cost of these Works, and their maintenance, would amount to a great deal more than the sum which could be saved by the closing of Glandovey Station, and we think any change is at present impracticable.'

Looking through the platforms, in the 'down' direction from Dovey Junction, and showing the two long pieces of timber shoring up the waiting rooms on the riverside (up) platform. 1963. *Author*

Signal box and station building from the Machynlleth end. 1963. *Author*

2–6–0 No. 6370 on an up passenger in August 1957. *P. J. Garland*

The up platform shelter. 1963. *Author*

Detail under canopy of up waiting rooms. Although this was, by any standard, a small rural station, better passenger accommodation was provided on the up platform than at Machynlleth, including a separate ladies waiting room. The all-timber construction suited the poor foundations available. *Author*

So the station was retained, and provided with interlocked signalling (controlled from the old cabin), brought into use on 20th April 1891, at a cost of £261 18s 7d. By the late 1880s, Glandovey had become a tourist station, but the trips into the hills beyond were subject to the running of rival tours by coachmen plying out of Machynlleth.

In 1899, the river bank was piled and reinforced at the suggestion and request of the agent for the Gogerddan Estate, at a cost of £100; and it had to be heavily repaired again in 1903, when another £120 was expended.

The committee voted for a change of name, to Glandyfi, in May 1904.

The increasing length of trains brought about another lengthening of platforms in 1910. In 1913, a tablet irregularity was dealt with extremely severely by the dismissal of the station master after twenty-five

A view across the station yard from the roadway above. The bridge over the Afon Dyfi on the Aberdovey line can be seen in the background. *Cyril Mountford*

GWR 4–4–0 'Duke' No. 3283 *Comet* waiting in the loop with an up train and a full head of steam. 16th August 1935. *H. F. Wheeler*

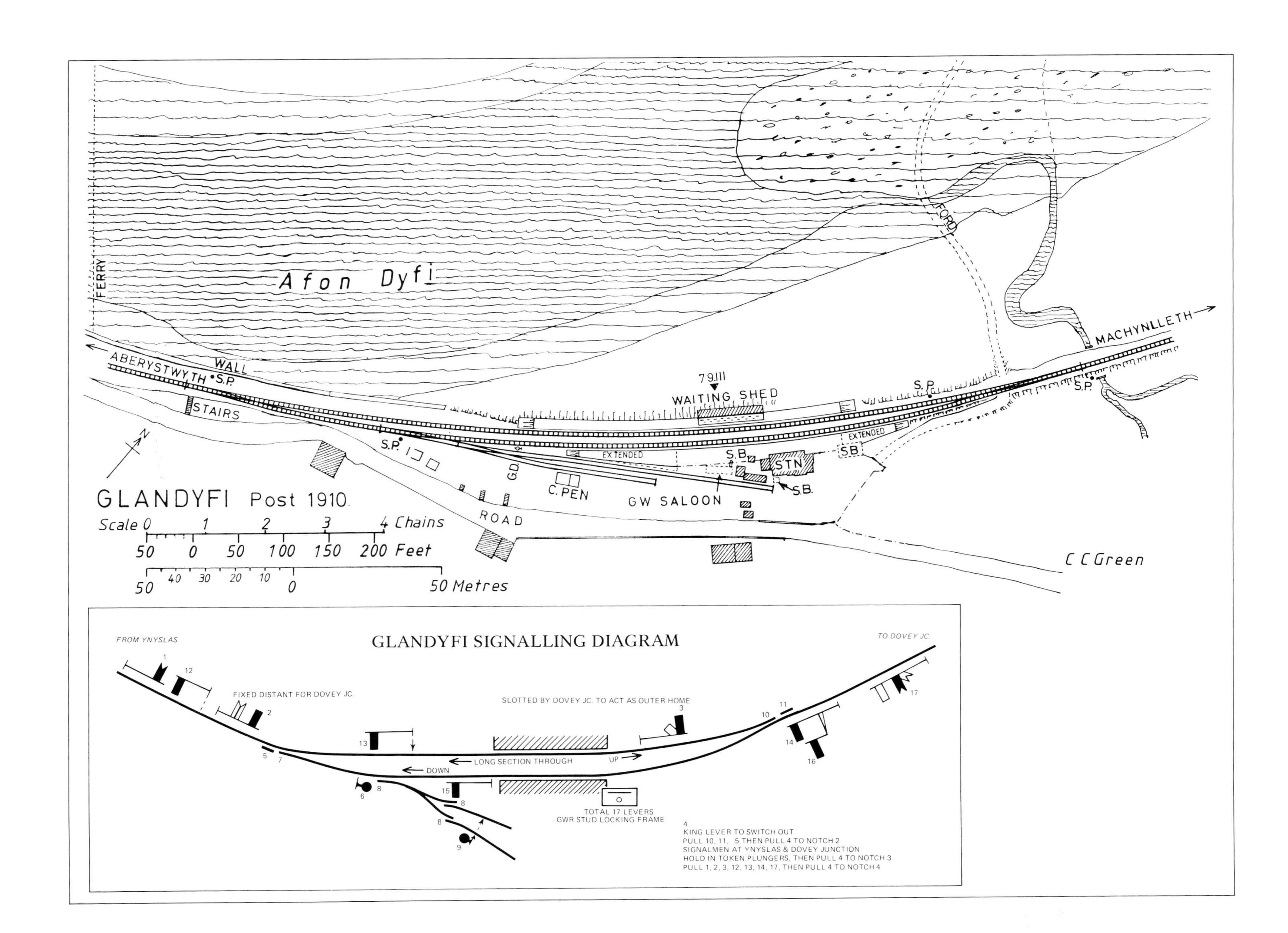

FERRY
Afon Dyfi
FORD
MACHYNLLETH
ABERYSTWYTH
WALL
S.P.
STAIRS
79.111
WAITING SHED
EXTENDED
S.B.
STN
G.D.
C.PEN
GW SALOON
ROAD
N
GLANDYFI Post 1910.
Scale 0 1 2 3 4 Chains
50 0 50 100 150 200 Feet
50 40 30 20 10 0 50 Metres
C C Green
GLANDYFI SIGNALLING DIAGRAM
FROM YNYSLAS
TO DOVEY JC.
FIXED DISTANT FOR DOVEY JC.
SLOTTED BY DOVEY JC. TO ACT AS OUTER HOME
LONG SECTION THROUGH
UP
DOWN
TOTAL 17 LEVERS
GWR STUD LOCKING FRAME
4
KING LEVER TO SWITCH OUT
PULL 10, 11, 5 THEN PULL 4 TO NOTCH 2
SIGNALMEN AT YNYSLAS & DOVEY JUNCTION
HOLD IN TOKEN PLUNGERS, THEN PULL 4 TO NOTCH 3
PULL 1, 2, 3, 12, 13, 14, 17, THEN PULL 4 TO NOTCH 4

The yard, looking in the up direction, showing the miniscule cattle dock and the Nissen-style hut on the right. The 'Duke' and its train were stabled apart because the longest siding was too short to hold a four-coach train and an engine.
G. H. W. Clifford

The yard, looking down, showing the original signal box, now a store shed, on the right. Both sidings had been shortened and provided with stop blocks consisting of nothing more than upturned rail chairs. The grounded coach body seen below had been removed. 1963.
Author

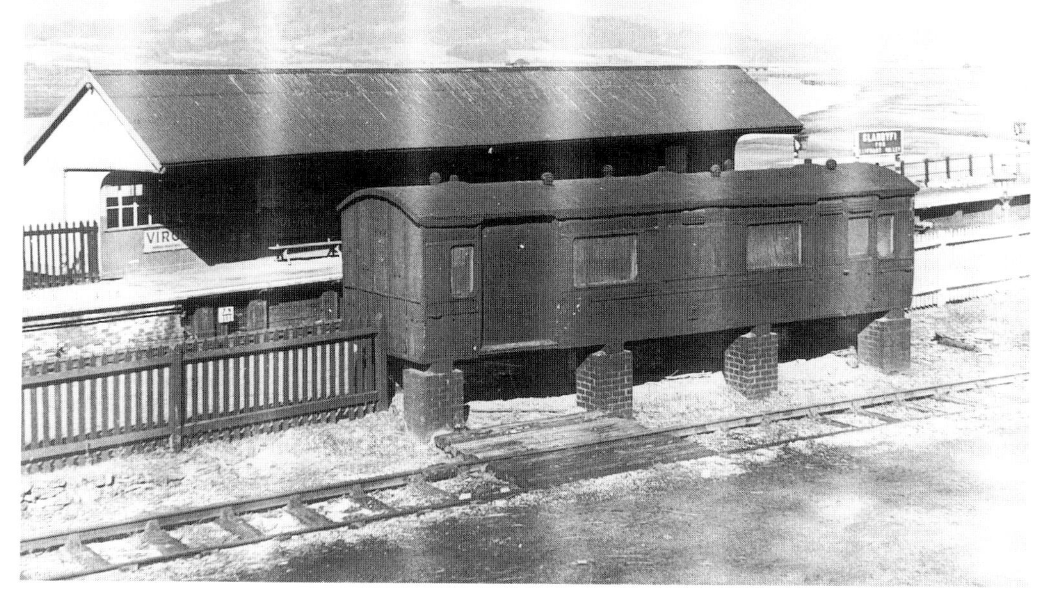

A GWR saloon used as a store shed c.1956.
P. J. Garland

A view across Glandyfi station, again taken from the roadway above, looking 'up' towards Dovey Junction. *P. J. Garland*

years service. The board refused to pay him the pension which he had nearly finished earning, but in view of his long service, they did award him £25. With much local support, he tried in vain to get himself reinstated.

In the early 1920s the Great Western perceived that there was a growing postwar boom in holidaymaking, and in anticipation, the loop was lengthened considerably towards Dovey Junction. The chief civil engineer was authorised to expend £1,800 on trackwork and the signal engineer £1,600 on a new signal box and resignalling. Part of the up platform and the retaining wall along the river bank were also rebuilt for another £1,650. The Cambrian had recorded in 1921 (after the Abermule disaster) that the tablet instruments were in the station because the signal box was too small (it was still the original Dutton structure), and that there was only a part-time signalman. The changeover between that old box and a temporary one had taken

Children on the wall of the roadway above the line, watching the fishermen on the River Dovey below. This view looking towards the junction shows signal 13, the 'wrong line' starting signal for the down direction from the up platform at clear, revealing that the signal box was 'switched out'. Both of the signals near the camera had concrete posts, which were extensively used by the GWR (on a trial basis) for the new work done in 1923/4 at Glandyfi and Aberystwyth. 1963. *Author*

place on Tuesday, 28th March 1922, and trains had been flagged through from 7.30 a.m. until 5.15 p.m.

The Great Western's policy of rescuing weighbridges replaced by new units at more important locations and re-using them at the newly-acquired stations, brought a 14ft x 8ft 15-ton cart weighbridge to Glandyfi, for which the capital 'charge' was £110 in 1924; the following year, they had to spend another £66 in putting right the defective manner in which it had been installed!

In 1931, signalling and trackwork were altered again at a cost of £660. It is believed this was in connection with adding facilities to allow the signal box to 'switch out' of circuit when not required for traffic purposes. In 1932, more of the up platform had to be retimbered at a cost of £120, and in 1936, loads of block stones had to be tipped onto the river bank to check scouring, at a cost of £500.

Working Notes

Drivers of up trains were instructed in 1903 'to run cautiously through the facing points'.

To relieve staff at Machynlleth, the tickets of two up trains daily were examined and tickets for Machynlleth collected.

In a good year, the yard would be holding a small stack of hay.

By 1963, Glandyfi was staffed only between 10 a.m. and 5.30 p.m.; freight in full truckloads, and parcels, was diverted to Machynlleth from 19th March 1963.

The public notice given out of one of the horse brake trips of the 1890s read: 'Llyfnant Valley, Glaspwll Cascade and Cwmrhaiadr Waterfalls by kind permission of Sir Henry Wiggins Bart. and Mrs T. Owen. From Glandovey by Road Conveyance to Cae'rhedyn'.

In 1928, goods and parcels were collected and delivered by porter, for whose services an additional charge was made.

Detail of embankment and road walling, looking down river towards Ynyslas. There was no fencing between the river and the railway here, so what constituted 'trespass' was a very moot point. 1963.
Author

A public stairway from the road above gave access to the river bank where the construction of the railway had cut across long-standing rights of access. The down starting and up home (with distant for the junction beneath) both stand 'off', for the box was switched out on this Sunday in 1963. Note the long bar inside the rail, working with the facing point lock, to prevent the points being unbolted once a train had passed the up home signal. The weight reducing slots in the concrete signal posts show up clearly.
Author

South-westwards from Glandyfi, the line crosses the Afon Einion on a timber trestle and then runs across what is now the Ynys-hir Nature Reserve to a rock cutting and Ynys-hir bridge beyond. The distant signal is the up distant for Glandyfi. 1967. *Author*

Cottage bridge, Afon Einion, showing another form of bracing used on very low timber trestle bridges. 1967. *Author*

GLANDYFI to YNYSLAS

– 79m 68c to 85m 00c

Leaving Glandyfi, the trackbed runs on a ledge, tightly squeezed in between the river and the road, which had to be pushed back to make enough space for it. A gentle curve takes the line westwards across the outfall of the Afon Einion, on over another timber bridge, thence the line runs across flat land to cut through the ridge of Ynys-hir (long island). Once in the open again, it curves back to its generally south-western trend to skirt the south bank of the Dovey estuary. In good weather, this is a fine scenic run with views of distant mountains on both sides, but close to the line it is comparatively featureless for we are on the Cors Fochno, also known as Borth Bog. Once dangerous and useless, it was drained and given flood defences before the railway came, and was put to use mainly as grazing. In rain or mist, and often in both together, it is a grey, mysterious land indeed; in high winds, it is the permanent way men's idea of purgatory.

Here, the construction of the line was delayed for more than a year as ton after ton of stone was tipped, and sank out of sight in the watery peat underlay; it was not until someone had the brainwave of layering sheep fleeces into brushwood to make a raft that any progress was made.

All the viaducts had to be deep-piled. Exactly how deep is not precisely known, but there is a point in such a construction when the friction between the timber and the peat precludes further driving, and the flotation tendency of the timber results in a slight buoyancy; heavy swivelling barbs affixed before driving commenced, rotated outwards, and locked themselves like arrow points. Then the raking cantilever beams were bolted on to bond each row of piles into one rigid structure, to which civil engineers have given the term 'bent-' or 'pile-frame.'

The elasticity of timber viaducts matches the natural spring of land such as this, and none of them have been rebuilt in steel or in concrete. Originally there were five such structures on the Cors Fochno, but three have been closed in; the two that remain are the three-span Pil Lodge over Afon Ddu (Black or Dark River) at 82m 48c, and the seven-span Tre'r-ddôl over Afon Cletwr (83m 31c).

Impressive flood bank and drainage work is visible along this next three-mile stretch of almost straight line. Having crossed Pil Lodge and Tre'r-ddôl viaducts on the way, the direction changes to a more westerly course at 83m 77c. On the south side of the bend once stood the ganger's house, $1\frac{1}{4}$ miles along the line from Ynyslas, or a two-mile walk via the track and along the dyke flanking Afon Cletwr, to the main road, a village store, and the nearest inn. There was no garden, for nothing but bog and sea grass would grow. Whether a married couple ever lived there, or whether it was a job kept for single men only, is not known. Life there can never have been remotely comfortable, and even the drinking water had to be brought from the station.

Another half-mile of straight brings us to the two alternative sites for 'Penmochno Junction', which would have been the location where the line to Aberdovey (across the great embankment) would have left the main line had it ever been built. Looking north, on a clear day, one can see the unattainable Aberdovey; we can imagine that huge $1\frac{1}{4}$ mile-long embankment stretching away across the Traeth Maelgwyn, blocking

Occupation way 30ft west of Cottage bridge. This was probably the route taken by Mr. Paddock's tramway (see page 106). 1967.
Author

Detail of tidal check and fencing on the north side (facing Afon Dyfi). When a serious high tide threatened, sandbags could be stacked on the cap stones to anchor the timbers down. 1967.
Author

The up distant signal for Glandyfi, with the occupation way and Cottage bridge beyond. *Author*

the tidal flow in fine weather, and causing tremendous floods in foul.

After a gentle curve,. crossing the erstwhile Black Pool and Brickyard viaducts, Ynyslas is reached. We have traversed one of the railway's most troublesome stretches. The painstaking researches and seismic surveys carried out by Messrs D. J. Blundell, D. H. Griffiths and R. F. King have shown that, in places, truly solid ground lies beneath up to three hundred feet of aqueous peat. There is a modern tale of a contractor who had a JCB delivered on site here for work next day – it is said that all that could be seen the next morning was the tip of the bucket in a pool of dark brown water.

The project to build and maintain a railway across this vast bogland area was ambitious indeed. Of course, everybody knew at the time that it would have been an impossible and unnecessary task to have built that great viaduct across to Aberdovey, and the truth of the matter was that it could not have been built with the money and equipment then available. Savin's former partner, David Davies, said that 'he could never see the necessity of it', but for a brilliant example of the heavy pontification of his time we might well look to Edward, Third Earl of Powis, who has been quoted as saying that when they saw the 'Crimean campaign' they seemed about to be engaged in against the sea, he thought it would have been very much to the advantage of the Welsh Coast line, if, on the formation of the Board of Directors, they had been put through

Ynys-hir road bridge, looking up. The double track formation was indeed the result of an over-optimistic vision of the possible success of the railway. 1967. *Author*

The outlook in the down direction past Ynys-hir to the flatlands of 'Borth Bog', the Cors Fochno. 1963. *Author*

a series of questions in early English history, and their engineer had been directed to report to them on the maritime events of the reign of Canute.

As to the maintenance of the line after it was opened to traffic in 1864, the engineer wrote on 23rd June 1869 that 'Gorsfochno embankment near Tre'r-ddôl is in a poor state. The Railway runs along it for $\frac{1}{3}$ of a mile and then keeps north of it.' On 18th December 1873 he reported the abandonment of another great and impossible scheme, that for the construction of a reclamation embankment stretching from Ynys-hir to the tip of Twyni Bach, which had been under consideration since before the line had been built.

In February 1877, after a severe storm, he had to report that 'the ballast is partly or wholly washed away, in many places it is perfectly wrecked. The Bridge near Ynyslas shifted because the Drainage Commissioners had sited the sluice for Gorsfochno enclosure

Looking down from milepost 81 showing how the formation has become an effective flood barrier despite the company's original refusal to make it so. 1992. *Author*

As the railway towards Dovey Junction curves to the right towards Ynys-hir road bridge, there is a line continuing straight onto the boggy ground (marked only by difference in vegetation and really only visible from the air) which shows where the ground was disturbed in the short-lived attempt at a straight-line formation across to Dovey Junction. In the old days the signals of Dovey Junction could be seen in the distance. Photo taken from milepost 81 in 1992. *Author*

so that it had dammed the river up and overflowing the line. Much of the problem caused by use of sand from Ynyslas for the embankments'. He also praised the work of the company's men.

In 1877, Mr Paddock, the agent for the Ynys-hir Estate, asked for a level crossing for the tramway he was laying in connection with a land reclamation scheme. Permission was refused, but he was allowed to run his line through 'one of the flood or river bridges'.

The engineer reported a problem with a batch of Dowlais steel rail in 1882, these had been laid along the estuary, and showed signs of 'blurring' because, he thought, 'sand had become embedded in the surface during rolling'. He also stated that Taylor, Pierce & Co. had supplied 'inferior quality sleepers of insufficient scantling'.

In 1891, the subsidence of the embankments was remedied by off-loading debris from a serious rockfall in the Talerddig cutting. Between 10th and 14th February, high tides submerged the rails up to a depth of three feet in several places, but there was no serious damage.

October 1896 brought 'furious gales and high tides during the night of the 7th – ballast washed out and the track suspended'; and the flooding of 1914 took out a quarter-of-a-mile of ballast.

The Tre'r-ddôl viaduct was almost completely renewed in the 1910 programme. In the 1915 bridge

Pil Lodge viaduct and the estuary shore. 1992.
Author

Pil Lodge viaduct, south elevation, at flood tide. 1992.
Author

A BR Standard 4–6–0 with a short freight for Aberystwyth in 1963. This view was taken along the Cletwr Cut, looking seawards with Tre'r-ddôl viaduct in the distance. The Cletwr Cut was made in 1834 to drain part of the Cors Fochno (Borth Bog). *Author*

Tre'r-ddôl viaduct, north elevation (spanning the Cletwr Cut). 1963. *Author*

The south elevation of Tre'r-ddôl viaduct with an Aberystwyth-bound train hauled by an unidentified 'Manor' class loco. 5th June 1963. *Author*

survey, Pil Lodge was reported 'very bad', and was repaired at a cost of £700. Tre'r-ddôl was 'good', Black Pool was 'fair', whilst the former three-span Brickyard (at 84m 74c) was also 'fair'.

Between Ynys-hir and Ynyslas, the Great Western over the years expended at least £2,365 on flood erosion and subsidence remedial work, and £6,188 on piecemeal repairs to the bridges. This was in addition to minor work that the civil engineer did not have to report in detail.

In January 1919, the Director of Land Reclamation wrote to the company asking for their support and co-operation in plans for reclaiming Borth Bog more effectively. In February he made it known that he wanted the whole of the railway embankment along the estuary raised so as to become a defence against the penetration of sea water onto the land. The company's reply was in favour, provided that the Ministry paid for the work and for its future maintenance. The ministry's response was that as the raising of the embankment was to the benefit of the company, then the company should be willing to bear that cost. It was then decided that a fixed annual payment should be settled by arbitration. By May 1921, the whole scheme was abandoned because of shortage of money.

A view along Tre'r–ddôl viaduct, looking 'up' towards Dovey Junction, and illustrating the use of gravel on the timber decking of the bridge to try to reduce the risk from falling ashes setting the bridge alight, always a serious consideration on timber bridges. The wide emptiness of the Cors Fochno, and the enormity of the task of building a railway across this bog, are amply evident. 1963. *Author*

Details of wide-brace pile frame. 1963. *Author*

The turnout at the Machynlleth end of the loop at Ynyslas was a 'gentle' one laid in by the GWR as part of the work done in 1941. This late 1963 view was taken as a gang commenced the task of removing the loop. *Author*

A general view of Ynyslas station from the east, showing the single siding behind the down platform. 1963. *Author*

Left: The platform side and the up end of the signal box now minus the roof tiles. *Right:* The yard side and the down end. Both photos taken in 1963. *Author*

YNYSLAS (Green Island)

– 85m 00c to 85m 24c

A general view, looking 'up' towards Dovey Junction, with the station mistress outside the station building, which had to have its upper storey removed before it sank into the peat bog. The very low height of the original platform could not be remedied during later improvements because of problems that would have been encountered with the doors of the station building. Drivers of down trains were instructed to stop with the coaches at the higher part of the platform if possible but not to stop so short as to leave the rear coaches off the platform altogether! 1954. *Author*

The only really firm ground around Ynyslas had already been used in the establishment of farms, and the station had to be built on boggy ground.

Two Manning Wardle 0–6–0 saddle tanks (*Merion* and *Cardigan*) were reported to have been working here by September 1862; it seems that they must have been towed on a barge from Derwenlas, and disembarked at what was later known as East Wharf.

The first indication of traffic at Ynyslas was the traffic manager's return of staff for 1867, which showed four at the station, plus a foreman and two timber loaders. Savin's landing stage had therefore already come into use as a timber yard by 1867. At that time, the station is believed to have been comprised of a wooden booking office and waiting shed on the down side, and a set of gates at the road crossing.

The second indication of the nature of the traffic offering was the refusal (in 1869) of permission for the Western Counties Manure Company to erect a manure shed. In 1871, cattle pens and a landing were authorised at a cost of £40, and these had been completed by January 1872.

The construction of a permanent station and residence for £500 was authorised on 26th January 1872, but by August 1873 the structures were subsiding. It was reported that the buildings 'will not stand through the winter'; the upper storey of the house was removed at a cost of £150.

(NOTE: 'Las' implies a deep green, a blue-green, or even a blue)
Station at 85m 17c
Signal Box at 85m 15c
Loop taken out of use 7th September 1963.

On 25th August 1876, four Welsh ponies strayed onto the line and were driven off by the porter and platelayers, the gates then being re-secured. Soon afterwards, 'a Boy drove across with a Donkey Cart and left the gates open again'; back came the ponies, and one was hit by an engine and killed. At this time the level crossing gates were not locked by the signalling in any way.

A rearrangement of running lines and sidings with interlocking (by a wire system) was approved on 2nd June 1888 for £254. It is believed that the Dutton signal 'hut' was put up as part of this work. Correspondence with the Board of Trade records the resignalling as completed on 11th May 1891 (cost £353 10s 10d).

On 15th September 1896, Colonel Yorke inspected and passed a longer loop, resignalling, and a new signal box on the down side. The platforms were also

The goods yard, viewed from the roadway gate, with the cattle pens just in view on the right. 1963. *Author*

This Great Western four-compartment brake third used as an extension to the station facilities and as a camp coach, was fully maintained and with a sound water butt in 1954, but by 1963 both had fallen into disrepair. *Author*

Below: End of yard and rear of station master's house, showing the corrugated-iron storm porch. *Author*

A general view of the station, looking 'up' towards Machynlleth in 1963. The station 'offices' here were in the form of an extension to the main building which was to have been two storeys high. The gentleman on the right has his hand on the top of the lever which locked the gates when open to the railway, and interlocked with lever 9 in the signal box, thus proving the gates open before signals could be cleared. 1963.
Author

Detail of station front, again featuring a storm porch to the house. The enamel sign showing that a telephone available for public use was inside the station office was a feature common to many Cambrian stations. It was a throwback to the days when often the only telegraph operator in a village was at the railway station. 1963.
Author

lengthened, and the station thereafter changed little until it was dismantled.

Trespassing on the line (one of the few routes across the bog) was always a problem. J. Taylor, a trespasser, was knocked down by a train on 2nd December 1899, and died later. However, it was an accident on 2nd August 1910 that inflicted the greatest shock to the local folk. Colonel Fielden, who lived at Borth, and had a walking permit for wild-fowl shooting along the estuary, was trying to pick up his dog from between the rails in front of an approaching locomotive; tragically he tripped and fell, and the light engine passed right over him.

A case brought against the company in 1910 made legal history as the first of its kind in this part of Wales. Six dead sheep had been 'found' on the railway and, with the support of his landlord, Sir Edward Pryse, their owner sued the company for their value. Often, sheep were drowned and carried up onto the railway by the tide, but this case hinged around the suggestion that these sheep must have found a weakness in the fence, strayed onto the railway, and been trapped and drowned there in the company's ditches. At the County Court, the Judge decided that there was no evidence to support such a claim. This was an essential decision for the company – its officers had been worried about the possibility of farmers for miles around pitching their drowned sheep over the railway fencing every time the Dovey flowed across their lands!

In 1915, the Board agreed to contribute up to £5 per annum towards the cost of maintaining the Leri embankments, provided that the other landowners paid their fair share; they later restricted the company's contribution to up to one-twelfth of the total cost.

From 1918, there was a plan to try to sell the land bought under the 1863 Act for the approach road to

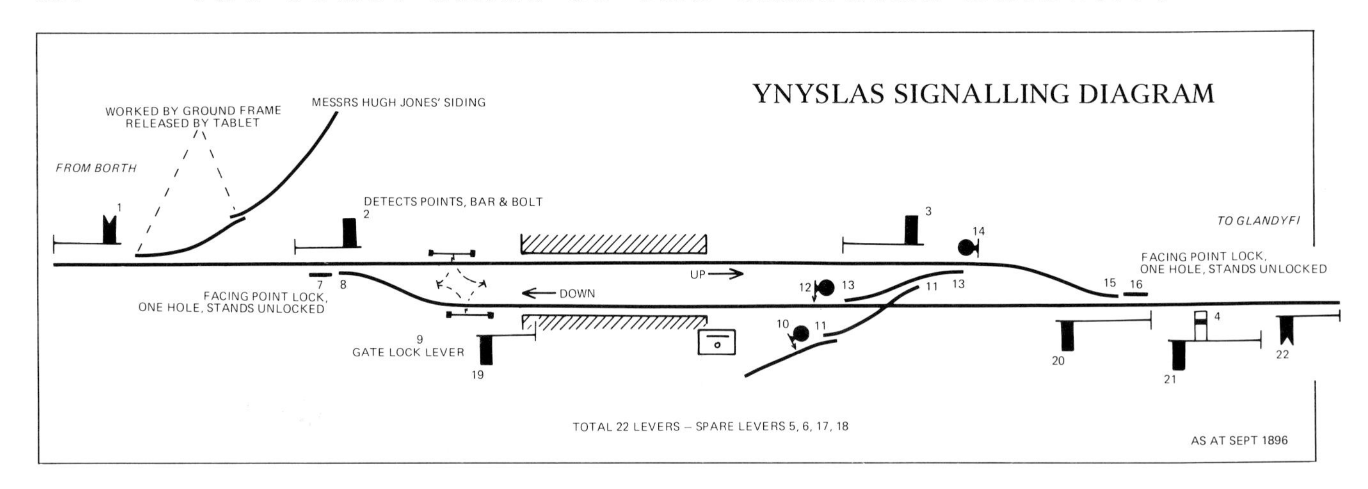

This view, looking east through the station, shows both the old signal box (on the left, with two windows in the end) and its later replacement put up in the summer of 1896, at which time the up platform was renewed. *Author*

The shelter on the up platform at Ynyslas was a miserly affair, but at least it retained the early style of displaying the station name in large letters on the front of the building (instead of 'running-in' boards). The sloping-roof 'extension' at the far end is the former signal box, believed to have been built to the design of Dutton & Co. 1963. *Author*

Down outlook to the gates in 1963. Note the little side-door to the porch marked 'Private', the slope between the two parts of the down platform, and the gravel covering to the timber-built up platform.
Author

the bridge, for not less than £42 10s 0d per acre, but nothing came of the proposal.

After the Abermule accident in 1921, it was reported that the tablet instruments were being held in the station because the signal box was too small. It was further stated that there was only a part-time signalman, and that the turnstile at the crossing was not locked from the signal box.

In 1922, the Board guaranteed a contribution of one third of £100 towards a Ministry of Agriculture and Fisheries scheme for the alleviation of unemployment by setting men to work on the repair of the embankments. Again, this assent was subject to others paying their share. The Ministry were to execute the work, and claim the cost back when it had been completed.

The Great Western spent £345 in April 1926 on renewing the up platform, and a year later they paid Porter R. E. Jones the sum of £5 for flood, mud and water damage to his household effects after an exceptional inundation of the whole area.

Goods and Parcels services had been withdrawn by 1938.

The loop was extended towards Glandyfi in May 1941 at a cost of £535, plus £233 for resignalling. At the end of 1944, repairs to both platforms were authorised, and in May 1945 the civil engineer reported that it had been necessary to expend £680 on this instead of the £575 he had estimated the year before.

One working instruction stated: 'Drivers of Down passenger trains scheduled to stop at Ynyslas must bring coaches to a stand opposite the Dovey Junction end of the Down platform, care being taken that the rear passenger vehicle is not left short of the platform.'

Ynyslas was a site for the accumulation of hay, and could show a 4 ton stack at the end of a good season (which was not very often).

The signal box was closed on 7th September 1963, and the loop was removed soon afterwards. The level crossing gates were thereafter protected by up and down distant signals, worked from a ground frame beside the gates and interlocked with the gates. This was one of the very few 'distants' only crossings on the former Cambrian lines; the Cambrian practice had been to provide stop signals only (at 440 yards or thereabouts from the gate) with no distant signals.

Ynyslas has an unenviable reputation for regularly having the level-crossing gates 'run through' by trains. The GWR replaced the original set of four gates with two long ones – less work for the signalman, who had to come down from his box to work the gates by hand. 1954.
Author

EAST WHARF SIDING (also called THE PENRHYN SIDING) – 85m 18c

This left the up side of the station loop via trailing points and curved along a slightly raised embankment to the east bank of the Leri. Originally, it was curved more sharply to give a 400 foot straight run of line next to the water's edge.

It was put down by Savin to enable materials to be shipped in using the *James Conley*, and barges; he could therefore tackle the crossing of the Cors Fochno from both ends at once, and push on towards Borth at the same time, as well as carrying out the exploratory work on forming the embankment for the bridge. This explains the 'tongue-in-cheek' claim that, in August 1862, the line was within two miles of Borth; nothing was said about the middle bit that was missing!

A properly-piled face for the wharf was driven in October 1863, but it is very doubtful that it was to the planned length of 400 yards, which was part of the undisclosed ambition of making Ynyslas a port to rival Aberdovey.

On 16th February 1871, the traffic manager reported that the Penrhyn siding and wharf were out of use, and that Jones & Griffiths, timber merchants of Aberdovey, would rent it for £10 per annum. It was then decided that no more rails could be taken up without destroying its potential as a wharf, that the company should retain all rights of import and export, and that the firm ought to be asked to pay more; and so they did – £15 rent per annum. In 1879 it was realised that the rent had not been claimed since the firm moved in, and £116 5s 0d was duly recovered.

The siding was closed and dismantled after April 1896, when Mr Hughes Jones transferred his business to a new works on the west bank. References seem to make a distinction between the two sides of the Leri by terming this one 'the Penrhyn siding', whereas the Aberdovey Ferry branch (on the west bank) had become 'the Penrhyn branch'.

Opened: by Savin, 1862.
Closed: April 1896

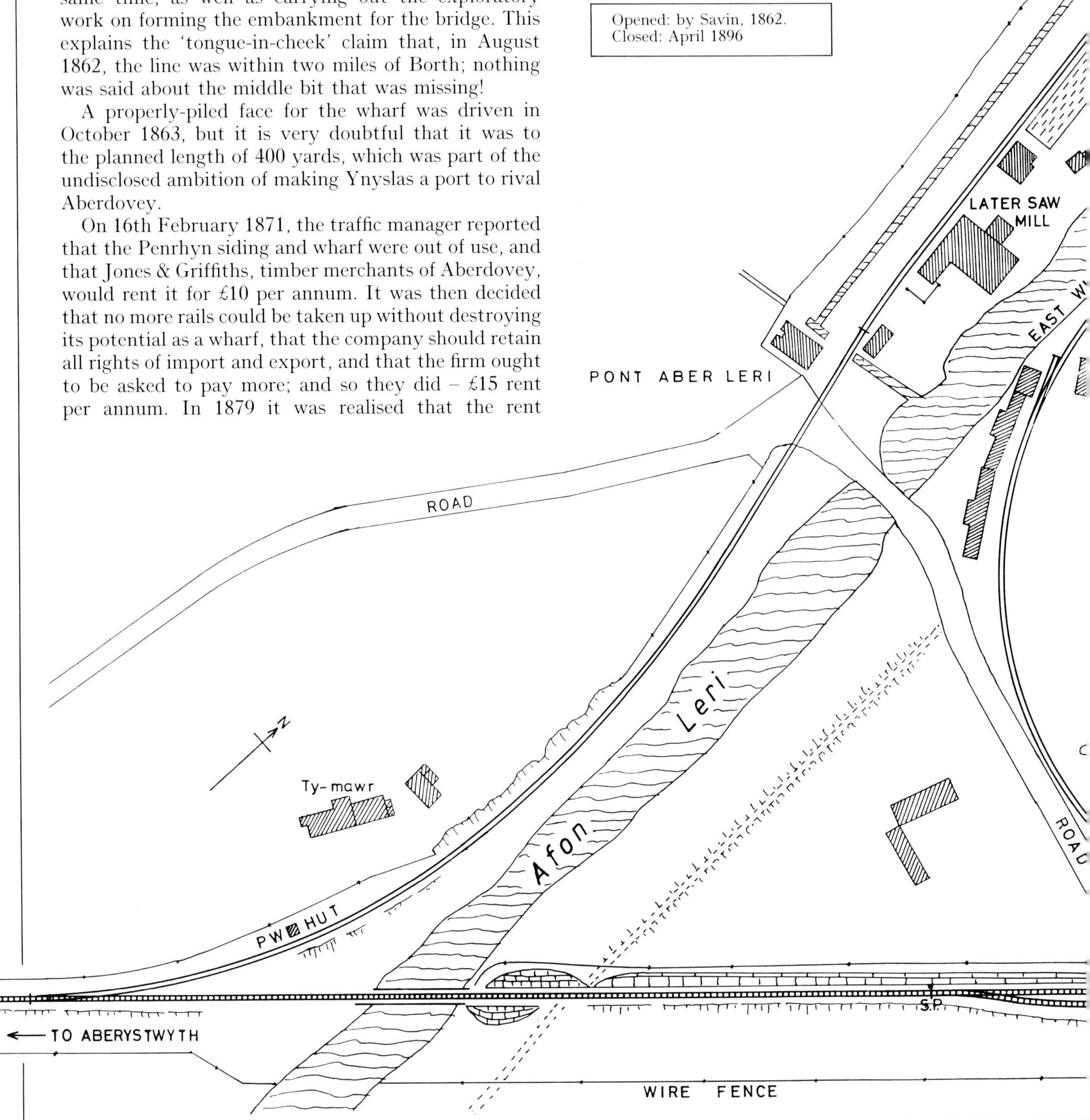

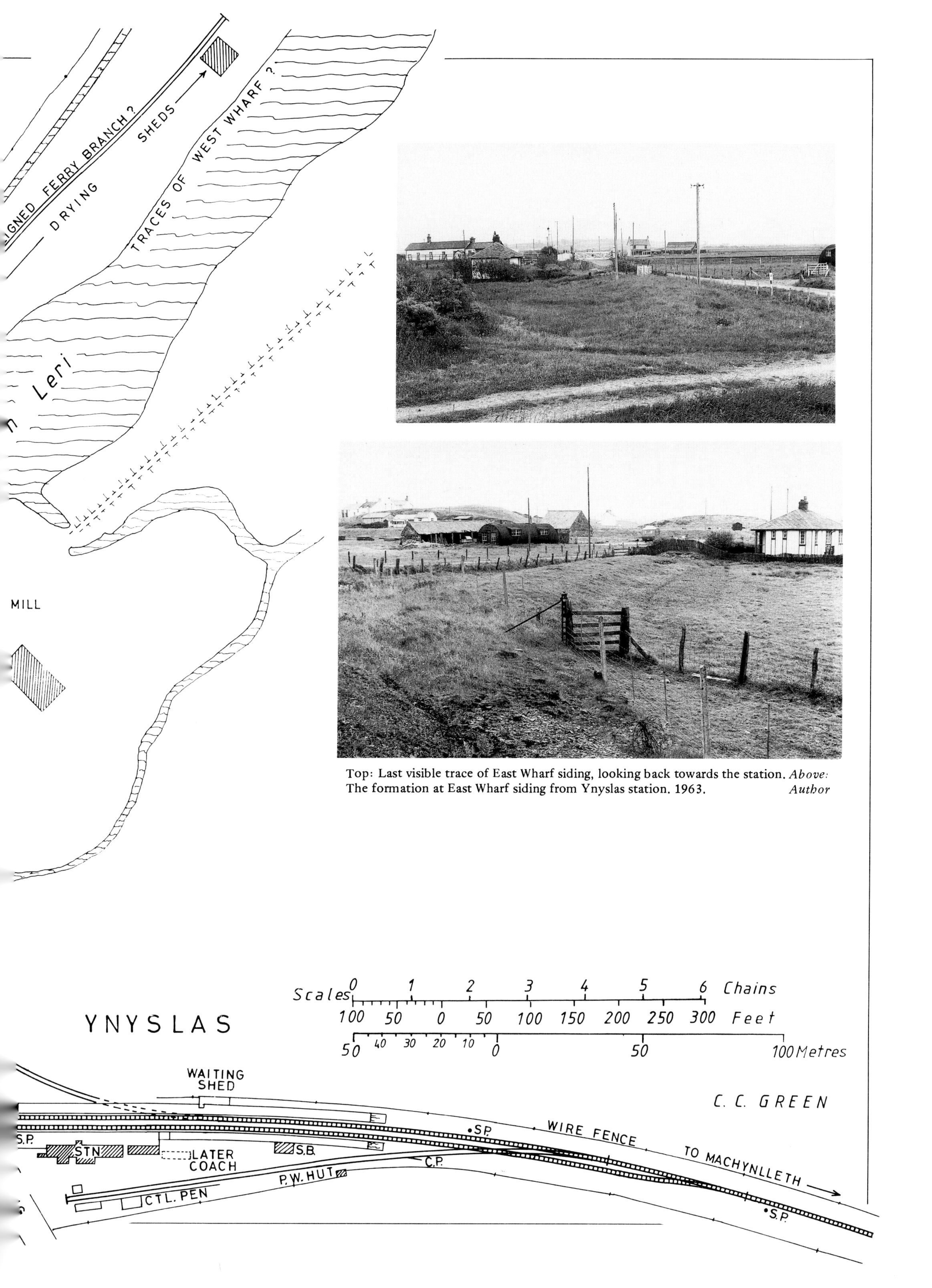

Top: Last visible trace of East Wharf siding, looking back towards the station. *Above:* The formation at East Wharf siding from Ynyslas station. 1963. *Author*

The site of 'West Wharf', on the left of this view, looking inland up the Afon Leri. From this view it is difficult to imagine how the 121ft long ferry *Elizabeth* turned round, but there was a turning point (the 'winding hole') now silted up. 5th June 1963. *Author*

Ynyslas station, viewed from the west, with a Dutton-made semaphore up home signal (so typical of the Cambrian system) in the foreground. The sharp turnout of the loop was very different from the 'gentle' point laid in at the east end. 1963. *Author*

THE ABERDOVEY FERRY BRANCH – 85m 38c

Opened: 1862, by Savin as a contractor's line.
Opened: 24th October 1863, for railway passengers.
Closed: 14th August 1867.

After leaving the station loop, the line runs straight along a rough-stone embankment and across the seven-span Leri Pile Bridge at 85m 30½c.

The promoters of the Plynlimon & Hafan Tramway wished to pass a line under the bridge, and the Board considered this request on 13th July 1893. It assented in principle, but added: 'Barges shall not be brought up the river beyond the road bridge or no arrangement will be made for the user of a quarter-of-a-mile of Company land' (i.e. there would be no avoiding the charge for using the company's wharf).

Just across the Leri bridge lies the site of a set of points (facing up trains) which served two distinct purposes at two widely-separated periods. The Aberdovey Ferry Branch commenced at the up facing points, and rounded a low hill (on which stands Ty Mawr – 'The Big House') to run along the west side of the Afon Leri. It passed the site of the future West Wharf where, later, there was to be a siding and a shelter. From here it curved north-west along the stony eastern rim of the low-lying hill, to reach the north-western tip of Cerrig-y-Penrhyn, just 650 yards short of Aberdovey Pier. From end to end, the branch measured 1 mile 53 chains.

At the time the branch was being built, the ferry service between Aberdovey and Cerrig-y-Penrhyn was worked by a ferry captain who held a lease for the

The Leri bridge, looking towards Ynyslas. Note the 'crown' in the trackbed. 1963. *Author*

The Leri bridge, looking south along The Cut from the road. The route of the Hafan Tramway proposed to pass under the right-hand span of the bridge would have been submerged at high tide. The course of the Ferry branch can be discerned on the right, with Ty Mawr on the low hill above. 1959. *Author*

Leri bridge, north elevation. 1961. *Author*

Detail of wide skewed pile frame. 1963. *Author*

Detail of timber trackbed, at this time with no gravel cover to the decking. 1963. *Author*

right to do so. Historically, the original owners of the right to operate a ferry were the Ynys-y-Maengwyn Estate, which had been in the hands of the Corbet family for a long time. There were three levels of service:

Y Fferri Fach, 'the little ferry', which took only foot passengers and what they could carry.
Y Fferri Ganol, 'the medium ferry', would take horsemen, passengers with luggage, and small animals; these were met at the point by carts.
Y Fferri Fawr, 'the large ferry', could take flock or herd animals, heavy carts, and carriages and horses.

All were powered by sail, and would work up towards the spot where the Leri mouth is today at high tide. On special and well-paid occasions, they would operate outside the normal regulations of the legalised ferry – this would happen more often after around 1836, when the Leri had been channelled to flow into the Dovey, instead of running into the sea by a more direct course. However, by the 1860s, road improvements had made it much easier and safer to drive round the estuary via Machynlleth; ferry traffic fell off considerably as a consequence leaving only the foot passengers and local farmers.

The fares in the 18th and 19th centuries were:

Foot passenger	2d.
Horse and rider	6d.
Wheeled carriage	2s 6d.
One-horse phaeton	4s 0d.
Two-horse phaeton	4s 6d.
Carriage and pair	7s 6d.

The high-perch phaeton was the sports car of its day, but just how many there were in West Wales at that time is unknown.

The Cambrian bought the lease of the ferry later, but, until that time, the railway ferry activities were all totally illegal. Savin was forced to apologise to the Board of Trade for omitting to apply for sanction, and he evaded the just penalty by pleading that the existing ferries were 'utterly unfit and dangerous' and quite inadequate for the transfer of large groups of men and large quantities of materials from one side of the Dovey to the other.

The appearance on the scene of the railway contractor must have seemed like pennies from heaven to the ferry captain, Edward Bell, who was soon working almost entirely for the railway to the detriment of the public service. The first (and most important) job was to get rails laid onto the end of the point so as to be able to work at all tides, and Savin planned a roll-on, roll-off landing stage there. Initially, there was some difficulty in getting the landing stage to stay put in the face of a westerly gale, but after the placement of some 40 tons of steel rail, it was sufficiently stable to be used by that example of modern technological advance – a steam-powered paddle tug. The company seems to have chartered one, possibly as a trial, or perhaps while waiting for the delivery of the tug it had arranged to purchase.

Looking east at 85 miles 38 chains. The embankment which once carried the Ferry branch diverges to the left. 5th June 1963. *Author*

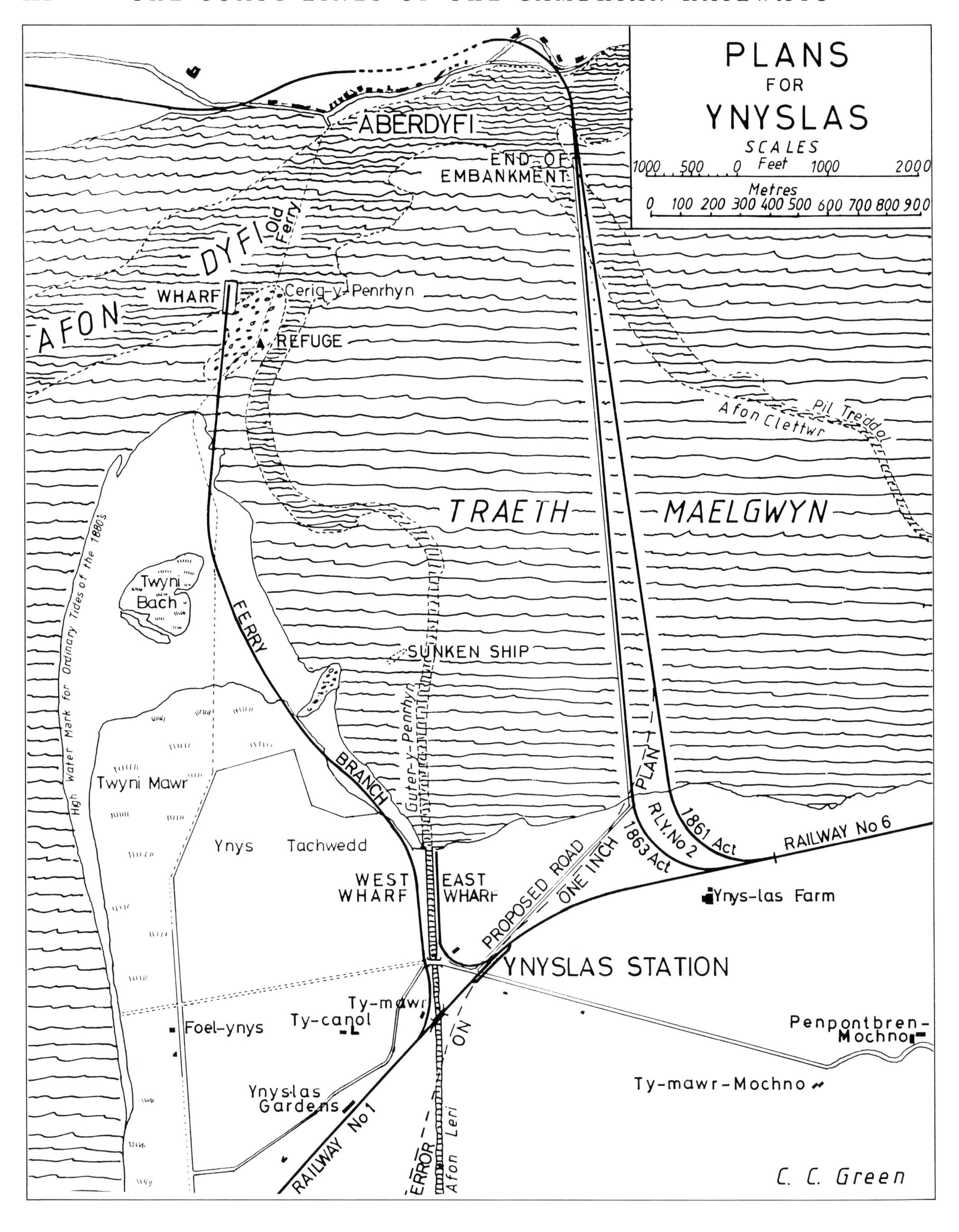
PLANS
FOR
YNYSLAS
SCALES
Feet
1000 500 0 1000 2000
Metres
0 100 200 300 400 500 600 700 800 900
ABERDYFI
END OF
EMBANKMENT
AFON DYFI
Old Ferry
WHARF
Cerig-y-Penrhyn
REFUGE
Afon Clettwr
Pil Tre'ddol
TRAETH MAELGWYN
Twyni Bach
High Water Mark for Ordinary Tides of the 1880s
FERRY BRANCH
SUNKEN SHIP
Guter-y-Penrhyn
Twyni Mawr
Ynys Tachwedd
PLAN RLY. No 2
1861 Act
1863 Act
RAILWAY No 6
WEST WHARF
EAST WHARF
PROPOSED ROAD
ONE INCH
Ynys-las Farm
YNYSLAS STATION
Ty-mawr
Ty-canol
Foel-ynys
Penpontbren-Mochno
Ty-mawr-Mochno
Ynys-las Gardens
RAILWAY No 1
ERROR ON
Afon Leri
C. C. Green

So near, yet so far. Aberdovey from Cerrig-y-Penrhyn in 1959.
Author

The last remains of West Wharf, with Aberdovey beyond. 1963.
Author

There has been considerable speculation as to whether or not the first engines to arrive at Ynyslas had been sent by road, but the author feels that had any of them been sent along the narrow and inadequate byways, it would have attracted some attention from the press with an exaggerated account of how these monstrous weights had been transported. So far, no such account has been found, and, in any event, the Dovey abounded with competent sailors. The two class 1 Manning Wardle 0–6–0 saddle tanks, *Merion* and *Cardigan*, are known to have been at Ynyslas by August 1862. They were admirable engines for the work as they weighed only about 15 tons when built, and had a drawbar pull of more than 3 tons. Soon, a third of that type, *Nantclwyd*, joined them, as did *Volunteer*, an 0–4–2 Sharp Stewart tender engine; the latter weighed over 24 tons with her tender, and had a drawbar pull of over 4 tons. One or two other slightly heavier (but more powerful) 0–6–0s and 2–4–0s may have followed, but all were well within the carrying capacity of the barges and the unloading capabilities of the sailors.

By these activities, Savin had set up the means of construction of the line for some time to come, with depots on both north and south banks of the Dovey estuary being connected by rail and tug; the tug was a seaworthy all-weather ship limited only by the effects of the weather on the tow. There is a tendency to credit Savin with the success of actually getting the work done, but it would be well to keep in mind that he was more the astute politician and schemer. However, behind him were the more dignified Piercy's, Benjamin and Robert, and it is far more likely that they had thought up these effective maritime arrangements. Indeed, once Savin had got rid of them in March 1864, his operations became more high-handed and less structurally sound.

In October 1863, the wharf received its proper piled facing in time to be ready for passengers using the ferry to Aberdovey when the line was opened between Aberdovey and Llwyngwril on the 24th of that month.

On 5th July 1867, George Owen, the Cambrian engineer, reported despondently of the West Wharf: 'it is a source of daily expense – the Leri changes course with every flood. If the Deviation cannot be opened soon piling will be needed.' The deviation line along the north side of the Dovey estuary was opened in haste on 14th August 1867, at which time the ferry branch could have been closed were it not for a hiccup – the Board of Trade Inspector closed the Deviation because he wanted more work to be carried out on the tunnels. Passengers were conveyed round the closure by road vehicle, but the goods trucks had to be put across aboard the *James Conley*.

George Owen wrote again on 27th May 1869 recommending that 'the old Landing Stage' be sold for its materials because 'Planking is being carried away and the Company is liable for damages if it is hit by a vessel'. Sailing directions for the west coast of Wales in 1870 still carried erroneous information under 'Aberdovey', that 'the railway station is on the opposite side of the river near Ynyslas and from whence a line of railway is laid down for the convenience of shipping slates. A ferry also crosses the river at the same point.'

A final footnote came with the authority for the sale of the 'Penrhyn Branch 3rd Class coach to Mr Buckley for the Mawddwy Railway'.

The course of the branch could still be identified in the 1930s, but storms have since washed all traces away.

WEST WHARF SIDING

In May 1895, it was proposed that Mr I. Hughes-Jones, the owner of the saw mill, should transfer his undertaking from the east bank of the Leri to the west, onto the site of the former West Wharf which would allow the up platform at Ynylas station to be extended. The proposal was 'to take up the present siding [on the east bank] and to put in a new one running from the Railway Bridge over the Lerry [sic] and by the side of the river to the land now proposed to be leased to him'.

The siding, locked by tablet, was inspected and passed by Colonel Yorke in April 1896, and actually followed the old course of the ferry branch for as far as was needed. Completion of the work laid the way open to remodelling the station layout at Ynylas through the summer of 1896.

In November 1912 the mill required a long drying shed, and the Board instructed the solicitor not to accept less than £50 an acre, and to reserve the right to repossess if the land was needed again for extensions of the siding facilities. The long shed was duly erected, with a smaller one about 350ft beyond it; the siding was extended to serve both buildings.

At a point where the road ran close to the railway (about 85m 47c), the Hafan Sett Quarry proposed, in 1896, to put in a level crossing over the Cambrian line instead of routeing their line under the river bridge. The Cambrian Board responded by stating that the Hafan line must cross the main line by a bridge. The abutments might be erected on company land, but had to be distanced for double track and allow 15ft clear above rail level. Having suggested a wayleave of £2 per annum, the Hafan promotors had to accede to a figure of £5 per annum, and the agreement was actually drawn up and sealed in September 1898; and there the matter ended.

Opened: April 1896.
Closed: ?

THE DOVEY STEAMERS

The first steamer to arrive, in 1862, was the paddle tug *Victoria*. She is mentioned just once in the company's minute books, and may only have been chartered until the arrival of the *James Conley*, also a paddle tug.

The *James Conley* was the reliable work horse, but her regular untroubled performance was eclipsed by the more elegant *Elizabeth*. No authorisation has been found for the purchase of the *James Conley*, though the *Carnarvonshire and Denbigh Herald* stated that she was owned by the 'Coast' company. She was a clinker-built seagoing boat constructed at Newcastle-on-Tyne, and after her use by the railway company was sold to the Portmadoc Steam Tug Co. Henry Hughes, in his splendid book *Immortal Sails*, has recalled seeing her arrive there: 'Painted black and green, with a tall lean smoke-stack and a barren-looking bridge, the craft had an appearance of something half-starved as it lay surrounded by the beauteous shapes of sails and spars'; the year would have been 1868. She had a hard and useful life at Portmadoc, taking the graceful slate schooners away from the harbour, and back home again after they had sailed halfway round the world. In 1884 or 1885, she was replaced by a more modern tug, the *Snowdon*, from the same shipbuilder.

A pencil drawing of Aberdovey in 1862. The steam yacht on the left is probably the *Elizabeth*.
Cty Aberdyfi Institute

The *Elizabeth* was more yacht-like in appearance, with cabins for the passengers (probably for the First and Second classes), and had been built by Lewis & Stockwell of London, with engines and boiler from James Watt & Company of Birmingham. She was of 86 tons register (30 tons exclusive of engine and boiler space), 121ft long with a beam of 20ft, and drew 6ft of water. The boiler was tubular in design; the two oscillating cylinders were 22in bore by 24in stroke, and produced a nominal 30 b.h.p. She barely fitted across the Leri at Ynyslas!

After being storm bound for a time in Milford Haven on her passage from London, *Elizabeth* duly arrived at Aberdovey. As the day of her arrival was 'exceedingly warm and fair', she promptly put to sea again with 'a select party' for a trip to Barmouth and back. She started ordinary service sailings on 24th October 1863 when the train service between Aberdovey and Llwyngwril commenced; it had originally been set for 26th September, and the *Herald* had announced a special excursion from Oswestry and intermediate stations for that date, and a public dinner at Aberdovey. *Elizabeth* was to operate hourly trips across the estuary at 6d a head. On the public opening day, a reporter wrote: 'we found the place gay with decorations, numbers of people were congregated at the stations, a band of music played merrily, and every sign of rejoicing, and mothers expressing satisfaction at the great event of the day. When the first train started it was crowded with Passengers.'

Although the *Elizabeth* seems to have been reliable enough, her captain (the ferrymaster Edward Bell), her mate and crew of five (plus one carpenter) had a pretty difficult time trying to keep up a good service. Most of her troubles were caused by going up the Leri at flood tide, then having to wait for the arrival of a delayed train, and so becoming stranded without adequate engine power to drag herself clear. She was so tight a fit across the river that she had to be turned by nudging the bank and letting the wind or tide turn her, as did canal barges in the 'winding holes'. When wind opposed tide, she would have to mark time accurately in mid-river with her two paddles revolving in opposite directions, and get round that way; either method was a risky, highly-skilled operation calling for instinctive seamanship, and the decision to appoint Edward Bell as skipper was a very wise one. While she was stuck fast, sometimes for a week or more, the old sailing ferries filled in, to the delight of the hardy and the dismay of the rest.

The sunken Derwenlas schooner shown on the map on page 122. It was one of the three sunk in 1868 to maintain the course of the Guter-y-penrhyn. It was uncovered by an easterly gale in 1962 and has not been seen since. *Author*

Her last days as a Cambrian steamer revealed a sad picture. On 18th August 1868, the directors were informed that she was 'resting on a timber gridiron which the owner wants back'; and 'Each spring tide the water rushes into her cabins which does her great injury'. Flat-bottomed, light timber-hulled ships were often laid up with full ballast and chained down onto a stout underwater frame, with a little water in the bilges to keep the seams tight. The ship's husband or shipkeeper checked the water levels and pumped as necessary, and a ship so laid up could rise and fall on the tide without getting her bottom stove in as she grounded. Unfortunately, the object of the practice was defeated by the excessive violence of the Dovey tides.

She had been partially repaired, but a further £50 was required to be spent on her before she would be fit to steam to Liverpool; she was therefore advertised for sale at Aberdovey. In April 1869, the Board heard that the auctioneer, Mr Dew of Bangor, had failed to dispose of her, but by September he had been successful, and she was bought for an undisclosed sum by a Mr Green of Londonderry. The amount realised was to be credited to the Owen and Quilter's Fund, and of this, £400 was to be spent in providing a station and accommodation at Barmouth Junction. Owen was the Cambrian's engineer, and Quilter was Savin's solicitor; this suggests that Savin might have paid for her, and that she had been seized by the Cambrian in connection with his debt to the company – and the same might be true of the *James Conley*.

A visit to Ynyslas can be a very rewarding exercise, and with a little imagination it is quite possible to picture what might have been: if the Dovey reclamation scheme had been followed through, the estuary would now be only half of its present width; if the railway bridge had been built, the view at ground level would have been blocked for the whole of its width by the long embankment, with the bridge on the northerly side; and if the postwar Dovey barrage scheme had not been turned down (because of the inimical effect it would have had on Aberdyfi), there would have been no tidal strand but just a vast lake to the east, penned in by a large dam stretching from Ynyslas to the Aberdyfi shore.

For those blessed with a really vivid imagination, this is a place to be at dusk. Here there was once to be heard the gentle murmurings of drivers and riders as they tried to calm their apprehensive horses on the ferry, the shouts of sailors as they sank the last Derwenlas ships to hold up the bank of the Leri, and the puffing of a small tank engine; for this is Wales where the echoes of things past linger.

Mr. Thomas Wynne Thomas and friends on the 'refuge', when newly completed in 1933 to stand above normal high tide level in the middle of the sandlands The navigable channel is just discernible as a dark band in the sand behind the tower and Ferry Branch Wharf projected out towards it behind the refuge. *Author's collection*

YNYSLAS to BORTH

82m 24c to 87m 18c

Between Ynyslas and Borth, the line runs just inland of a bank of sand dunes which form a barrier between the sea and the great Borth Bog — effectively a sand spit pushing out into the Dovey Estuary. Behind these dunes the railway builders found it easy enough to build a nearly-level formation. This picture shows the 9.45 a.m. ex-Whitchurch coasting towards Borth. Note the last traces of the original course of Afon Leri in the foreground. *Author*

From the site of the Aberdovey Branch points, the line runs straight for a few hundred yards. Here was the site of Ynylas Gardens. This was one of Savin's speculative ventures, believed to be a curious combination of holiday homes for visitors and a market garden producing fresh vegetables for the chain of hotels he had expected to build. The precise use may be uncertain, but the fate of the houses is not – like Ynyslas station they sank, and had to be demolished.

Continuing on the journey, the line bends gently to the south near 85m 60c, and traverses an area which was levelled by the use of carts, wheelbarrows and shovels after Afon Leri (Eleri on some old maps, and Aberdovey River on others) had been recut to flow into the Dovey at Ynyslas. The entire scheme by which the Cors Fochno or Borth Bog (once known as Henllys or Old Mire) was drained had been carried out by local landowners working together under an Enclosure Act of 1813. The Leri had been diverted by 1826, after the Calettwr had been recut and the embankments finished; however, the legal and financial settlement arguments continued until 1847 (*The Enclosure and Drainage of Cors Fochno (Borth Bog) 1813 to 1847* by R. J. Colyer). Without this drainage scheme, it might not have been possible to have made the railway. The first chart to show the new course of the Leri was the OS 2in draft of 1833/34, made for the production of the OS 1in map of 1837 – this still indicated a deep indentation in the coastline where the outlet of the river, and a tiny harbour had been. Soon afterwards, coast defence works banked it off in a straight line.

Just past the golf course crossing (now an automatically operated level crossing known as Aber-leri) a dense patch of reeds shows where the Leri once flowed; the railway crossed the old course by the three-span timber Black Bridge at about 86m 50c. As the area dried out, this bridge was replaced by a small culvert through the embankment, which had been laid to keep the line above this wet ground.

On the other side of the road, an attractive golf links was laid out. At a Board meeting on 25th May 1895, the decision was made to donate a Challenge cup to the golf club. The cost was not to exceed seven guineas (£7 7s 0d), it was to be presented annually, and be renewed as necessary as a winner in two consecutive years would keep the trophy (does one still exist?).

After a very minor crest, the embankment returns to the general ground level. Somewhere around 87m 00c, Sands Siding was to be found. The use made of the sand extracted is not certainly known.

Continuing straight and level, the line reaches Borth, which lies on a slight ridge, which is actually the crest of a hill submerged to the west by the sea, and to the east by the Cors Fochno.

Looking southwards into Borth station in 1963. On the left is the long down refuge siding, with the down platform on the loop beyond. If a freight train was too long to ascend the bank beyond without assistance, part of the train could be left in the refuge siding, which was long enough to take 38 wagons plus an engine and brake van. One of the two goods yard sidings behind the main station building on the up side platform was close enough to the back of the platform to act as a loading dock (and in later years a camping coach site). The houses of Cambrian Terrace, erected as a private venture by Savin, can be seen in the right background. 1963.
Author

A view towards Ynyslas, showing the up platform starting signal, the long shunt neck serving the goods yard, and the down refuge siding. 1963. *Author*

The up advanced starting signal (No. 14 lever) was a Dutton product, although by 1963 the finial had been replaced by one of GWR pattern. The buffer stops (with dismounted lamp!) were at the end of the goods yard neck. *Author*

BORTH (Port, or Haven) – 87m 18c to 87m 38c

A general view looking towards Aberystwyth, including the camping coach in the siding behind the up platform. 1963. *Author*

Station at 87.28
Signal Box at 87.30
Opened: as a terminal, 1st July 1863;
fully, 23rd June 1864.
Loop taken out of use 4th November 1973.

When the railway came, Borth was a village of offshore fisher-folk. It possessed a broad stretch of fine sand backed by a hard shingle bed (called Gro'r Borth), where the boats were drawn up, although other Borth sailors walked to the Cerrig-y-Penrhyn ferry to join their ships at Aberdovey.

Before the Leri was diverted, boats were moored above the inlet at Aber-leri and along the banks of the river, which was tidal up to the back of the old village of Morfa Borth (Sea Marsh Harbour).

It was not surprising that the villagers could not see any value in the railway, and believed that it would bring ill rather than good; they certainly could see no use for visitors, either. Indeed, there is a story of four tourists who went there before the line had been joined up, and could find no place in Borth willing to put them up for the night. Eventually, they settled down under a tarpaulin in a contractor's wagon on the embankment to the north. Person or persons unknown gave them a gentle push in the night, and they coasted away down to Ynyslas with no prospect whatever of any breakfast!

As soon as the line had been connected back to Machynlleth, a passenger and Royal Mail service was started (from 1st July 1863), and excursions were run to try and get people addicted to the joys of a day at the seaside. In that delightful old book *The Story of the Cambrian*, C. P. Gasquoine (of the *Border Counties Advertizer*) has left us with a marvellous account of the 'goings on' at Borth beach before the bathing machines arrived. He described lithe urchins 'naked as unto earth they came', and 'There was a bevy of females in a state of ... shall I go on? No; but I will just say we saw them waddling like ducks to the water. The porpoises were alarmed and betook themselves off', and more besides. During this first year, those from inland came by train, but a lot of people from Aberystwyth came by horse and brake to join in the fun. Goods were carried as consigned, as all trains were run as mixed goods and passenger, however they were designated in the timetables.

On 7th June 1864, Savin was commended for his foresight in having constructed an additional platform and two long sidings in anticipation of the impending Board of Trade inspection, and Borth commenced its intended role as a passing station when the line to Aberystwyth was opened on 23rd June.

Again, excursions were run, and of the trains from Aberystwyth it was related that 'In the carriages the passengers shouted, talked, ate, drank and ... sang hymns.' When the Oswestry, Ellesmere & Whitchurch Railway was linked up on 27th July 1864, there was an inaugural through run, onto which occasion Savin

The seafront at Borth, with Savin's 'speculative venture' hotel (in the centre) marking the entrance to Cambrian Terrace, the roadway down to the station. This view shows how much coastal defence work was needed to prevent the sea from washing away the houses built along the sea front. *Collection M. Christensen*

tacked the ceremonial opening of his new Cambrian Hotel. By this date he had completed, or nearly completed, the existing station buildings and the houses of Cambrian Terrace. This terrace of houses and the Cambrian Hotel were part of Savin's extensive operation of speculative property development, made in the hope that the opening of the railway would lead to a demand for new properties.

On 13th August 1864, an official train from Welshpool drew up; from it, the entire Cambrian board of directors descended to look around and to hold their first meeting. Perhaps the station, which replaced an old timber farm building that had been used for those first twelve months, had been completed. They passed one most important resolution, that the contract for building the workshops at Oswestry should go to Mr Savin.

By 7th February 1866, Savin had overreached himself and on that day he suspended payment of accounts. The ensuing searches arising from his impending bankruptcy revealed some engines of his in a shed at Borth; they carried the names *Ant, Bee* and *Dart*.

In 1867, Borth possessed a staff of four, plus the gatekeeper at Capel Soar level crossing. One of them, the stationmaster, went off without authority and subsequently came back drunk; he was dismissed.

An account of the letting of refreshment rooms at the station in 1869 shows that they consisted of a front kitchen, a back kitchen, a pantry, a cellar and three bedrooms. In those times, there were no prepared or pre-cooked supplies, everybody lived on the job, and had to provide good, freshly-cooked meals. The first tenant had been paying £25 per annum, which the manager considered inadequate; he was therefore allowed to put it out to tender, and secured £35 per annum. This licensed facility, so conveniently located at or near their places of work, was the downfall of more than one railwayman. The first of such casualties was the foreman drainer who, with another drainer, passed a November afternoon there in 1871. When they left, walking up towards Ynyslas, he was stated

It was at Savin's hotel that the scholars of Uppingham took refuge from the typhoid scare which threatened the school's survival. It was seldom fully occupied. *Collection M. Christensen*

to be 'not intoxicated', but his companion had drunk 'as much as he could take'. The foreman was found dead on the line, and his companion was 'not knowing anything had happened'.

On 26th June 1873, distant signals for the level crossing were approved at a cost of £65 19s 3d.

In May 1875, matters were arising which explained why the company needed to employ drainers. The Inspector of Nuisances to the Rural Sanitary Board of Aberystwyth had laid complaints about the accumulation of stagnant water in the drainage ditches. 'The Climate of Borth is considerably damaged by such sources of dampness and malaria', he claimed. A broken sluice was repaired for £20 4s 0d, after which 'the remainder of the nuisance is on the lands of Sir Pryse Pryse Bart.' The Engineer was instructed to 'resist clearing or covering the drainage ditch on the south side', and an outlet was to be protected (from animals?).

Another item, dated July 1876, shows how some managers tried to help older members of staff for whom there was no pension, and the loss of a job meant, for old married couples, separation into the male and female sections of the workhouse: 'Mr Robinson, the Stationmaster at Borth, is now incapable of performing his duties and I propose to remove him to act as Clerk or in some similar capacity.'

In October 1877, two signals were blown down 'by the Cyclonic Storm an intimation of which was telegraphed from America'. Just before Christmas in that year, it was found that the inhabitants were proposing to cut off the course of a brook, which had been diverted to flow directly into the sea. This action would have caused the water to run into the drainage ditching, and 'great damage may be possibly caused to the Company's Station and Buildings'.

In 1881, the Gogerddan Estate (Sir Pryse Pryse) was complaining that sewage from the station and hotel was discharging into their drainage, and it was found that the company's pipe by the level crossing had become blocked; this was cleared, and a new trench was cut from Bontddu into the Leri. Two years later, a local enquiry found that flooding in the lower village was being caused by the company's failure to maintain its sluices; this was firmly denied, and the council had to look again at its own drainage arrangements. Here the drainage saga ended, but would be replaced later by other drawn-out disputes.

On 17th October 1881, an accident occurred which may have been a warning that the Stevens indicators at facing points were clearly unreliable. This mishap involved the small Sharp Stewart 4–4–0 *Beaconsfield* and the Sharp Stewart 0–6–0 *Snowdon*, with ten coaches and vans from Aberystwyth; *Beaconsfield* struck the points, though she remained on the rails until she reached the siding, where the bogie dropped into the 4ft and the 'trailing wheels into the 6ft'. It was stated that the distant signal was not fully 'into its sheath' (i.e. was only partly cleared to 'off'), and in that position the points could have been partly open. Nobody was hurt, but the crew had a good shaking.

Another accident occurred at the station on 7th April 1884. The 1.40 p.m. ex-Whitchurch was being shunted to allow a special cattle train to pass through; however, the latter turned up sooner than had been expected, and clipped a corner of a Brecon & Merthyr coach – this cost the Cambrian 6s 11d for an iron step and part of a footboard. Driver J. Cunningham received a commendation and £5 for his alertness in slowing his train in time to avoid a major disaster.

There was a further accident on 22nd August 1889, when Mrs Williams, the gatekeeper, was trying to close

A photograph showing the graceful ironwork of the station canopy at Borth. This view was taken prior to 1894 (when the down loop platform was added). Photography was then only just becoming really practicable and any photographer was assured of the full and respectful attention of passengers and staff.
Cty. M. E. M. Lloyd

The five 4–4–0 Stephenson 'Big Belpaires' were the pride and joy of the Cambrian's locomotive superintendent, Mr. Herbert Jones. The fireboxes followed Great Western practice, the outlines were pure Stephenson, but the frames concealed valve gear of LNWR derivation, for the valve events led left in advance of right. This photo, taken c.1920, shows No. 96 on an Aberystwyth-bound train in the down platform.
G. H. W. Clifford

and secure one of the gates blown open by the wind and was hit by an engine. She 'received severe injuries but is now recovering slowly'.

It was reported in October 1884 that the Borth Improvement Committee were erecting 'Sea Groins'. The general manager stated: 'The Line is a considerable distance from the shore and sheltered by a double line of housing. I cannot therefore recommend that any subsidy be granted unless taking a more general view that the safety and retention of Borth as a Watering Place may be considered as a valuable adjunct to the Traffic of the line and would on these grounds justify a subscription.' By the turn of the century, a more direct and enlightened approach was recommended by A. J. Collin, the new engineer, backed by the new general manager, C. S. Denniss. There was an interesting consultation with George Owen, the retired engineer, who advised that the groins should be extended down to the low water mark to cause the silt to be deposited more effectively. After this, a happy partnership formed between the company and the council to further these protection schemes, which were based on 'Mr Case's System' (Case was the engineer to the Dymchurch area). The company donated regularly when asked, and the contribution for 1908 was £100. The payments continued right up to the Great War, when shortage of money forced the company to decline further support.

The year 1893 saw the first moves in the great water supply saga, which was to trickle on for the next 18 years. Back in 1863, when Savin's men were digging near Tyn-y-Parc, they had cut into a good spring, and Piercy had the flow piped back to a reservoir near Pen-y-Wern and to a header tank in the cutting below. A 4in cast iron pipe was laid, from which the crossing house and the stationmaster's house were each supplied by a ¾in pipe, whilst the lavatories and refreshment rooms shared a third. Savin's Cambrian Terrace had one 1¼in pipe between all thirteen houses, while the 4in main continued right into his Cambrian Hotel, although the engine water tank had first call via a 4in tee. To his houses, he had given a water supply 'in perpetuity', but with no guarantee of rate of flow or renewal of pipes; he had been bankrupted anyway, and now the pipes were furring up.

The company's immediate solution c. 1893 (because they had not the power to compel these other users to contribute towards the cost of replacing the pipes) was to decide to install a force pump for £37, to get them through the approaching summer. However, this was probably not installed, and a warning was sent to all that the locomotive supply would be given priority. Then the whole village made an application for a water supply, addressed to 'The Directors of the Cambrian Company and the owners of the Cambrian Hotel and Terrace at Borth who at present monopolise the water supply from Penwern cutting near Llanvihangel Station.' By 1897, they were filling the locomotives by hand, pumping from the adjacent drainage ditch. Repiping would then have cost £643, and the Board approved a layout, proposed by the council, though only if the council were prepared to pay for it. But the council wanted the project to be at the company's expense, and subsequently prepared an independent scheme of their own. The engineer warned the Board: 'I shall have to ask you before very long to permit me to renew the pipes for our own purposes', but the Board ignored this because they wished to manoeuvre

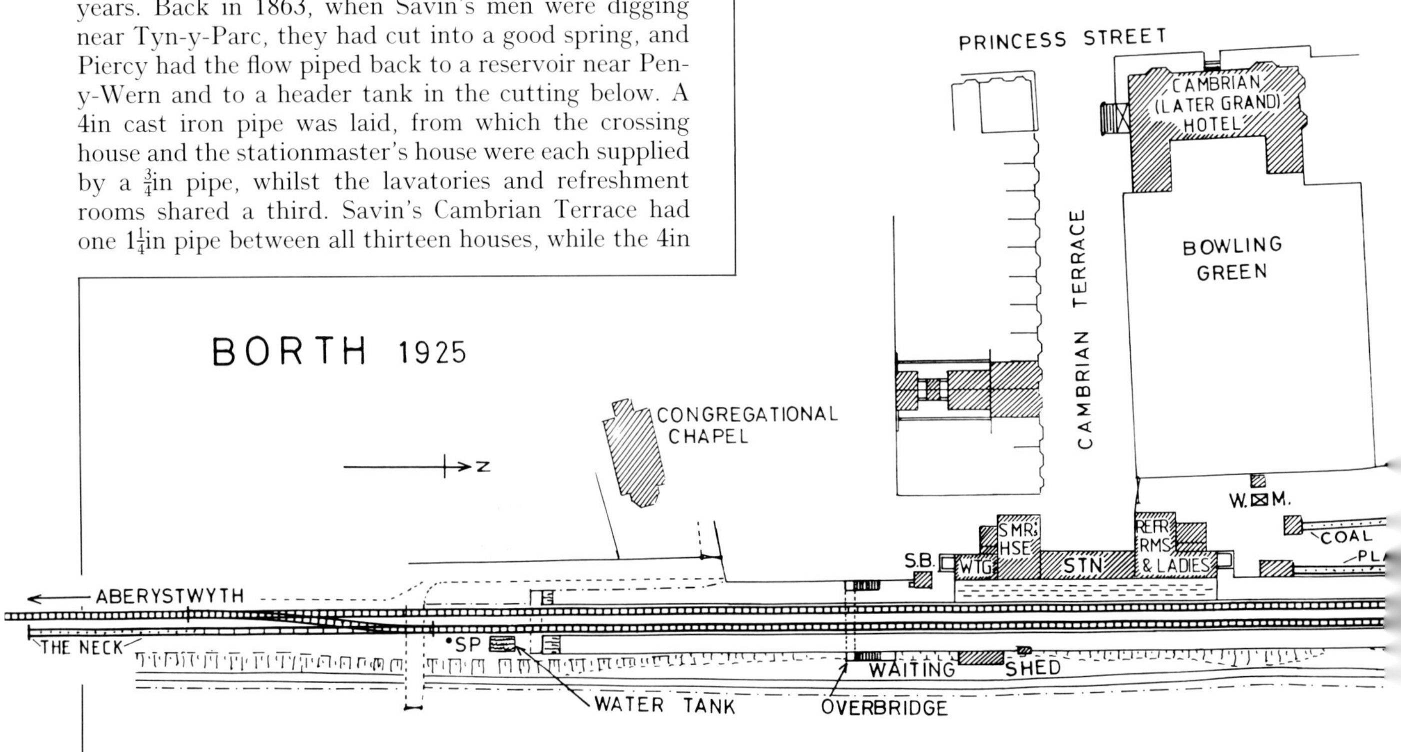

others into paying for the pipework. By 1899, the estimated cost had risen to £860, and by 1900, with a new reservoir, the cost had risen further to £1,000. The subject of the pipes to the terrace and hotel was still being deferred, and the company took solicitor's advice as to the true legal position; another clear notice was sent warning that, in the event of a shortage that summer, all outside supplies would be cut off as all water available would be required for the engines. Despite this, in 1906 the Borth Parochial Council asked for a water supply from railway sources. By 1908, when the price had come down, the Board had won; the pipes were renewed at a cost of £604 13s 5d, of which the hotel and terrace contributed £600. In 1911, the terrace owners and the hotel evaded the new district water rate because they already had an adequate water supply.

Although Borth had the capability of crossing two passenger trains, it only possessed one platform. It was therefore still the practice in 1894 for the train held in the loop to await the departure of that in the platform before pulling forward onto the main, and backing into the vacated station. In the unfounded hope that there would be a Board of Trade grant to pay for work required by the 1889 Act, a 200-yard-long down platform with a waiting shed and a footbridge was authorised, but at their own expense the company could only afford to construct a short platform. The footbridge did not arrive until May 1900, and it was a further eleven years before a long down platform was provided, when £1,000 was expended on this and some other work.

In 1895, one of Thomas Savin's ideas was revived. The London & South Western Railway had just announced the promotion of combined rail and hotel bookings to their Ilfracombe Hotel. The Cambrian proposed to charge £5 5s 0d for a similar scheme, with visitors staying at the Cambrian Hotel at Borth. However, the London & North Western refused to issue the tickets from Euston.

On 26th July 1902, the 6.15 a.m. down goods halted in the loop after shunting, with 26 wagons, 5 coaches and 7 passenger vans. The points had been left set for the neck, and the crew, who had spent the half-hour waiting in a public house for the section to be cleared before they could proceed, quite failed to notice this; they 'demolished the stop block entirely'. The general manager reported: 'The Stationmaster has always been unsatisfactory but I have never been able to find adequate ground for removing him to a less important place. I regret however that the usual petition (for his reinstatement) has been received signed by the

The load gauge was above the siding behind the platform. The siding served as a loading dock. 1954. *Author*

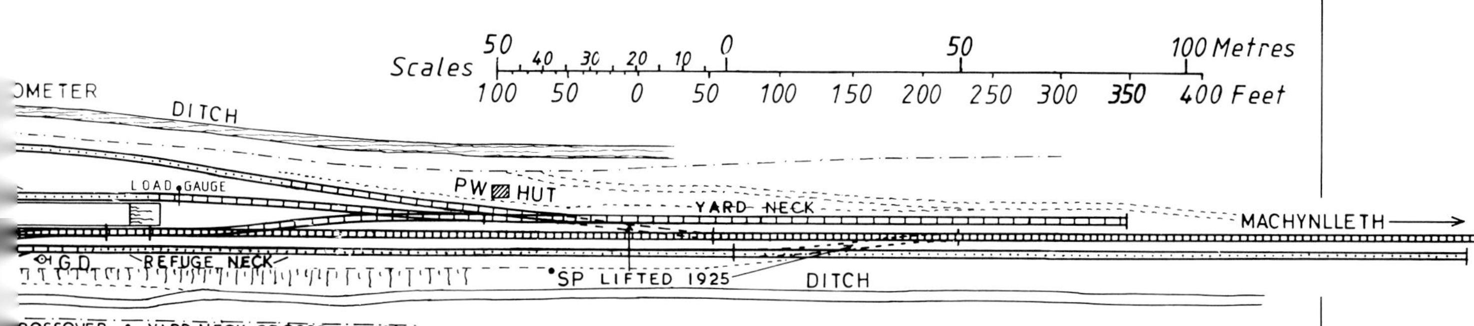

Chairman of the District Council and, probably, a large proportion of the inhabitants of Borth.'

At midsummer 1902, the company applied to the magistrates to have the licence reduced, to allow the closure of the refreshment rooms from October to April each winter; the facility had been closing by 7.30 p.m. for several years. In 1915, the police opposed the renewal of the licence and won their case on the grounds that 'it was not required to meet the wants of the neighbourhood and if granted would make the number of public houses in the neighbourhood excessive.' However, the general manager made an appeal to the Quarter Sessions and won the licence back. Soon after the outbreak of the Great War, the Cambrian Hotel was offered for sale to the company, who declined.

In 1921, the tablet instruments were still being held in the stationmaster's office as the box was stated to be too small, and the turnstile at Capel Soar level crossing was noted as not being locked with the gates. The signalman at the station was only engaged part-time on signalling duties.

The Great Western kept the station well, and made little alteration. The tablet instruments were moved into the box, and in 1925 the old ground frame working

The station approach road, looking down Cambrian Terrace. The row of terraced houses built by Savin is on the right. 1963. *Author*

The GWR renewed the canopy over the up platform at Borth. Compare the sturdy but rather spartan ironwork with that shown in the picture on page 131. 1963. *Author*

The canopy erected by the GWR did not extend the full length of the building, as this view demonstrates. 1963. *Author*

The signal box, looking towards Dovey Junction. This box was provided as part of the 1891 resignalling, which was completed on 23rd February at a cost of £1,253 4s 7d – a large sum to spend on a relatively small station. 1963. *Author*

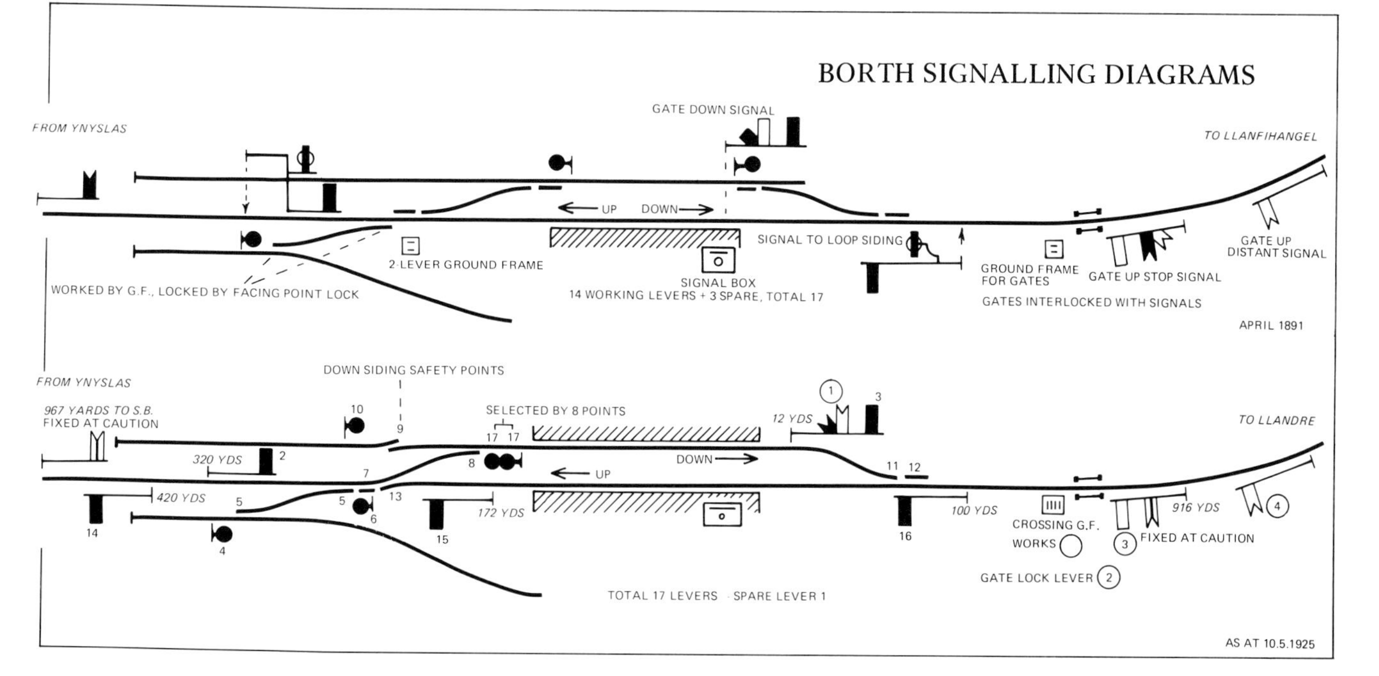

the points leading to the goods yard was removed, and single levers put into the sidings – this work cost only £150, as 1925 was a year of poor wages. In 1930, a second-hand 15-ton cart weighbridge measuring 16ft by 8ft, and costed at £110, replaced the old one. In time for the summer season of 1932, £700 was expended in erecting a standard Great Western-style awning to replace the old Cambrian pattern.

Electric lighting was installed in place of oil lamps in 1936, at a cost of £150.

The Great Western took over the refreshment rooms from Spiers and Ponds in 1926, but they put them back to tender again in 1943. F. W. Hughes & Sons tendered 3% on the gross takings.

In 1954, the old footbridge was replaced by a reinforced concrete structure.

Working Instructions

In Cambrian days and later, banking engines were often taken off up trains at Borth for return to Aberystwyth.

From the advent of GWR ownership, if a goods engine was required to assist a passenger engine and it had to run tender first, it was to be coupled to the train, with the train engine leading.

When moving from the up loop to the yard, the train or engine had to be brought to a stand at the Up Starting signal. After this

Looking along the up platform towards Dovey Junction, showing the reinforced concrete footbridge erected in 1954 to replace the one put up in 1900. 1963. *Author*

The down side waiting room – a modest affair compared with the substantial building on the opposite platform. 1963. *Author*

Borth station from Morfa Borth, showing the construction of the timber platform on the down side. 1963. *Author*

2–6–0 Mogul No. 4377 on a seven-coach down train. *P. J. Garland*

had been lowered, the train could move forward to a point short of the locking bar governing the points leading to the yard neck. Then the Starter was put back to danger, the points were set for the yard, and the disc was lowered to allow the final movement.

No. 2 (down) platform was lower than standard, and portable steps had to be kept available for the assistance of passengers.

General Notes

Borth was a haystack point, but holding barely three tons.

The water tank measured 9ft 6in x 5ft 6in x 4ft 9in and held 1,488 gallons. In Cambrian times, the frost precautions were the responsibility of the Traffic Department.

The Great Western had installed a camping coach by 1934.

A note of 1888 showed that horses and carriages belonging to visitors were being unloaded and reloaded at the end of the platform siding.

In 1991, only the main station building with a little ticket office remained, next to the single running line. The refreshment rooms were being made into a private house, and the remainder housed a marzipan factory.

In 1938, goods and parcels were collected and delivered free of charge by cartage service.

Recollections of Cambrian Days by Bill Owen (Stationmaster in the 1950s)

I had to go to Oswestry for the interview, and I remember being sent into the awful presence of the secretary, Mr Samuel Williamson, who told me that if I worked hard and behaved myself I would have a fine future in front of me.

My first stationmaster lived in the station house with his wife and mother, who were always quarrelling. He might be sitting at his desk when they started, and he would put his pen down with a grim, resigned gesture, and go round and make them shut up as the people at the station could hear them. Often he could be away for more than an hour trying to persuade them to keep themselves peaceable.

Once, I heard the rumble of a train approaching down the bank when there was no train due; on rushing outside I saw five loaded wagons bearing down on the station. I raced to the box and set the points for a straight run through, just in time. The wagons rushed past me and slowly came to a halt at the top of the slight rise towards Ynyslas. I then rang the stationmaster of Llandre, who was a very dignified man of the old school, and very caustic towards junior porter/signalmen. 'Have you lost anything Mr Partridge?', I asked him.

'What do you mean, have I lost anything? – are you being impudent, young Owen?'

At the south end of Borth station there was not only a barrow crossing for the railway, but also a footpath crossing. The down starting signal on the left carries the distant signal (there was no down stop signal) for Borth Capel Soar crossing beneath. *Author*

At length he withdrew to look round his yard, and then rushed back to the telephone.

'Is old X there?'

'No, he's in the house'

'Does he know?'

'No'

'Well, I'm sending my shunting engine and a brake – you hold everything and let them through, and if you breathe a word to anyone about this day's business I'll make you smart, d'you hear me?'

Borth bank could be difficult on a wet day with a single engine and a heavy train, and the drivers considered it below their dignity to ask for a banker. On one occassion, Tom y Borth had two goes, and was back in the loop for the third time, so I asked him if he wanted a banker. 'Duw no! – you open the points behind me, the stationmaster isn't about, and I'll back down and get a good run.' I did what he asked, as juniors then did not argue with drivers either; he fouled the up main for a good two trains length, but came storming through the station loop and made it clear away that time.

UPPINGHAM-BY-THE-SEA

The Reverend Edward Thring, the progressive – and sometimes aggressive – headmaster of Uppingham School (which he had built up from barely thirty boys in 1853 to three hundred by 1875) was facing the possible ruin of all for which he had worked so hard. Sewage disposal and water extraction in Victorian days were still a long way from being exact sciences, and gravity, seepage, and the use of brook courses and wells often caused the two to intermingle. The little township of Uppingham had all these problems, and

The small water tank alongside the down loop line was used mainly by assisting engines waiting to return up the bank and back to Aberystwyth light engine. *Author*

also a reactionary Sanitary Board headed by the Reverends Barnard Smith and William Wales. Thring openly blamed them for the outbreak of typhoid fever which had occurred in the town, and they blamed him for its spread amongst his scholars; and parents were considering the removal of their sons and heirs to safer places, nearer to their homes.

At this time, Savin's roomy Cambrian Hotel at Borth was in one of its frequent periods of disuse, and there were empty houses in his Cambrian Terrace. On 27th March 1876, an eighteen-van special train arrived at Borth carrying the Reverend Thring, some of his masters, three hundred bedsteads, much lesser equipment, and the massive school lawn roller. As there was insufficient local labour, Thring is said to have 'made a descent upon Aberystwyth and returned with the required number', and a large shed was put up in the hotel grounds to function as the assembly hall. On 4th April, only ten short of the three hundred boys detrained and were conducted to their lodgings.

The boys loved it, and set to work with great enthusiasm in their unusual surroundings. Out of school there was the beach, the sea, walks, and even expeditions into the mountains. For sport, there was a large field near Bow Street, let for a nominal rent by Sir Pryse Pryse; this had been levelled by that great roller, set in motion by 'fag-power'. The Cambrian made a special rate for the train journey to the sports field, and helped in many other ways to further those more distant expeditions, earning the title 'the ever-helpful Cambrian Railways'.

Facilities for private study were virtually non-existant, and it seems a shame not to be able to relate that they adopted the bright suggestion that two hundred bathing machines should be loaded onto the London & North Western Railway at Llandudno for transfer to Borth, via Afon Wen. Imagine two hundred boys studying in bathing machines on Borth promenade in a freezing north-westerly gale!

It was after an exceptionally powerful south-westerly gale that the masters and boys distinguished themselves by their efforts with hands and shovels in helping to straighten and resettle the piled sleeper wall along the back of the beach, in time to hold off the worst of the effects of a second high tide. After this, they helped the distressed villagers more directly, in moving the piles of stones which had been driven up against the backs of the houses near the sea, and assisting in the clearing up and drying-out of flooded and damaged homes. No-one in Borth was even injured, nor one single animal drowned, whereas Ynyslas went twelve feet under water in places, and one farmer lost all but eleven of a flock of one hundred and fifty sheep.

The Cambrian was put out of action in many places for some time, and after a day's attempt at conveying passengers round the breaks by road, the solicitor decreed that the storm had been 'an Act of Providence and the Company was not liable'. They telegraphed 'all parts of the Country' to stop sending passengers, hired 'Conveyances' for the mail, and waited while George Owen and his men cleared up the mess. He paid a glowing tribute to the way the masters and the boys had conducted themselves at Borth.

Although the school's stay at Borth had been intended for one term only, Thring had refused to bring the boys back to Uppingham until he had his promised new water supply, and the Sanitary Board had admitted and remedied their mistakes.

One outstanding incident illustrates well the devious ways of Victorian petty authority. The news came to Borth that the voting papers for the absent masters in the coming election for seats on the Sanitary Board were to be posted to their Uppingham addresses, too late for them to be redirected to Borth and posted back again. Doctor Bell, both an enlightened local doctor and the School Medical Officer, telegraphed Thring at Borth, had the voting papers collected, and handed them to a Mr White. This gentleman rode with all possible speed to Rugby station, and joined a train north-west to Crewe. Thence he took another train to Whitchurch, and therefrom jolted south-west in a four-wheeled carriage behind one of the Cambrian's cabless Sharp Stewart engines, eventually arriving at Borth station. Here, on the platform, the masters were duly assembled and waiting with a desk, an inkwell and a pen. The worthy gentleman then caught the next up train, retraced his tortuous route, and the voting papers were back in time to be counted.

The last term at Borth ended on 10th April 1877, and Reverend Thring took his charges safely back to Uppingham and their own new and unpolluted supply of water, to a town which had properly cleaned up its sewage system, and to a new Chairman of the Sanitary Board, for the Reverend Barnard Smith had died (of typhoid!).

They had left a grateful Borth after a farewell of song and speeches that only Wales can give.

NOTE. Compiled in the main from *By God's Grace* by Bryan Matthews, and from the *Borth Centenary Magazine of 1977*, with the kind help of Mr J. P. Rudman, the school Archivist.

BORTH to LLANDRE

– 87m 38c to 89m 54c

From Borth, the line runs due south over Capel Soar level crossing and climbs into the hills by means of an impressive, curved embankment. On a south-easterly course the railway heads inland, crossing the three spans of Pont Wern, the last timber bridge on this section, and the Cwm-cethyn bridge over the B4353. Now the climb continues in cuttings, along short embankments, and across several bridges of varying character until, after recurving back to a southerly course again, Llandre is reached. The whole climb is known as Borth Bank in working instructions, and is 1 in 60 at the lower end. In the 1870s, the old 0–6–0 goods engines were allowed 20 wagons plus carriages, and the 0–4–2s only 16 wagons plus carriages, without a banking engine. By 1911, the small 4–4–0s were allowed 18 wagons whilst the 0–6–0 goods engines could take 30, but this was often exceeded 'off the record'.

The crossing keeper at Capel Soar Crossing and his family with the Borth station master c.1895. He diligently cultivated the narrow strip of ground on the up side right up to the sleeper ends – potatoes earthed up on the left, then young seedling onions, spring cabbage, rhubarb, more onions, rhubarb again, and lastly possibly young brussels sprouts. *Cty Mrs. Glenys Gratton*

Left: The gate on the Borth side of Capel Soar Crossing, with the slate-clad crossing keeper's house behind. The device on the right-hand gate post was the equipment which locked the gates against the road when signals were at clear – the interlocking rod from the ground frame lever can be seen coming up from the wooden cover over the ground-level trunking. *Right:* The GWR renewed the ground frame for the signals at Capel Soar Crossing with this standard product from the Reading Signal Works. 1966. *M. Christensen*

Capel Soar Crossing, with GWR gates, looking inland. The pedestrian wicket gates on the right were not locked by the signalling. 1956. *Author*

In 1923, the Great Western rated the bank for the steam railmotors at 16 wheels in addition to the motor.

An old Cambrian instruction provided for a banking engine to be placed ready in 'the neck' at Borth if the guard had advised the driver at Moat Lane that this train might require such a banker, and the driver had agreed, and Moat Lane had telegraphed the requirement onwards.

In July 1893, the engineer asked for around $2\frac{1}{2}$ miles of bull-headed steel rails 'For the steep incline between Llanfihangle [sic] and Borth'. He was authorised to purchase 320 tons.

A wet summer caused a build-up of water over the bed of clay where the spring had been piped at the top of Pen-y-wern cutting; in September 1896 the overlying rock slid off, and the cutting had to be widened out.

Pont Wern, looking north to Borth. The wooden-post Cambrian era signal shown below had been replaced by a standard GWR tubular post signal by the time this picture was taken in 1959. *Author*

Pont Wern bridge, looking east. 1959. *Author*

Cambrian up home signal for Capel Soar Crossing. The GWR fixed the distant arm below (for Borth signal box) at 'caution'. This picture, taken in 1956, shows how this signal had been reduced in height compared with the photo on the next page. *Author*

LEWIS

A postcard view, looking down Borth Bank towards Capel Soar Crossing, probably around the turn of the century. In the foreground is the Cwm-cethin road underbridge in its original form. Beyond lies Borth, a 'ribbon village' spread out along a single seafront road. Just to the right of the nearest signal is the largest chapel in Borth, but further to the right, beside the level crossing, is the Capel (chapel) Soar from which the crossing took its name. The signal in the foreground is the up distant for Capel Soar Crossing. The arm is painted red, with the deep white chevron which characterised Cambrian signals. This was destined to be the last survivor of the Dutton signals provided for the Cambrian. Further down the bank is the up stop signal for the crossing, with the distant for Borth station signal box beneath. The arms are set high on a tall post, so as to provide a clear sighting – above the confused background of the houses – from a distance. The problem with this was that the signal lights would have been too high for easy focusing. This was dealt with by having the lamps and spectacle glasses lower down the post. The telegraph pole route was later renewed by the GWR with one carrying more wires – an expensive operation but essential to the extension of the telephone network. *Pope/Parkhouse Archive*

Cwm-cethin bridge, looking north in 1968. The original girders of the bridge had been replaced by concrete beams. *Author*

A view of the Dutton-made Cambrian up distant signal for Capel Soar Crossing, 1968. The curve here limited vision of the up stop signal, and trains were wont to run quite fast down this bank — all good reasons why the GWR left this as a worked signal when distant signals were made 'fixed' along most of the Cambrian lines in 1923/1924. *Author*

The Great Western placed a 'Sound Whistle' board for up trains approaching an occupational crossing at 'Llan Deri Farm Crossing' i.e. Glan Leri.

During the summer of 1929, Pen-y-wern farm bridge had to be entirely reconstructed at a cost of £290. Also in 1929, Pont Wern was treated to an interesting bit of surgery by splicing fresh timber into the main piles before renewing the upper parts. This was a common form of repair to a timber bridge, but it was unusual to find it so described. The cost was £770.

To enable the B4353 to be widened in the summer of 1939, the Parc-Back bridge also had some unusual treatment. After the abutments had been set back, the old Piercy suspended-deck girders were rebedded after having extra panels grafted into the ends to save expense for the County Council, who paid £6,000 towards the total cost of £6,664.

In December 1959, there was a spectacular incident at Capel Soar level crossing. A double-headed up goods, with 13 fitted vans followed by a string of loose wagons, a well wagon and the brake van got there in three minutes less than the fastest booked passenger train, and before the gates had been opened. There was a full emergency brake application which saved the gates, but there was one casualty. On the well wagon, Vale of Rheidol engine No. 7 (en route from Aberystwyth to Swindon works) broke all eight anchor chains, jumped a

9in baulk, and slammed hard up against the front of the well.

Capel Soar level crossing was unusual on the Cambrian system, in that it had both home and distant signals in the up direction. The distant signal gave the extra braking distance required by trains on the descent at 1 in 60 from Llandre. The crossing was to have been converted to an AOC (L) automatic crossing with lights but no barriers (hence the term 'open crossing') by the end of September 1988, but an unexpected difficulty in remodelling the cattle grid delayed the change until January 1989. The last crossing keeper was a highly popular lady known to all, of course, as 'Glenys The Crossing'.

Cwm-cethin concrete bridge, looking south up the bank to Glan-leri and Llandre. 1968. *Author*

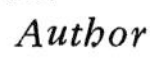

Cwm-cethin concrete bridge, looking west in 1968. The massive brick abutments had been made to carry a double track line had traffic ever required the widening of the line. *Author*

No. 7819 *Hinton Manor* with the 10.25 Oswestry-Aberystwyth excursion climbing Borth Bank and approaching Glan-leri bridge. 18th May 1959. *Ifor Higgon*

Glan-leri bridge, looking uphill (but in the down direction!) towards Llandre. 1968. *Author*

The lane ascending from the main road to Glan-leri bridge. 1968. *Author*

Glan-leri bridge, looking north-east, showing the corrugated-iron palisade. *Author*

Looking towards Llandred in 1968 from the lineside, the Round bridge on Borth Bank seems insignificant. *Author*

But from below (this is the east elevation) the height and grace of the arch is revealed. *Author*

Parc-back bridge, looking towards Borth in 1959 before replacement. *Author*

Parc-back bridge, looking west in 1959. The original Piercy underslung deck was slightly lengthened for road widening in 1939. *Author*

Parc-back bridge, looking up towards Borth, after rebuilding with new girders. The name may have been intended as Parc-bach (Little Field) but the railway draughtsman misunderstood and printed 'back'. 1968. *Author*

This 1992 view of Parc-back bridge makes an interesting comparison with that on page 149 and shows the new girders erected in place of those extended during the 1939 road-works. *Author*

Near the top of Borth Bank is Pen-y-wern bridge (reconstructed in 1929). The water tank providing the supply to Borth, described in the text, was just past the bridge on the right. 5th June 1963. *Author*

Looking downhill (the up direction) from Tyn-y-parc bridge with Pen-y-wern bridge in the distance. The springs which provided the water supply were on the right. The Ballast Hole siding from which construction material was taken in the early years of the railway, is believed to have been located in this cutting. 5th June 1963. *Author*

2–6–0 Mogul No. 7309 in lined green livery with the Aberystwyth portion of the down Cambrian Coast Express, nearing the top of the climb from Borth. 30th August 1957. *Ifor Higgon*

Tyn-y-parc bridge, the south elevation, looking downhill towards Borth. Like Pen-y-wern bridge, this has a timber palisade on steel girders. 1963. *Author*

This view through Tyn-y-parc bridge towards Aberystwyth reveals the down home signal and level crossing gates for Llandre station. *Author*

4–4–0 'Earl' No. 9015 (intended to have been *Earl of Clancarty*) leaving Llandre on an Aberystwyth to Machynlleth up local. The horse is grazing on the site of the terminal loop of the Plynlimon and Hafan Tramway, and the formation of the line descending to the Cambrian's siding can be seen above the leading carriage. 30th August 1957. *Ifor Higgon*

LLANDRE (Churchtown) – 89m 54c to 89m 68c

For the first few months of operation, there was a 'ballast hole' and siding below Tyn-y-parc bridge and the man in charge was responsible for train staff working, since the 'ballast hole' was in such regular use that it was a train staff 'station'. The station was originally called Llanfihangel (St Michael's Church), though the village also had Gen'eur Glyn (at the head of the Valley) as part of the name. In 1916, the name was altered to Llandre at the request of Cynallmawr Parish Council, 'as Llanfihangel is a very common place name in Wales and much confusion is causing considerable inconvenience.'

Initially there were only two employees, but traffic from lead mining increased, and by 1871 a 5-ton crane (for loading timber) and a cattle pen had been authorised, the latter costing £25. On 27th June 1873, the committee heard that the Esgair-Hir Mining Company wished to rent land at a nominal figure for the erection of an ore shed.

The engineer, George Owen, reported in July 1874 that it had become necessary to lengthen the 160ft platform by another 100ft at a cost of £46 8s 4d, and this was approved. In 1876 the cattle pens had to be paved, and this cost £9 7s 0d.

Station at 89m 61c
Signal Box at 89m 63c
Opened: 23rd June 1864
Closed: 14th June 1965

In 1882, the question of erecting a goods warehouse and an ore shed came up. The ore shed was deferred, but the goods warehouse was built at a cost of about £200. The matter of the ore shed dragged on ineffectively until the Bryn-yr-Afr Mining Company took it up in 1885, and it was left to the newly-appointed secretary, John Conacher, to arrange construction at a cost of £96 1s 0d, the shed to be let for £5 per annum. The mining company was forecasting traffic of between 450 and 480 tons of lead ore per annum.

During the summer of 1883, another siding, 107 yards long, was laid down at a cost of £115 11s 6d.

On 6th December 1883 Emma Hughes, servant to Mr Baker of Rhyd-y-prennan Farm, was going to post a letter at the station letterbox when she stepped in front of the non-stop 1.40 p.m. ex-Whitchurch passenger train, and was killed. The Coroner's Jury recommended that all stations should be secured during the times when trains were passing. Nothing was done

A view of Llandre station, from a location close to where the siding provided for the Hafan Tramway trailed into the up loop line. The signalman had to work each of the four level crossing gates, separately, by hand. 1963. *Author*

Llanvihangel c.1895. The loop is clearly in use as a loop siding rather than a crossing loop, as evidenced by the dumb-buffered five-plank drop-door wagon standing on the left. The white-painted paling fences were typical as were the Cambrian's standard pattern of crossing gates hinged to swing across both rail and road. The carriage body is clearly definable as an Ashbury four-wheeler, originally a first or a second, possibly downgraded later to third composite. The small shed, with a sloping roof, at the top of the platform ramp, is the signal cabin shown in the upper drawing on page 160. The Inspecting Officers of the Board of Trade were constantly demanding that clocks be provided where they could clearly be seen by passengers. The clock here was prominently displayed on the front of the station.

Cty. Cambrian Railways Society

about this, however, and the pedestrian wicket gates beside the level crossing were never locked up from the signal box as was common on many other railways.

During the Whitsuntide week of 1885, a block telegraph was installed temporarily to facilitate the working of the heavier traffic. This was so successful that £40 12s 0d was spent in making the arrangement permanent. Later in that year, the stationmaster, Mr Richard Gough, was awarded the £3 prize for the best-kept station.

On the 12th October 1888, Porter John Joseph Gough was running alongside the engine of the 6.25 ex-Machynlleth mixed train to speak to the driver when he fell over a barrow and under the train, 'receiving such injuries as led to his death the same night'.

During the 1889 economy review, Llanfihangel was considered for a reduction in staffing level because the block and telegraph equipment had been removed when tablet instruments were introduced to control single line working and Llandre ceased to be a 'block post': 'While the gates were too heavy to be worked by a woman the place could be attended to by an old servant for whom a light place was required or a Station Master who could not work a Telegraph.'

The station was resignalled to conform with the Regulation of Railways Act, and the new layout was approved by Colonel Rich for the Board of Trade on 18th April 1891.

Elizabeth Jones (aged 86), mother of Mr William Jones of the Hafan Sett Quarries, failed to hear the whistling of a train on 18th February 1894 when on her way to church, and was run over on the level crossing by the Vicarage. The Coroner's Jury recommended gates across the railway, and the provision of a footbridge. Colonel Yorke from the Board of Trade disagreed, and advised that the gates, which were hung as for an occupational road and thus opened away from the railway, should be rehung so as to swing across both road and rail, and be provided with red target discs and lights. The wicket gate could remain, but a warning notice should be displayed. The committee approved both these arrangements and also, at the son's request, that the company should pay for the funeral.

On 3rd June 1893, the committee approved the installation of a siding to serve a narrow gauge tramway. Soon afterwards Richard Brayne, the general manager, reported that a siding for the Hafan Tramway would be required in the next few weeks at a cost of £183 4s 0d, of which the narrow gauge company was to contribute £100, and that a wharf was to be provided. The history of the Plynlimon & Hafan Tramway

Llanvihangel station c.1890. The station nameboard behind the WILLIAM MORGAN LLANFIHANGEL BORTH wagon No. 3 had white letters on a green board. The engine, a Sharp Stewart 0–6–0 'Queen' class goods, was unaltered except for the addition of a roof and side sheets to form a cab over the footplate. The wagon on the left, with only its end showing, was a lime wagon in use for lead ore, and the wagon beyond was a Cambrian three-plank. The one behind the coalman's tip cars was R. WILLIAMS & SONS No. 134. The road vehicle in front of the station was a light tip cart.
John Thomas, cty. National Library of Wales

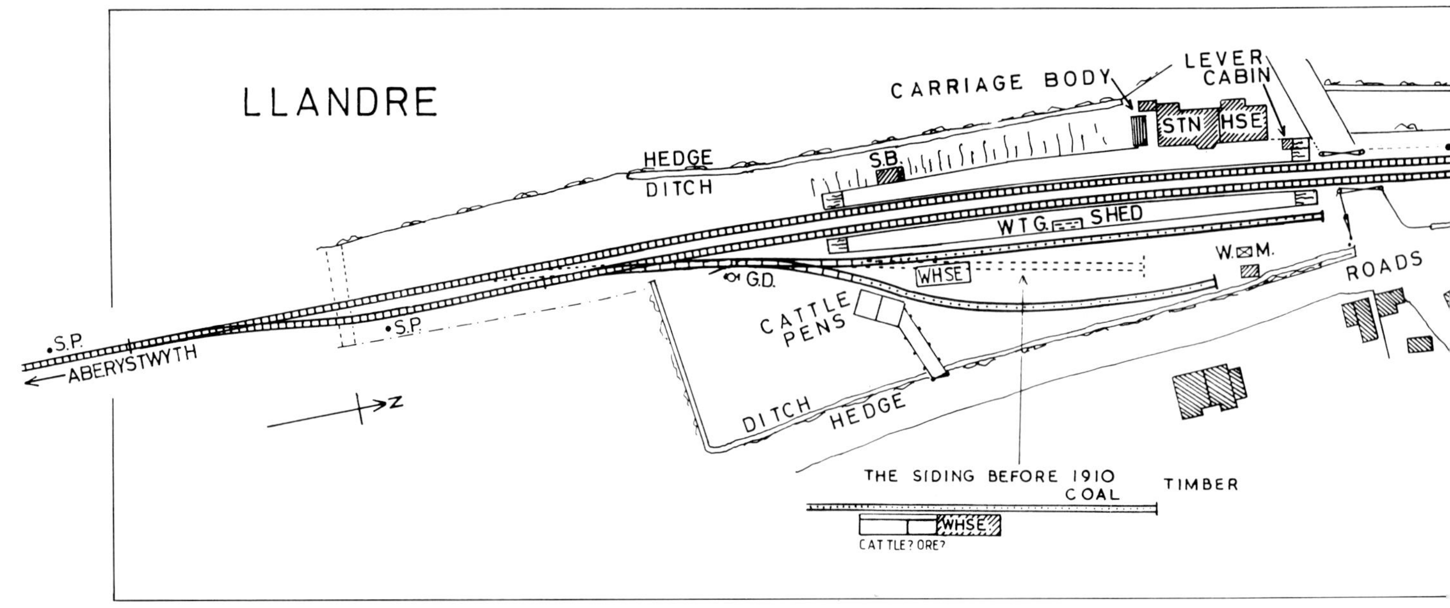

Llandre, looking towards Borth, with the site of the Hafan siding on the right. The tramway butted to it at the gap in the fence visible between the right-hand leg of the stop board and the adjacent telegraph pole. The rails at right-angles to the track, in the foreground, were provided to allow maintenance trolleys to be removed from the line. Tyn-y-parc bridge can be seen in the distance, beyond which the falling gradient steepens from 1 in 127 to 1 in 75. 1963. ***Author***

is comprehensively described in E. A. Wade's book about that line. Molyneaux, the promoter, was determined to secure an outlet to the sea without being 'throttled or choked' by the Cambrian's restrictive practices, and stated in one of his reports that 'The negotiations with the Cambrian have produced nothing'. He had then considered constructing his line to Ynyslas (already referred to in the section on Ynylas – the tramway was to pass under the Cambrian line there), with a branch to Llanfihangel, or building it to the high tide limit of the Leri at the back of Borth Station, or even of laying the line down to Clarach. He seemed obsessed with the idea that having his own direct access to the sea must increase the volume of his traffic; but it never would have been so, and the hoped-for flood of orders for his setts never came. One full year's output was recorded as 1,690 tons 4 cwt., which might average at around 4 to 5 eight-ton trucks a week. So the Hafan Tramway was dismantled in late 1899, and the siding taken up in 1911 when the layout was altered in connection with the provision of a down platform.

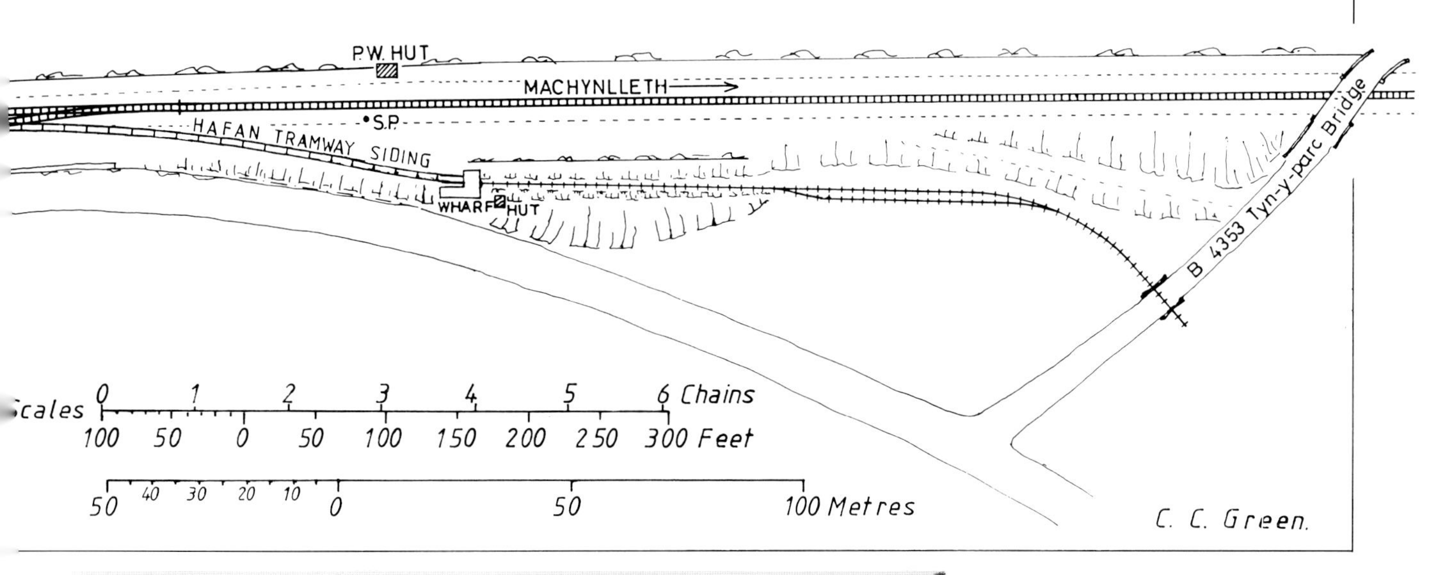

The station building, looking towards Aberystwyth. Without any awning over the platform, its appearance was always very austere. The space under the platform was formerly occupied by the rodding from the first signal box. *Author*

Left & right: Details of the Machynlleth end, and rear, of the station buildings. *Author*

The yard from the road, looking towards Borth and Machynlleth. The gate on the left gave access from the roadway to the cattle pens. 1963. *Author*

Looking south, towards Aberystwyth. The public telephone box, which superseded the public use of the telegraph instrument at the station, was effectively on railway property. 1963. *Author*

There were several attempts at revival of the P & H system, in 1907, 1909, 1910 and 1915. Of the last proposal, Samuel Williamson, the Cambrian's last general manager, wrote that while he felt it was his duty to acquaint his Board of the nebulous scheme put forward by Sir Edward Pryse, he hardly thought that the company would be justified in undertaking any financial responsibility or of entering into a working arrangement. All that now remains of the project at Llandre are part of the bed of the siding and, hidden in a stand of pines, the lower end of the descending ridge and ledge which carried the Hafan line to its end-on junction with the Cambrian.

In June 1898, the Reverend Evans asked for permission for himself and members of his congregation to walk along the line to Bow Street, but this, to the great relief of a horrified general manager, was refused. As a further safety measure, the level crossing gates

A view of the cattle dock and roadway side of the goods warehouse. ***Author***

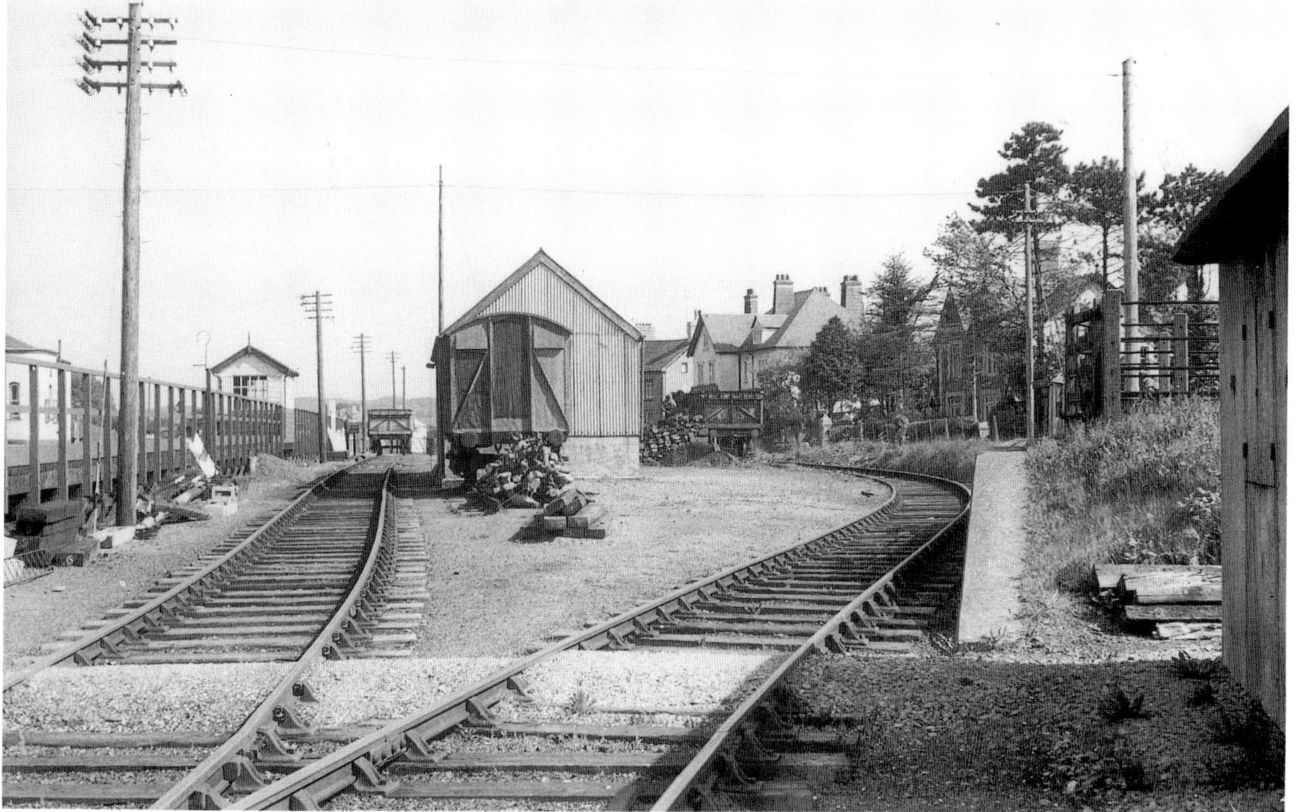

Looking into the yard past the cattle dock, showing the tiny waiting shed on the timber-built down platform and the 'stationary' van used as storage. 1963. ***Author***

A view of Llandre station, looking towards Borth. It was unusual to have a point within the goods yard worked from the signal box – the use of lever 9 to work these points is believed to have been because of the close proximity of the trap points at the exit from the yard. The posts for the token exchange apparatus are prominent in the foreground. 1963. *Author*

were left locked across the road, which aroused a local protest in 1899.

To act as additional counterbalance, and probably to enable the weight of the load being lifted to extend beyond the crane's rated 5-ton capacity, a stack of old rails were added to the back of the unit. These fell off on 18th May 1906, and crushed the foot of timber loader Lewis. He initially lost his foot, then a part of his leg and, two weeks afterwards, he died of blood poisoning and congestion of the lungs. At that time, timber loaders were casual labour, under no contract, and free to seek other work when not required. The pay was 11d per ton per gang (usually four), but the fewer there were the greater was each man's share.

Approval was given in 1911 for the station to be provided with a down platform. At the same time the siding behind the platform was slewed and the

The signal box provided by Tyer & Co for the 1911 resignalling. After the Abermule incident in 1921 the tablet (later token) instruments were moved from the station office into the box. One can clearly be seen through the open window. *Author*

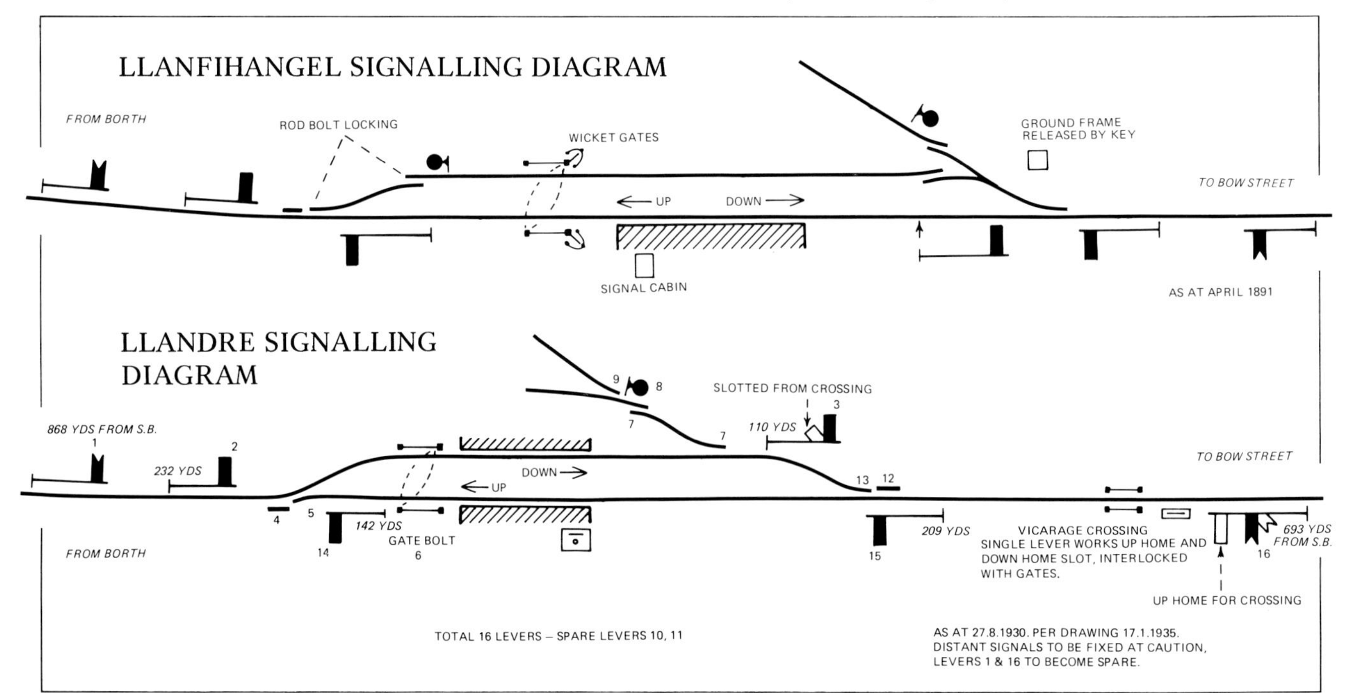

Looking towards Aberystwyth from beside the ramp of the down platform, with the house for the keeper at Vicarage Crossing in the middle distance. The gate (normally left open for the railway) can just be discerned. 1963. *Author*

warehouse was moved to suit. The whole station was resignalled as a crossing place, at a cost put at £1,600. By 1911 Dutton & Co. had ceased business, and Llandre was one of the few stations on the Cambrian to have a signal box fitted up by Tyer & Co.

Before the 1911 alterations, Llandre had been a station with a loop, in which a goods train could stand while a passenger train passed on the platform line, but at which two passenger trains were not allowed to pass. The rule was, of course, broken in emergencies. After the alteration, the station assumed the appearance which it retained until closure.

In 1921, the North Cardigan Farmers' Co-operative offered to lease the ore shed for £3 per annum, and to put it into order themselves – it had ceased to be let to the Hafan Mining Company (at £2 per annum) in 1915. A 5-year lease was arranged. In the same year, the tablet instruments were noted as being sited in the stationmaster's office, although there was room in the signal box for them to be moved to that location.

The station was not in an acceptable state of repair on takeover by the Great Western, and they had to spend £208 on putting matters right in 1923. The warehouse had to be replaced entirely for £300 in 1930, and in the following year, the old cart weighbridge was replaced by a second-hand model measuring 16ft by 8ft, with a capacity of 20 tons, at a cost of £250. The cattle pens were rebuilt in 1946 (£215).

Working Instructions

1943, Rule 114 (c): 'Up trains may be allowed to set back outside the Home signal provided there is a brake van in the rear and a Guard attending to it or an engine at the rear end and the Signalman has withdrawn the token for the Llandre – Bow Street Section.'

Up goods trains were to stop and have their brakes pinned down before descending Borth Bank (and were to be unpinned before leaving Borth).

General Notes

The Hafan Tramway ran a passenger service meeting main line trains on market days.

A note of 1888 shows that a facility existed for horse loading, but not for carriages.

The last Cambrian Weekly Notice advertised a vacancy for a 'Station Agent' (stationmaster) at '5th class Salary', and that the station house would be rented to him for £9 per annum.

There were no goods or parcel delivery services by 1938.

In 1966 the signal box was closed, and a replacement 3-lever ground frame provided to work the protecting signals and gate lock for the station level crossing. This work was undertaken by the LMR using LNWR pattern levers. This ground frame was taken out of use on 26th January 1989 when the crossing was converted to an 'automatic open crossing'.

GWR 4—4—0 'Duke' No. 3268 *Chough* pulling away from Llandre with a stopping train for Aberystwyth. 15th August 1935. *H. F. Wheeller*

LLANDRE to BOW STREET

– 89m 68c to 91m 15c

Vicarage Crossing, looking towards Aberyṣtwyth. The single-storey keeper's 'lodge' was typical of those found on the Cambrian lines and the square 'targets' on gates were another typical feature. 1963. *Author*

The line continues straight on, falling at 1 in 197 and 219, to Vicarage Crossing before descending into the gentle upland valley of Nant Ceiro. Beyond the crossing the gradient steepens to 1 in 94 and 1 in 75 as Bow Street is approached. The only engineering works on this section are the bridges by which two minor streams are crossed.

One woman had a very narrow escape from death about half-a-mile north of Bow Street in July 1884. She was walking along the line with two other women when the driver of the 6.20 p.m. ex-Machynlleth sounded his whistle, and 'one woman in her alarm ran across to the other side of the line in front of the Engine and fortunately succeeded in getting clear. The practice of trespassing upon the line appears in many places to be much resorted to – I would suggest that Platelayers be authorised to put a stop to it as much as possible'.

Looking east towards the main road (now the A487). 1963. *Author*

General Notes

The wickets at Vicarage Crossing had still not been locked by lever by 1921 and never were.

Vicarage Crossing, from a vantage point alongside the main A487 road. 1967. *Author*

Looking up towards Llandre station, the home signal (and signal box) for which are in the distance. The single lever in front of the keeper's house worked both up and down signals, and the gate lock. 1963. *Author*

A feature extensively found on the Cambrian Railways was the single-lever ground frames provided by Dutton & Co at level crossings. Two chains round the two large wheels simultaneously pulled to clear both the up and down home signals. A rod connection off the tail of the lever below surface level proved that the gates were open to the railway before the lever could be moved to clear the signals. When the signals were pulled 'off', the lever moved over 'top centre' and lay nearly parallel to the ground. 1963.*Author*

BOW STREET

– 91m 15c to 91m 36c

An up stopping train from Lampeter to Barmouth (tender first with 9017 from Lampeter to Aberystwyth) pausing at Bow Street. Beyond, the line climbs (from the level section through the station) at 1 in 75. The goods yard was served by a facing point from the down loop. 1959. *Ifor Higgon*

Station at 91.28
Signal Box at 91.29
Opened: 23rd June 1864.
Closed: 14th June 1965.

The village was originally known as Nant Afallen (Applebrook). The story runs that, in the early 19th century, a London lawyer had a house built there, and other friends or relatives did likewise. The acerbic wit of Wales soon had the little row of houses dubbed Bow Street, after the celebrated Magistrates' Court which was also the headquarters of the predecessors of the police force, the Bow Street Runners; and the name stuck!

The original Coast Act of 1861 required 'A First-Class Station for Passengers, Cattle, Goods, with a Siding and all the usual proper Accommodation for the loading and unloading of Goods and Cattle to be provided at Bow Street or at some other point on the line convenient to the Gogerddan Estate; and the Company might not erect any Inn or Eating House within one mile from such Station.' This explains why the station building was more handsome than many of the others, and why the station had two platforms from the beginning.

At first, only three staff were employed there, but more were needed before very long. The Pryses of Gogerddan had been making sure that they would have a good outlet for the lead ore from Blaenceulan and other mines, and for the produce from their great acreages of timber; by 1873, a siding was needed for a travelling crane to load 800 to 1,000 tons of timber, and this was provided.

For a short time early in February 1875, traffic had to be worked by flags or handlamps as a gale had blown

Bow Street bridge. A several-times-failed brick ogee arch finally settled by an ingenious prefabrication of old rail. This view was taken looking towards the 1 in 75 gradient in the direction of Llandre. 1984. *Author*

High summer and Bow Street is surrounded by the Territorial Army. Note the impeccable alignment. No company sergeant-major was ever satisfied until all the bell tents were in line diagonally as well as along and across the rows. The down refuge siding in the right foreground was full of stabled vehicles as was the No. 1 siding (visible below the smoke from the loco). *Pope/Parkhouse Archive*

down one of the signal posts carrying both a Home and a Starting signal.

In March 1879, a permanent way man had both his legs broken while unloading rails, and his Inspector had called a doctor. After ascertaining that the doctor had been told just 'you will be paid', and not 'The Company will pay you', the solicitor advised the Board that they were not liable for the payment of fees.

On 3rd August 1885, Mr David Edwards, a tailor from Bow Street, claimed for injuries he had sustained when, along with several other passengers, he had jumped down from a carriage which had not yet arrived at the platform. It was contended by the company that he had failed to wait for the over-long train to be pulled up further, and that the name of the station had *not* been called at his carriage. During the next

Territorials detrained and marching to camp in fours. Note the officer on the left with his drawn sword shouldered.
Cty. Mrs. T. Daniels

year, the platforms were lengthened to 400 feet, at a cost of £150.

The traffic manager, Mr Edwin Liller, reported that on 5th February 1887 Porter David Owen, while in charge of shunting, had been run over by two wagons. He was severely injured, but no-one had seen how he came to be under the wagons, and 'his condition in Aberystwyth Infirmary renders it not yet possible to question him.'

In 1888 approval was given to a proposal that access to the sidings were to be locked with the signals from a ground frame at the up end. This work was then deferred but may have been completed by the summer of 1889, when train tablet instruments for the section

This picture of cavalry remounts for the Boer War features the North 'signal box', usually referred to on plans as a shelter cabin because, despite its substantial structure, it was no more than a ground frame (released from the signal box) to work the points at the Llandre end of the station. It did not operate any signals and only contained four levers!
Cty. R. C. Riley

Bow Street with tents all about. A rare photograph, showing the era immediately following the 1910 layout alterations when there were connections to the goods yard from both the up line (the original connection) and by way of a facing lead from the down line. Note the up starter signal painted with the Cambrian disc instead of the more usual stripe.
Cty. M. E. M. Lloyd

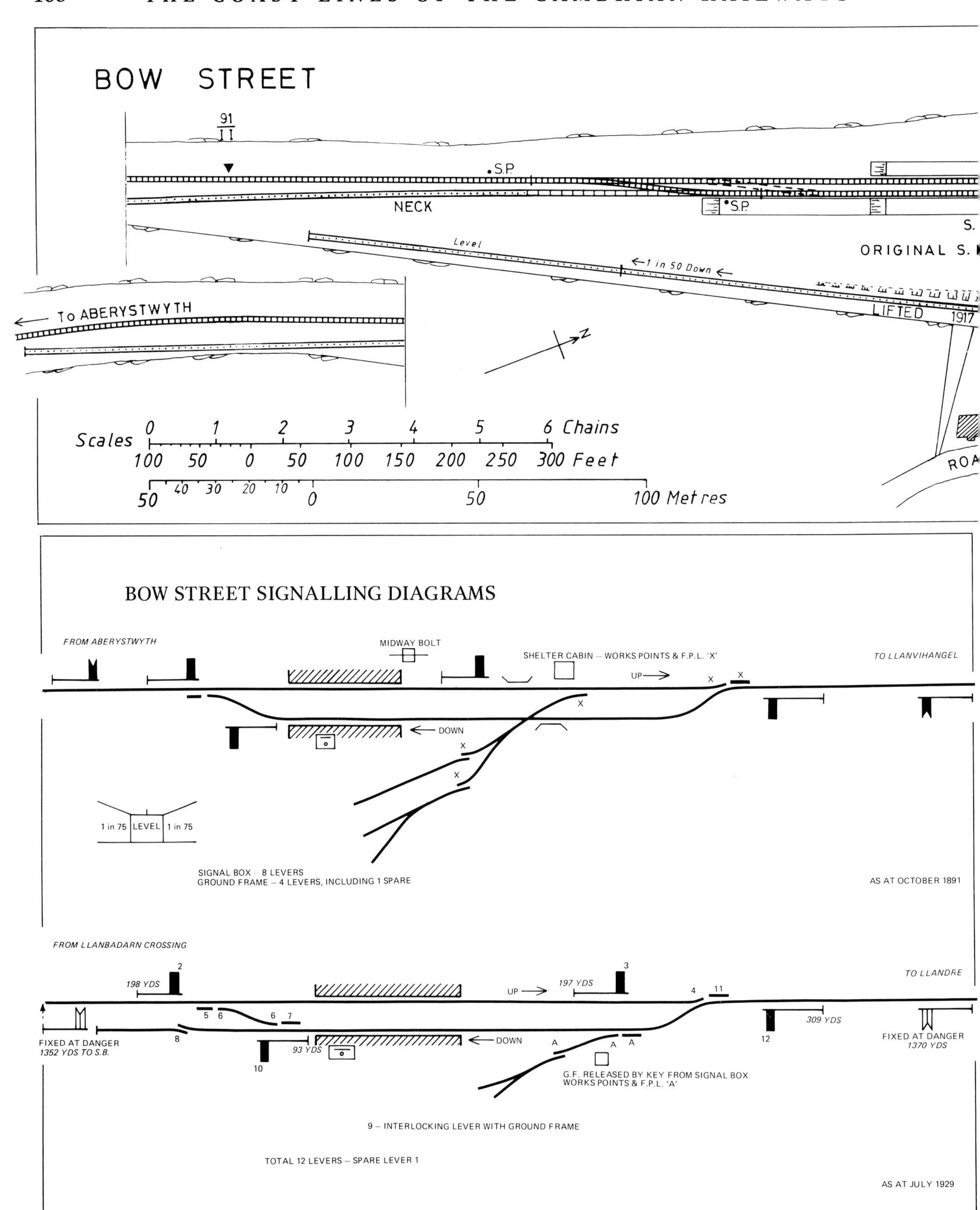
BOW STREET
91
S.P.
NECK
S.P.
S.
ORIGINAL S.
Level
← 1 in 50 Down ←
LIFTED 1917
← To ABERYSTWYTH
N
Scales
0 1 2 3 4 5 6 Chains
100 50 0 50 100 150 200 250 300 Feet
50 40 30 20 10 0 50 100 Metres
BOW STREET SIGNALLING DIAGRAMS
FROM ABERYSTWYTH
MIDWAY BOLT
SHELTER CABIN – WORKS POINTS & F.P.L. 'X'
TO LLANVIHANGEL
UP
DOWN
1 in 75 LEVEL 1 in 75
SIGNAL BOX – 8 LEVERS
GROUND FRAME – 4 LEVERS, INCLUDING 1 SPARE
AS AT OCTOBER 1891
FROM LLANBADARN CROSSING
198 YDS
197 YDS
TO LLANDRE
309 YDS
FIXED AT DANGER
1352 YDS TO S.B.
93 YDS
FIXED AT DANGER
1370 YDS
G.F. RELEASED BY KEY FROM SIGNAL BOX
WORKS POINTS & F.P.L. 'A'
9 – INTERLOCKING LEVER WITH GROUND FRAME
TOTAL 12 LEVERS – SPARE LEVER 1
AS AT JULY 1929

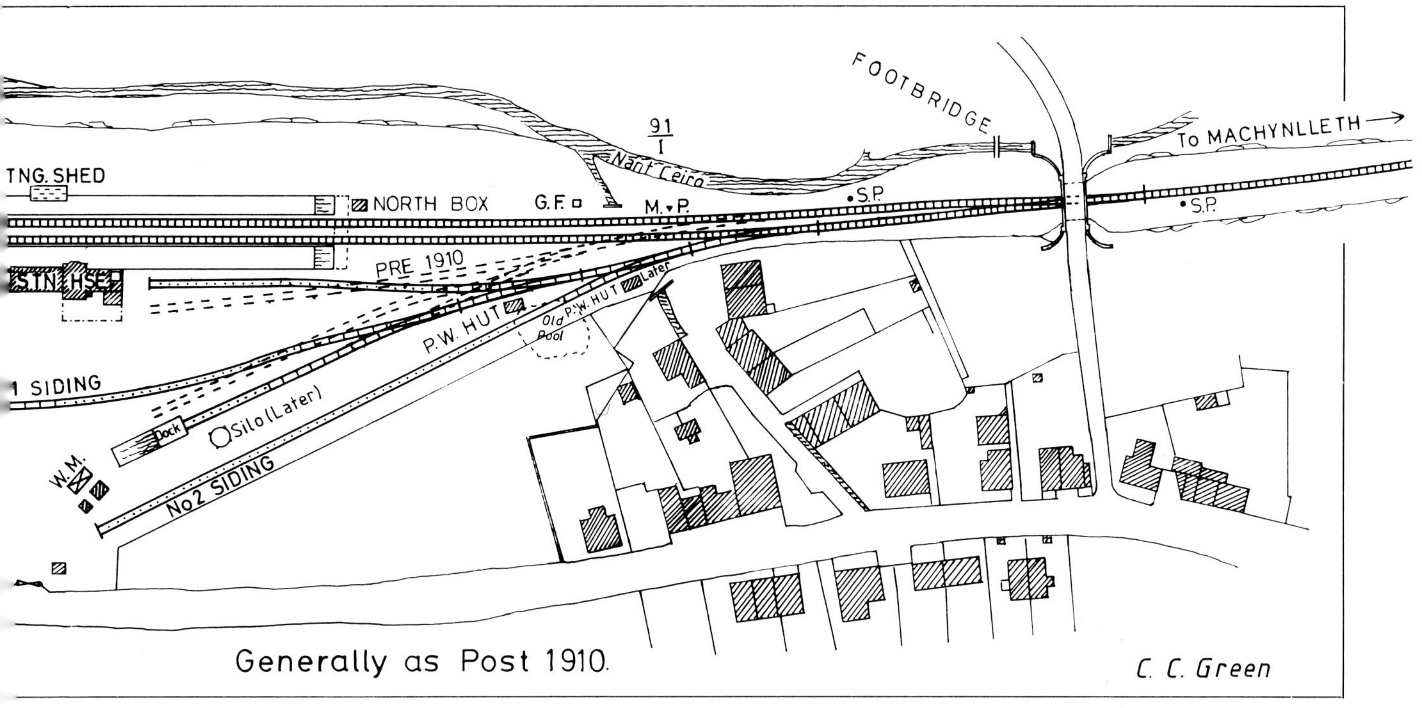

The back of the station master's house c.1900.
Pope/Parkhouse Archive

to Aberystwyth were installed. On 10th September of that year, the 2.10 p.m. ex-Whitchurch passenger train came off the line at the facing points, and ran for 87 yards along the sleepers. The porter was suspended from his duties. The report reveals an interesting train make-up: 'Engine No. 17, a 4–4–0 Small Sharp Stewart and 6w Tender with and L&NWR Break Van and 3 Carriages, 2 Cambrian Carriages and Break Van.'

On 19th February 1889, Dutton's tender for resignalling and interlocking for the sections between Bow Street and Glandovey was approved by the Committee. But, in October, the combined secretary, general manager and traffic manager, John Conacher, reported, as instructed, on the possibility of closing Bow Street. He wrote that 'it is conveniently placed for a considerable extent of country and there is a fair amount of Mineral and Timber Traffic at it', and he went on to remind his Board of their legal obligation under the 1861 Act to keep it open. The new signalling at Bow Street was brought into use on 6th April 1891.

During shunting on a wet day, 9th September 1895, Acting Goods Guard Watkins pinned down the brakes

Looking in the down direction from Llandre, and into the yard showing the cement silo used during the construction of the Nant-y-moch reservoir. 1963. *Author*

of some wagons parked on the uphill grade towards Llanfihangel. However, he omitted to place a scotch block, and they ran away into the sidings, where three Cambrian cattle trucks were badly damaged as a result. He was demoted to Porter.

Also in 1895, it was approved that a footbridge over the brook and a footpath should be built on the up side, provided that the local people paid for it. It was built as a 14in x 14in baulk of timber spanning 7 feet with handrails, and it remained there until it became too rotten to use (probably in the 1950s).

As the timber traffic had much declined, the spacious yard was found to be ideal for the detraining and entraining of recruits destined for the Boer War during 1899 and 1900. Afterwards, it was thought that some of the spare land could be sold off, and on 27th February 1901 the Board consented to the sale of two plots to Mr J. Meurig Edwards. Then a suggestion was made that the Army might need to use the station again, in anticipation of a war with Germany. So, in 1908, when Mr J. T. Rees of Bronceiro wished to buy a piece of land for 1s 6d per square yard, he was refused; although he rebid at 4s 6d no details of acceptance have been found.

At the end of 1909, there was an urgent 'flap' on about providing facilities at the station for the Territorial Army so that the old training areas on the Gogerddan Estate, which had been used for the troops at the time of the Boer War, could be put to good use once more. The chairman personally approved the expenditure of £1,228 on 5th January 1910, and the committee endorsed his action on the 16th. The result was that the sidings were extended in length way beyond that normally required at a country station.

There must be quite a few stories about the ensuing four years. In one fortnight in 1912, 45 trains brought 13,000 men and 800 horses of the North Midlands Territorial Division, with over 1,000 tons of stores and equipment. In his report to the traffic and works committee, C. S. Denniss struck a very satisfied note: 'for this large share of the traffic we have to thank General Lloyd who has always favoured this Company's route in every possible way'. Of the general time-keeping, he smugly claimed that 'time was well maintained on the whole, the principal delays being due to late running on other systems. One train followed at midnight but this was received four hours late from the North Western Company'.

On one occasion, 7,000 men were sent on a route march to Machynlleth for manoeuvres, and the Cambrian laid on special trains to bring them back to Bow Street. The bill to the army for the 16-mile journey was £350.

In 1917, it was suggested that a length of the now unused sidings should be taken up for relaying at Gogarth; the middle siding was shortened, the rails

General view with the 10.40 a.m. goods approaching from Aberystwyth. Note the change in platform height. *Author*

The signal cabin erected by Dutton & Co for the 1891 resignalling at Bow Street was a small affair, with only 10 levers. This was not big enough to work the enlarged layout brought into use in 1910, so it was replaced by this box recovered from Dolwen on the Mid-Wales line. The box was later extended to accommodate the token instruments – the extension (at the far end) later sagged a bit, as can be seen in this view. The hinged access door in the front of the box (it opened downwards) allowed access to the locking on the lever frame. 1963. *Author*

The station, looking across the yard past the dock. It was a feature of the yard at Bow Street that the No. 1 siding ran across the whole width of the entrance roadway. 1963. *Author*

Rear view of station. Such was the influence of the Pryses of Gogerddan that it could well pass as the country house of a well-off Victorian family. 1963. *Author*

being re-used. Another proposal was made in 1919, by the Gogerddan Estate, for the reopening of the Bronfloyd [sic] copper mine and the Loveden zinc mine, though nothing came of it.

The Tablet Instruments were still installed in the office in 1921, but there was room for their removal to the signal box. In the same year, the Territorial Army was back again, with 3,000 men, 200 horses and 50 vehicles of the Welsh Infantry Brigade.

The Great Western kept the station in good order, and brought in a second-hand 16ft x 8ft cart weighbridge, costed at £215. Someone put their hand in the till during 1933, and the Guarantee Fund had to balance the station account by producing £24 7s 9d. The Great Western also altered the signalling arrangements during the winter of 1938/9 at a cost of £235, though details of the work done have not survived.

The construction in the early 1960s of the great Nant-y-moch dam by Sir Alfred McAlpine & Sons for supplying water to the hydro-electric power station in the Vale of Rheidol gave Bow Street goods yard a new (though short-lived) lease of life, and a steel silo tower was erected for transhipping bulk cement.

In the 1960s, the sagging road overbridge was reinforced by a concrete saddle, and when this started to fail, five arcs of old steel rail were neatly inserted.

On the platform side, the station building was extended to form a small awning over the down platform. The sign advertised that a telephone was available for public use. 1963. *Author*

The up shelter or 'waiting shed' – a handsome structure reflecting Bow Street as a 'First Class' station. 1963. *Author*

The 10.40 a.m. ex-Aberystwyth goods dividing the train prior to shunting the yard. 1963. *Author*

The porter walking alongside a loose-shunted wagon ready to push the brake handle down at the right moment. The mineral wagon is rolling into the short siding which ended with the loading dock, whilst No. 2 siding is on the right. 1963. *Author*

With shunting finished and the engine 'blowing off', the train pulled forward and set back onto the remainder of the train left in the up side of the loop. 1963. *Author*

The end of the truncated No. 1 siding, the section beyond having been lifted in 1917 so that the rails could be re-used elsewhere. 1963. *Author*

Working Instructions.
'When the Up Starting Signal cannot be lowered to permit a train to proceed into the Llanfihangel Section Up trains must be halted at the Home Signal which can then be lowered to permit the train to enter the Station.' (Seen for 1911 and 1921).

Tickets for six trains (daily) were collected at Bow Street to relieve the staff at Aberystwyth, and also of the 'Down Mail' on Sundays. (1911 onwards.)

SHUNTING OPERATIONS ON THE MIDDLE ROAD (Camp Coach Siding):
'The Camp Coach is stabled on the stop block of the Middle Road and as the gradient falls towards the stop block the greatest care must be exercised by all concerned during shunting operations over the siding. Before a shunting movement is made towards the Camp Coach the hand brake must be pinned down on the leading vehicle. Vehicles must not be loose shunted on the siding but must remain attached to the engine and brought to a stand well clear of the Camp Coach. Each vehicle placed in the siding must be properly secured by the hand brake being tightly applied.' (1943)

The down neck beyond No. 8 points was rated as a refuge siding for down goods trains, accommodating up to 25 wagons plus engine and brake van (1943).

General Notes.
As in 1888, horses could be dealt with, but not carriages.

The camping coach was placed in 1931.

Hay from Llandre to Aberystwyth was collected into a stack of 5 tons and more.

The writers of Victorian guide books treated the name as a joke in the ponderous style of their time, e.g. 'travellers will be much surprised to find they have to go through Bow Street – not the police-court by the way – before they can enter the Queen of Cambrian watering places.' (T. Booth, in 'Wild Wales', *The Railway Magazine*, 1898).

In 1938, goods and parcels were collected and delivered by porter, for which a charge was made.

4–6–0 No. 7820 *Dinmore Manor* on the 4.20 a.m. ex-Oswestry goods going away from Bow Street. The neck in the foreground was nearly level, which gives a good impression of how the 1 in 75 gradient began immediately beyond the loop points. 1963. *Author*

Looking down the 1 in 75 gradient to Bow Street from Black Lion bridge. 1963. *Author*

BOW STREET to ABERYSTWYTH

(Llanbadarn) – 91m 36c to 94m 56c
(Plascrug) – 91m 36c to 95m 25½c

The climbing curve to Rhyd-tir bridge over Afon Clarach, viewed from the Black Lion bridge. 1963. *Author*

On leaving Bow Street, the line climbs at 1 in 75, crossing the head of Dyffryn Clarach on a high embankment. Here, two streams (the Bow Street Brook, and Afon Peithyll) join the Clarach to form a wide hinterland surrounded by hills on three sides, and falling away to the sea to the west. The Rhyd-tir road underbridge (A487) presents a fascinating feature – a skew bridge crossing a road at a point where both rail and road cross Afon Clarach, which is joined on the east side by Afon Peithyll.

A long, curved cutting completes the climb to a brief level section at Wern Phillip, before the line falls at 1 in 75 (finishing at 1 in 76) all the way down to Llandbadarn. At first, it goes with the lie of the land on a ledge cut into a curving bank, giving a lovely view across to the south-east. Then, the line plunges into a deep cutting, to emerge in the Vale of Rheidol, where the A44 is crossed by Factory Bridge. Another embankment carries the line down to level at Llanbadarn Crossing. From here the track runs parallel to the Vale of Rheidol line for half a mile, passing the gas works to the north-east, then Plascrug Crossing, before entering the terminal station of Aberystwyth.

On 24th June 1875, the north-west slope of the cutting behind Nantcaerio slipped, and a ballast train had to be called out to clear the obstruction.

The 6.20 p.m. mixed ex-Machynlleth, on 3rd April 1882, struck 'a Tressel placed on the line which broke to pieces', with the further note: 'I offered a reward of £10 but have been unable to discover the offender'.

Black Lion bridge, west elevation. A simple baulk timber bridge with pairs of baulks bolted together under each rail. 1972. *Author*

Rhyd-tir bridge, looking towards Aberystwyth. The Afon Clarach passes under the road here. Its course lies beyond the fence on the far side of the field, then in culvert under the road bridge abutment and embankment. Note the stone-built milk churn stand beyond the bridge. 1963. ***Author***

On 6th October 1884, Mr Edward Hamer (a former locomotive superintendent and traffic manager of the Manchester & Milford Railway) was travelling in a carriage attached to the rear of a special cattle train. He woke up, thought that the train had stopped at a station, and jumped out, falling heavily onto the ballast. As a result, he dislocated his shoulder and badly bruised his face.

Rhyd-tir Bridge had originally been constructed in lattice girder format, and 'had been too light for the strict requirements of the Board of Trade'; further 'despite a close watch and the addition of tie rods [it] is now oscillating and buckling.' It was replaced by a wrought iron plate girder bridge in 1890.

On 21st September 1892, Ganger John Hughes was killed near Factory Bridge when the lorry (trolley) on which he was kneeling was struck by a train. A lazy platelayer had placed the warning flag only 250 yards out instead of at the three-quarters-of-a-mile distance as required by the company's rules.

During a December storm in 1919, a tree crashed down across one of the cuttings, and Thomas Davies received an honorarium of £5 for bringing warning in time.

The Great Western overhauled a number of the bridges on this section (notably Fronfaith) in the spring of 1930 for £190, and later in that year Nantcaerio was totally reconstructed for £680; in 1933, Coach Road Bridge had £310 spent on it.

Royal Oak bridge, looking towards Bow Street. 1963. *Author*

Wern Phillip bridge was made wide enough for a double line. The formation here is level for a short distance, falling away at 1 in 75 on either side. 1968. *Author*

Wern Phillip bridge, eastern elevation. A neat little stone bridge with a stone parapet, but brick centering to the arch. 1968. *Author*

The GWR introduced 'motor economic maintenance' over much of the Cambrian system, and installed trolley 'run-offs' beside most of the lengthmen's cabins. The box in the foreground contained the instrument for the ganger's occupation key, which was electrically linked with the key token system that ensured safety on the single line. 1968. *Author*

Tanfanfagel bridge, looking towards Bow Street, with pre-British Rail reinforced concrete beams and block parapet. 1968. *Author*

Tanfanfagel retained a strange mixture of poor-grade stone and old brick in the approach walls when the rest of the span was renewed. *Author*

Left: Fronfaith or Bonsall bridge, looking uphill towards Tanfanfagel and Bow Street. 1968. *Right:* Bonsall bridge is an occupation way with farm gates. *Author*

Coach Road bridge, looking downhill towards Llanbadarn and Aberystwyth. 1968. *Author*

Coach Road bridge, the eastern elevation. 1968. *Author*

Left: This platelayers hut was sited at the top of the cutting side with a narrow path leading up to it from a bit of board spanning the drainage ditch. 1968. *Right:* Nancaeris Road bridge, looking downhill. This bridge has a thin plate parapet bracketed onto the main girders. 1968. *Author*

Looking up the Nancaeris Road from the south. 1968. *Author*

The down distant signal for Llanbadarn Crossing. The signal was 'fixed at caution' and thus had no spectacle plate with coloured glasses in front of the lamp. The glass in the lamp itself was coloured yellow. 1957. *Author*

Pendre (or Factory) bridge over the A44, looking uphill (and in the up direction) towards Bow Street. To the right is the valley of the Afon Rheidol, with the narrow gauge Vale of Rheidol line just in view. *Author*

Pendre (or Factory) bridge, southern elevation, looking towards Aberystwyth along the A44. 1968. *Author*

The sweeping descending bank down to Llanbadarn Crossing, viewed from beside the Factory bridge. 1968. *Author*

Glandewi bridge, near the foot of Llanbadarn Bank, seen from the south side. 1963. *Author*

Between Glandewi bridge and the crossing is Llanbadarn Fawr bridge. Again this is a view from the river (south) side. 1968. *Author*

Llanbadarn Crossing, looking in the down direction to Aberystwyth, with the last few hundred yards of track beyond. This view was taken after the double line to Aberystwyth and the down starting signal had been taken out of use. The fixed distant for Aberystwyth box, previously under the starting signal 9, was then replaced by an arm under what had been the down home signal (No. 10). The top of the pump house building can be seen above the gate, and the old crossing keeper's house on the right. 1968. *Author*

The keeper's house, seen here in 1968, dated back to the era when there was no signal box at Llanbadarn, just a level crossing on the single line. The house was built in 1872 at a cost of £140. The signal box was opened in 1924 in connection with the doubling of the line into Aberystwyth in 1925. *Author*

The 'lead off' in front of Llanbadarn box, shortly after it had been taken out of use. The gate here was worked from the box (unusual on the Cambrian lines) and the long bar in the centre, connected to large angle cranks, operated the drive to the gates. 1968. *Author*

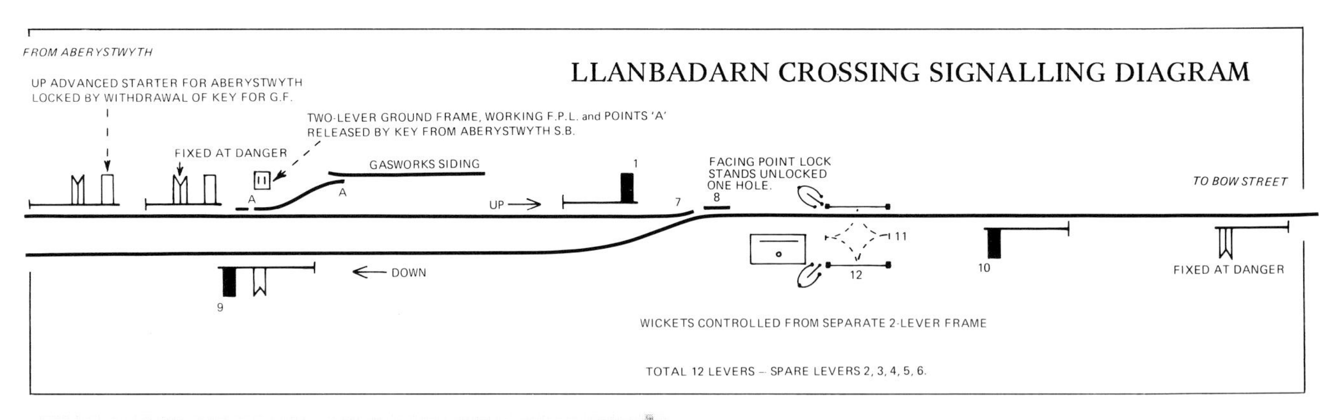

The crossing, viewed from the south in 1968. The 3-lever ground frame installed a couple of years before to work the stop signals protecting the gates, and the interlocking of the gates (after the signal box and double line into Aberystwyth was abolished) can just be seen in front of the keeper's house. *Author*

A fireman leaning from the cab to collect the token for the section on to Bow Street from the lineside exchange apparatus. The token was fitted into a carrier with a hoop-shaped handle, to facilitiate the exchange. The carrier was put up in the exchanger, the back of which was spring-loaded to open and allow the carrier to be taken away. Exchanging was a skill – especially in the dark – the oil lamp provided giving only a feeble light! *Author*

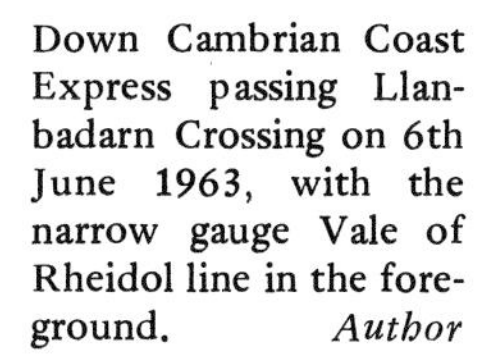

Down Cambrian Coast Express passing Llanbadarn Crossing on 6th June 1963, with the narrow gauge Vale of Rheidol line in the foreground. *Author*

Taken from the same location as the photo above, the train is seen approaching Aberystwyth. The gas works is barely visible behind the train. The pump house is on the right and the flood plain of the Afon Rheidol on the left. *Author*

The pump house, seen in 1963, looking towards Llanbadarn. *Author*

The pump house as it was in 1906, with a heap of coal in front, unloaded from a wagon standing on the main line. At this time the line was single here, and the space allowed for the coal heap was later used for the down main. This fortunate arrangement meant that the pump house did not have to be rebuilt for the 1924 doubling of the line, hence its survival to the end of steam days at Aberystwyth shed. When the Loco Department had material or coal to drop off here, the wagons were hauled on the up line to Llanbadarn Crossing and then propelled back 'wrong line' to the pump house. On completion of the work, the train was propelled the rest of the way, on the down line, back to Aberystwyth. *Cambrian Railways*

The J. J. Lane horizontal steam engine and the three-cylinder pump designed and manufactured in the Oswestry Works. 1906.
Cambrian Railways

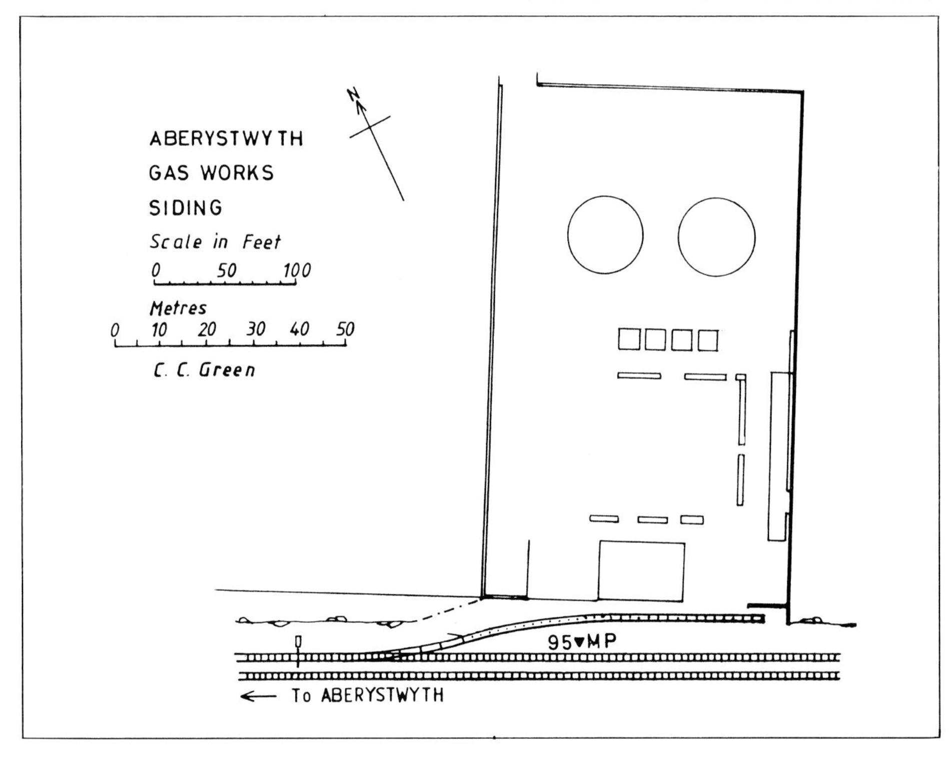

The Aberystwyth Gas Works, viewed from the trackbed of the Vale of Rheidol line, in 1963. In the days before the introduction of a 'grid' for natural gas, most towns had a municipal gas works, usually on an edge-of-town location beside a railway. The Aberystwyth Gas Works was relocated to this site in 1899. *Author*

Looking towards Aberystwyth, with the Llanbadarn Crossing down starter (No. 9) and Aberystwyth down distant in the centre of the picture. The gas works siding, on the right, was laid in during May 1899, when the main line was still single, so that it was inevitably 'facing' to one direction of traffic. This arrangement was retained after the line was doubled – a rare example of an 'in-section' siding served by a facing point. The two-lever ground frame (of Tyer's pattern) for the siding points was originally unlocked by the tablet for the single line section. In 1924 this was changed and the siding was unlocked by a key withdrawn from the lever frame in Aberystwyth box. The siding was shunted by propelling wagons on the up line from Aberystwyth, and then drawing the wagons in the down direction on the up line, back to the sidings at Aberystwyth. While the key was out of the frame in Aberystwyth box, the advanced starting signal on the up line was locked at danger to protect the shunting movement. The gradient falls gently towards the terminus, at 1 in 371 to just beyond the gas works siding, then at 1 in 966. 1963. *Author*

Turn-of-the-century Aberystwyth, looking northwards along the promenade from a location beside the pier, with Constitution Hill and its cliff railway in the background. All the men are attired in dark suits and most of the ladies are also soberly dressed. White blouses with long dark skirts were permissible and umbrellas were often used as sunshades. Bathing for ladies was a matter for great propriety and the machines could be drawn down into the water by a horse so that female forms were secure from ogling masculine eyes.

Cty. Mrs. Margaret Evans

ABERYSTWYTH.

94m 56c (Llanbadarn Crossing) 95m 25½c (Plascrug Crossing) Signal Box at 95m 45c Buffer stops at 95m 60c

Opened: Aberystwith & Welsh Coast Railway, 23rd June 1864.
Manchester & Milford Railway, 12th August 1867.
Closed to Steam Locomotives, 10th April 1965.
Signal Box closed 25th April 1982, layout and yard reduced.
Yard closed to rail traffic (except for Petroleum Siding) after May 1983.

The name Aberystwyth is derived from a description of the location of the first castle, built in 1109 by Gilbert Fitzgerald on the south bank of Afon Ystwyth – 'At the Mouth of the Winding River' or 'Ystwyth mouth'. The town was granted its Charter by King Edward I on 28th December 1277, when the present castle was being built.

Early publicity lauded it as 'The Queen of Welsh Watering Places', and C.S. Denniss, in a press interview, repeated other early claims of 'the Brighton or Scarborough of Wales' and went on to add 'and is being increasingly patronised by a very good class of families who wish to combine the attractiveness of a Welsh mountainous countryside and seaside resort with a really invigorating and bracing climate.' The Great Western, in its 1923 publicity campaign, having designated Central Wales as 'The British Tyrol', went on to call Aberystwyth 'The Biarritz of Wales'.

The sea front at Aberystwyth c.1905. *Cty. Mrs. Margaret Evans*

Aberystwyth had taken little notice of the railway 'mania' of the 1840s and 1850s. The gentry and the lawyers had their carriages, farmers and merchants went on horseback, and the poor did not travel. The main route to England was that of the Royal Mail, the turnpike road eastwards to Rhayader (via Devil's Bridge), whilst a second ran southwards to Carmarthen, which became the nearest station for a train to London. The northern way across the Dyfi ferry was much less used than the turnpike road to Machynlleth and the north-east.

The first attempt to serve Aberystwyth by means of a railway had been made by the Great North & South Wales and Worcester Railway in 1845; this prophetic proposal would have used much of the routes which were eventually constructed.

During 1859, the promoters of the Manchester & Milford Railway had envisaged a line to Aberystwyth, but had deferred detailed consideration until their main line from Llanidloes to Pencader had been secured. This was duly authorised under their Act of 23rd July 1860.

In November 1860 the Mid-Wales Railway, with their main line from Llanidloes to Talyllyn Junction empowered under their Acts of 1st August 1859 and 3rd July 1860, sought a Bill for a western extension from Rhayader to Aberystwyth via Pontrhydfendigaid. After all the costs and other implications had been ascertained, they withdrew this Bill of their own accord. However, they kept up a running battle of proposed duplication of lines with running powers over the Manchester & Milford to Aberystwyth until, by 1863, common sense had prevailed.

Aberystwyth's first introduction to its railway came at the end of April 1861. C. P. Gasquoine wrote of the public meeting led by the mayor, Mr Robert Edwards, being 'borne on the wings of Mr Whalley's eloquence', and of a second meeting at which Mr Benjamin Piercy (the engineer-to-be) outlined the plan, and bade the inhabitants to look forward to the day when the railway would enable them to compete with successful rivals on the North Wales coast, and once more justify the proud name of 'The Brighton of Wales'. Here he was alluding to the overnight prosperity brought to Rhyl, Colwyn Bay and Llandudno by the Chester & Holyhead Railway.

The Manchester & Milford's branch from Devil's Bridge to Aberystwyth via the Vale of Rheidol was authorised by their Act of 11th July 1861. They opposed the Aberystwith & Welsh Coast Railway Bill, which was passed on 22nd July, and were responsible for the insertion of the clause which required that the Machynlleth to Aberystwyth line should not be completed before that to Barmouth.

The Manchester & Milford again opposed a 'Coast' company's Bill, this of 1863, which included a harbour branch and a connection to the Manchester & Milford; the M & MR wanted it to be laid in such a manner that their trains did not have to reverse at the junction.

The Swansea & Aberystwyth Junction Railway (previously the Llandilo & Teifi Valley Railway) proposed, in 1864, to build its own independent line to Aberystwyth, or to take running powers to get there over the Manchester & Milford's proposed new route from Ystrad Meurig. The Mid-Wales company also sought similar running powers from the end of its western extension at Trawscoed. The Manchester & Milford presented its first Deviation Bill for a more direct line from Aberystwyth to Pencader, but this was defeated.

However, as already related in other contexts, it was the Aberystwith & Welsh Coast Railway, under an Act authorised on 22nd July 1861, which arrived first. It had been planned to complete the line before the opening of the Newtown & Machynlleth (on 3rd January 1863), but it was more than a year later when the first trainload of enthusiastic celebrants steamed triumphantly into Aberystwyth on 23rd June 1864.

The excitement of that first day of trains has already been described in the chapter on Borth, and more celebration followed on 27th July when, after the opening ceremony for Savin's Cambrian Hotel, the

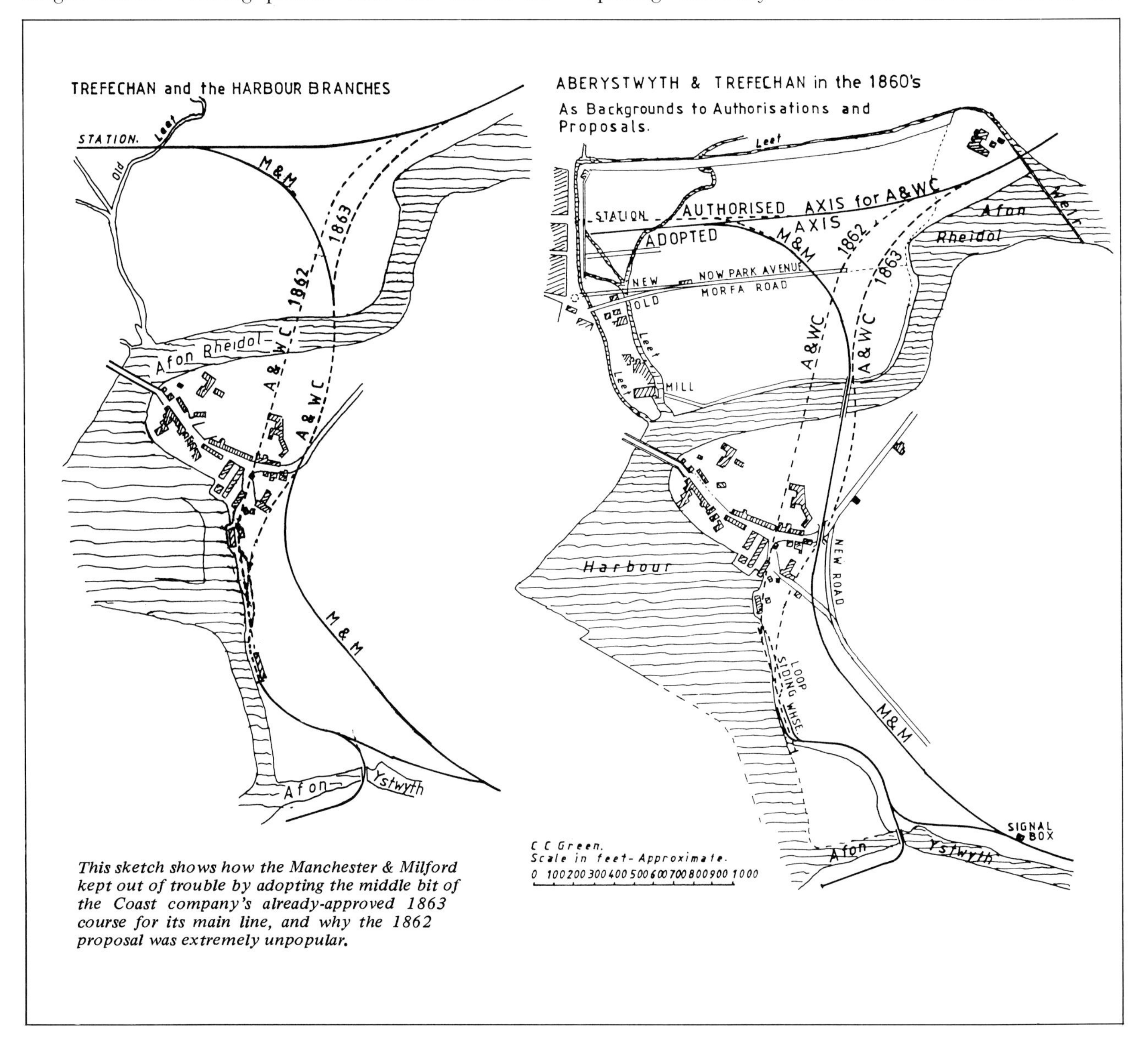

This sketch shows how the Manchester & Milford kept out of trouble by adopting the middle bit of the Coast company's already-approved 1863 course for its main line, and why the 1862 proposal was extremely unpopular.

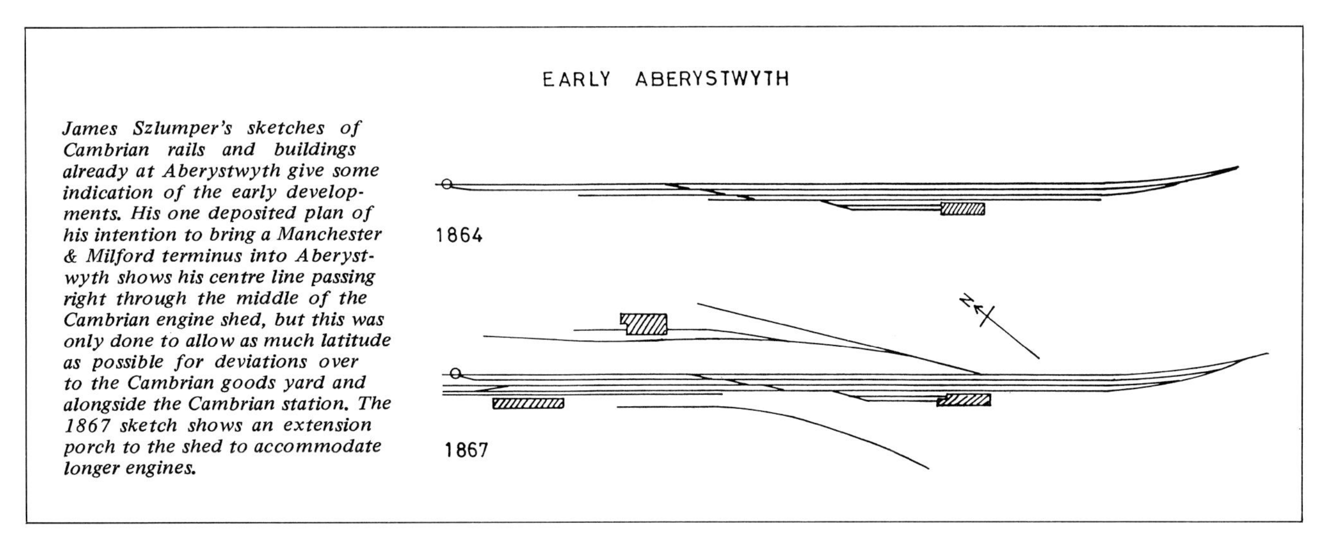

James Szlumper's sketches of Cambrian rails and buildings already at Aberystwyth give some indication of the early developments. His one deposited plan of his intention to bring a Manchester & Milford terminus into Aberystwyth shows his centre line passing right through the middle of the Cambrian engine shed, but this was only done to allow as much latitude as possible for deviations over to the Cambrian goods yard and alongside the Cambrian station. The 1867 sketch shows an extension porch to the shed to accommodate longer engines.

special train came on to Aberystwyth. From Mr Gasquoine again:

> 'The train was given a civic welcome and at the promenade the Lady Mayoress, Mrs Edwards, drove the first pile for the new pier and, after much processioning, the great assembly sat down at the Belle Vue Hotel for a banquet of which, surely, the like has never been seen in the town since. His Worship presided over a flow of oratory, the report of which occupied over five columns of newspapers.'

He also advised that 'visions of a new Aberystwyth swam before the eyes of the guests, wonderful and beautific'. All that summer, horse brakes and wagonettes brought visitors from Rhayader, from Llandrindod and from the south to sample the journey to Machynlleth on the new marvel.

The menu of that inaugural dinner in July 1864 at the Belle Vue Hotel was as follows:

SOUP	Turtle, à la Reine, Printemp.
FISH	Salmon, Stewed Trout, Turbot, Fillet of Mackerel.
ENTRE	Sweetbreads, Mushrooms, Compote of Pigeons, Civet of Rabbit Fenances, Olives, Lobster Paté, Lamb Cutlets, Cucumbers, Sauté of Kidney, Vin Madeira, Vol au Vent.
ROAST	Saddles of Mutton, Fore Quarters of Lamb, Suckling Pigs, Turkey Poults, Ribs of Beef, Fillets of Veal, Roast Ducks.
BOILED	Legs of Lamb and Spinach, Stewed Rumps of Beef, Calves Head à la Tortue, Raised Pies, Tongues.
ENTREINETS	Dantzic Jellies, Maedvine of Fruits, Victoria Jellies, Suidoise of Cherries, Suidoise of Strawberries, Coffee Creams, Carlot à la Parisienne, Canapes of Apricot, Peu d'Amour, Gateaux à la Bohemian, Mayonnaise d'Homward, Aspic of Prawns, Levrets, Green Gesse, Plum Puddings, Ice Pudding, Cheese, Lobster Cheese, Kippered Herrings, Biscuits.

With the speeches, it took four hours to eat and digest!

Although the intention of the Manchester & Milford Railway had been to construct a line connecting Crewe with Milford Haven, its dream had largely collapsed by 1865, at which time an Act was acquired which authorized the construction of a branch from Strata Florida to Aberystwyth. In the Act, the proposed Devil's Bridge line was abandoned, but a triangular junction with the 'Coast' company's harbour branch was included, together with the right to build its own line into Aberystwyth if the A & WCR failed to do so.

The Manchester & Milford published its first timetable for trains between Lampeter and Pencader on 12th January 1866, together with a claim that it formed a part of a trunk route from Liverpool to Milford (provided that one stayed overnight at Aberystwyth and took the morning stage coach thence to Lampeter, having made a total of five changes of railway company en route). Later in that year, the M & MR was extended northwards as far as Strata Florida.

The line from Strata Florida to Aberystwyth was opened on 12th August 1867, and the first Manchester & Milford service was to be seen at the station on that day. The arrival of this train was celebrated in a very much quieter way than the arrival of the 'Coast' company's first service had been.

At the dinner, the main speech was made by David Davies, who had built the Newtown & Machynlleth Railway, and had now 'finished' the Manchester & Milford where others had failed. He was presented with a clock, said to have cost £40. In his speech of appreciation, he added:

> 'You must not think I am hard with you because I will not go on and finish the old railway over the hills to Llanidloes. You say it wants finishing; so it does, but we must see our way where to get the money from because, perhaps if it was done it would not pay, and then where would be the result to you and me?'

He is further reported to have said in 1869 that 'he would not put a farthing of his own money on the line.'

And so, by 1867, Aberystwyth had its basic framework for its future railways. But, reading the *Cambrian News*, the *Welsh Gazette* and other newspapers in that wonderful great library at the top of the hill, one is guided inevitably to the conclusion that the efforts of its railway men to give good service over those miles of single lines, winding their way through the mountains, were never valued as they should have been. Nevertheless, Aberystwyth was destined to become the

Cambrian Railways' most important station in every way. The station masters would have the dignity of wearing a top hat.

After some experience of managing the 'Coast' company's assets, and with the departure of Savin (after February 1866), the Cambrian Board added a left luggage office and a landing for gentlemen's carriages at a cost of £53 17s 0d, and arranged some alterations to the platforms. There was a staff of seven, and a gatekeeper at Llanbadarn Crossing (which always came under the direction of the Aberystwyth station master).

When the Manchester & Milford Railway's line from Strata Florida opened for traffic on 12th August 1867, it shared the Cambrian station at Aberystwyth. On 28th August, the Cambrian's traffic manager (Mr Elijah Elias) reported that he had discussed an agreement with the Manchester & Milford for dividing the running costs of the station. The passenger facility expenses were to be shared equally between the two companies, goods costs were to be shared in proportion to value, whilst the Manchester & Milford would pay 5% of the costs of sidings put in for their use. The Cambrian Board approved an agreement with the Manchester & Milford to pay the full cost of their sidings, and the intention seemed to be that this should be capitalised at 5% per annum.

By April 1867, the Cambrian had to hire two horses from a livery stable run by Mr Morgan at Llanidloes for the shunting. Also in that year, an action was threatened by a Mr Hargreaves for injuries he claimed to have sustained while riding in a van, because there was no room for him in any of the carriages, and the company had to settle for £80.

In 1868, the Manchester & Milford were complaining that they were being asked to pay more than their fair share for the facilities they were using, and asked if they might buy land from the Cambrian, or a part of the station, or a platform. The Cambrian's engineer, Mr George Owen, advised against this, stating that 'they have the full and uninterrupted use of our Station, platforms and sidings. Should any difference arise this platform might be used in a manner adverse to the interests of the Cambrian Company.' The request was therefore refused. It was decided that, on their own land, the M & MR would erect locomotive repair and blacksmith's shops, and also allied smaller buildings, mostly alongside the approach curve. Beyond they put in sidings for the use of the Aberystwyth Harbour Trust for which a station master and a pointsman were appointed, thus providing their own harbour branch (the 'Coast' company and the Cambrian having failed to do so). The turnout from the main line was interlocked with the signals. The M & MR were also masterminding the promotion of a standard gauge line up to Devil's Bridge, and considering further the promotion of a Bill to obtain land and build a station at Aberystwyth.

By 1868, the railway was increasing in popularity with the public, and another £74 had to be spent in lengthening the arrival platform. In 1869, the need for public refreshment rooms was apparent, and these were completed by 2nd September, being let to Mr David Prodger for £160 per annum (one Jesse Deakin had apparently expected to get the tenancy for only £30). Being of brick, instead of wood as first approved, the cost had soared to £280.

The access bridges to the station over the leet or mill stream belonging to Sir Pryse Pryse had to be strengthened; later, when out of use, the leet was stopped off and filled.

The gas company was reported to be putting up the cost of its product to six shillings per 1,000 cubic feet. This could be around 350 therms in modern measure, but it may have been of only 200 therms in comparative quality. Mr Elias, the traffic manager gave the order that gas should only be used on the platforms and in the offices.

Figures under review in July 1869 showed that passenger and parcels traffic was earning £400 for the Cambrian, but only £127 for the Milford, who were naturally claiming the unfairness of the fifty-fifty agreement; they did obtain some alleviation.

In March 1870, there was a dispute over coal prices to the public, caused by the Cardiganshire Coal Company, supported by the Manchester & Milford. First, they had agreed not to undersell the other Aberystwyth dealers, but in June they had cut their price by two shillings a ton from the 7s 6d for ordinary and 8s 6d for best house coal. Mr Elias gave them notice to quit the coal yard 'as soon as the Law will allow.' From 1st January 1871, the Cardiganshire company put their price back up by one shilling per ton, and the Cambrian

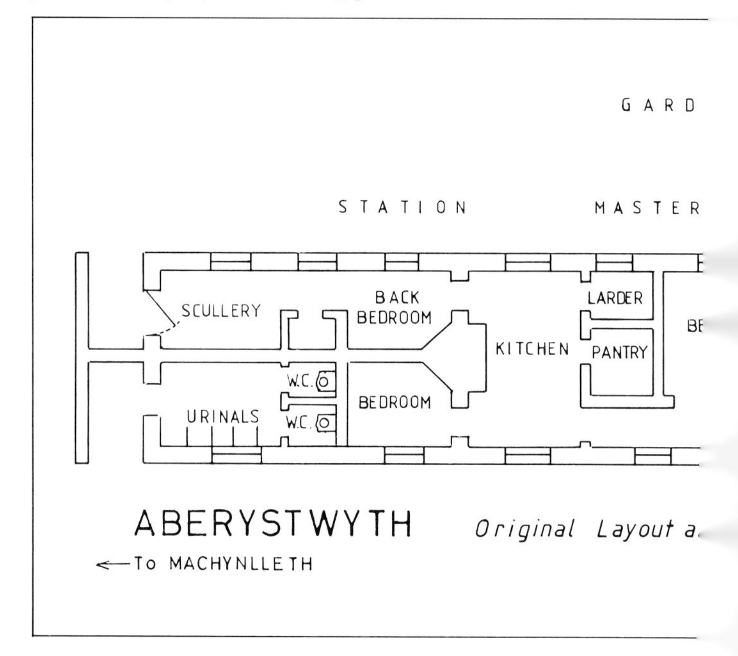

were able to stop giving a toll allowance, designed to keep the other users of their yard in business.

In June 1870, a booking clerk stole some of the takings, which were subsequently recovered. This was the Cambrian's first experience of such a defalcation, and in future 'Security was to be obtained from all Booking Clerks handling money.' To prevent 'a deal of Trespass' the yard was enclosed using second-hand material (ex-Savin) for £36 7s 6d.

Aberystwyth's first train accident occurred in 1870, when a Manchester & Milford driver stopped his goods train at the Rheidol bridge in order to run around, before propelling it into the main station. The train ran away, one wagon demolished a buffer stop, and jumped into the new refreshment rooms, though without seriously injuring anybody. The Cambrian's bill to the M & M was £13 2s 4d.

By 1871, the Cambrian had bought the two shunting horses, and it was reported that the brown, which had been there since the station had been opened, was sixteen-years old and would need to be replaced shortly, but the eight-year old roan that had been there for only a year-and-a-half was 'Very fresh'.

Mr James Maconochie, a fish merchant, was given a lease for a plot of land in the yard at £6 per annum to enable him to erect his own 20ft × 40ft warehouse, between thirty and forty feet from the end of the company's warehouse. On 22nd October 1871, approval was given for the extension of cattle loading facilities. The Manchester & Milford had provided some right on the end of the Smithfield Market, which was beside that company's line, and the Cambrian facilities for loading cattle had come to look rather inferior.

On 19th October, the engineer outlined a proposed scheme for a verandah (awning or canopy) over the arrival platform, whilst a heating boiler for eight footwarmers (at a cost of £8 10s 0d) was approved on 20th December.

It was agreed on 26th January 1872 that the shed abandoned on company land by the North & South Wales Coal Company was worth £70, should be bought for £50, and be let for £5 per annum to their successor, Mr D. A. Evans. At the same meeting, the expenditure of £2,816 12s 6d was passed for paving the ash and dirt platforms, and for erecting a verandah (after obtaining the permission of the Milford company 'for covering a portion of their line'). They assented, but asked that the work should be left until after the end of the summer season; nonetheless the project had been completed by the end of July. The sum of £140 was also approved for the construction of a crossing keeper's house at Llanbadarn.

In February 1872, Mr Jehu (an ironmonger of Welshpool) wrote to the company offering to sell them fourteen gas lamps, left on his hands after Savin's bankruptcy, for 58 shillings. The deputy chairman was authorised to approach him with an offer of 40 shillings.

During that year, the Manchester & Milford were planning the promotion of a branch from (near) Trawscoed to Devil's Bridge in a Bill for the 1873 session of Parliament, with the addition of powers to acquire land and to build their own station in Aberystwyth. On 19th September, the Cambrian committee were considering the report of their engineer that the Milford Company's request for an alteration in the use of platforms would cost £1,281 7s 3d; this may have been the construction of the Manchester & Milford bay on Cambrian land (and under Cambrian control). It was also stated at that meeting that the *Cambrian News* had just published a notice that the Manchester &

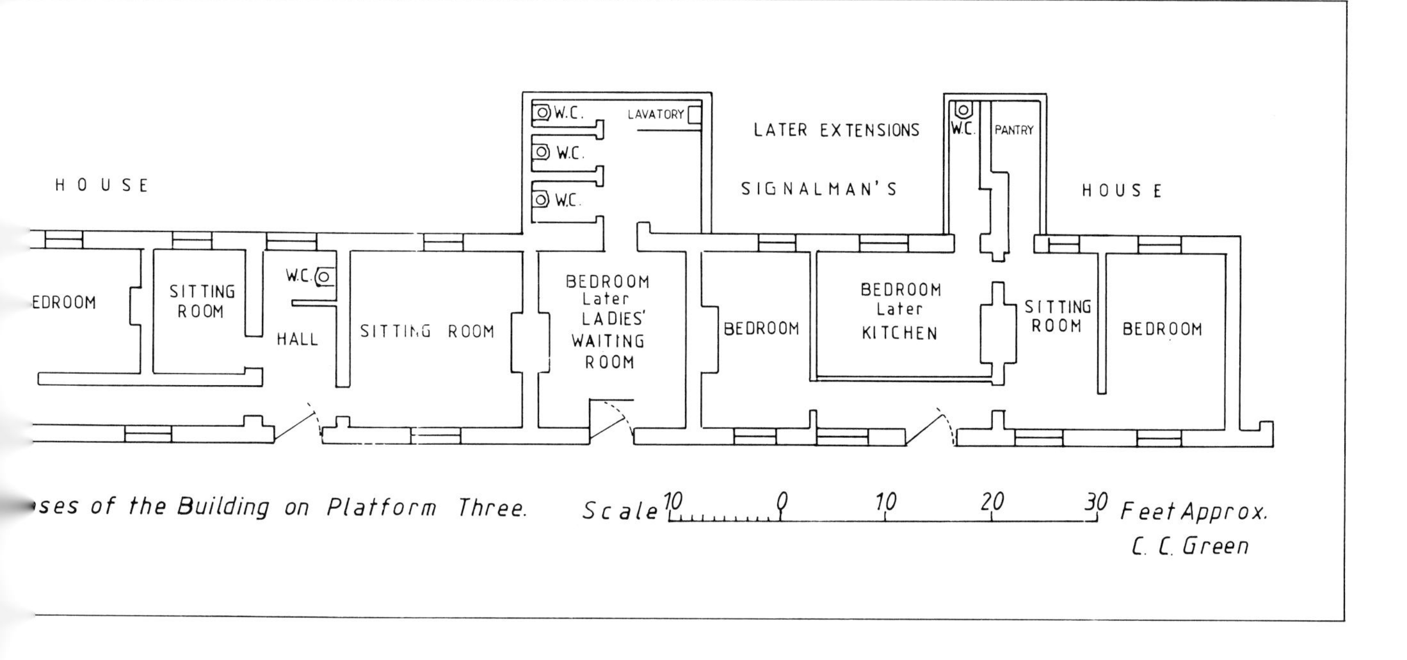

…ses of the Building on Platform Three.

Milford were expecting to have the Midland Company in Aberystwyth, and wanted to buy land for their own station in the town.

As the station was working with separate arrival and departure sides, water closests and urinals for the down platform were authorised in 1873 at a cost of £138 19s 0d. In the same year, a private owner wagon belonging to Mr I. Jones had caused an accident at Cemmes Road, and the remainder of his wagons were stopped in Aberystwyth yard until after the Board of Trade enquiry.

A Mr Harvey was given a site for a lead ore storage shed for £5 per annum in 1874, to enable the mineral to be dispatched by railway instead of by sea.

For the summer traffic, barriers were erected in 1875 at the end of the 'excursion platform' in order 'to keep the large crowds coming to the station at the times of departure of the Trains separate from the Passengers'.

The Corporation asked that two iron turnstiles should be set up at Llanbadarn Crossing, but the Cambrian installed two wooden gates instead. It was also decided that, as stabling the horses in the town was costing £10 per annum, it would be cheaper to build the company's own stable in the goods yard for the sum of £60.

By 1875, the Manchester & Milford were defaulting on their payment for the use of Aberystwyth station, and the Cambrian brought a law suit against them; this action also included a similar default involving the Llanidloes arrangements, but was rendered abortive by the appointment of a receiver.

In 1876, the siding to the Rheidol Foundry was laid, at their cost, off the Manchester & Milford line.

There were still only two cattle pens at Aberystwyth in 1876, and at the last Fair no less than 63 wagons had been loaded out from them. The existing pair were to be paved and three more were built, all for £103 6s 1d.

Allsopps (the brewers) had a store at the end of the goods warehouse, and were offering £10 per annum to rent an office in the station. Later, the Manchester & Milford offered better facilities, and the brewers moved over. Mr Thomas, a coal merchant, was given permission to have his own permanent coal office built in brick to replace his existing timber shed.

During the late 1870s a suggestion came from the town's inhabitants that the trains might be speeded up by omitting the stop at Bow Street; naturally, this did not please the villagers, and the request was refused.

By 1879, Aberystwyth Harbour station was deleted as a stopping place for northbound M & MR trains to improve the running time.

The London & North Western was found to be acting 'awkwardly' in 1880 by sending as much excursion traffic as possible via Afon Wen, instead of down the Cambrian main line.

The cast iron water pipes leading from the town mains were said to be 'bad castings very unequal in the cores', and the new higher-pressured supply from the Plynlimon range was making them leak; 375 yards of 3 inch pipe were therefore relaid at a cost of £73 15s 0d.

In 1880, the council surveyor suggested that there ought to be 'a proper wall and fencing to the yard', and £94 10s 0d was so expended.

On 22nd December 1880, severe storms in the mountains, allied to off-sea winds and an exceptionally high tide, caused the Rheidol to flood the whole area from Llanbadarn seawards. The water rose to within two inches of the platform tops, the approach lines had two to three feet of water over them, whilst the engine shed at a slightly lower level was affected even more. The 6.0 p.m. Mail was stranded at the platform, and the engineer's rescue train was held up outside Bow Street. As the flood ebbed on the following day, the 8.35 a.m. from Machynlleth was brought into the station by packing old sleepers under the rails to raise the line.

For the sum of £250, the booking & parcels office and the refreshment rooms exchanged places in 1881. The corporation granted permission for the erection of a verandah over the entrance.

A lady visitor had suggested that there should be an attendant in the ladies' waiting room. The acting traffic manager (secretary George Lewis) recommended that 'we adopt a system generally in use on so many railways of making a charge of 1d', and it was approved that this should be done, but during the summer months only. This seems to have included access to the lavatory accommodation as well.

In 1882, there were disputes between the two companies over the charges for water and about the joint station account generally, and in December the Manchester & Milford agreed to withdraw their claim that they should be consulted over the appointment of staff.

The bay horse was seized with colic, and died on 14th May 1883; now the Cambrian was three horses short, and another three were 'worn out.' On 15th September, Henry Evans Tan-castell was unloading timber from his carriage under the large crane in the goods yard when an unsecured horse from his team strayed onto the line, to be knocked down, run over and killed instantly. One of the company's wagons was also thrown off the line.

By the end of that summer, it had been found that 'the Provision of Lavatory Accommodation had more than recouped the cost and the practice ought to be extended to other stations'.

In February 1884, the Board ordered the provision of better ladies' and gentlemen's water closets and urinals, and the engineer reported that the cost would be £310 18s 9d; the idea was deferred. Also in that February, difficulty was being experienced in collecting

Aberystwyth, probably taken in July 1872 to show the improvements. The expression 'a verandah' in the minutes appears to have included the coverings over both the arrival platform on the left and the departure platform on the right. All four roads can be seen. 0—6—0 Sharp Stewart goods engine No. 6 *Marquis* is shown, slightly angled, on the crossover leading to the loco 'escape' road. The third road was used as an arrival road for goods trains, particularly off the Manchester & Milford, preparatory to shunting and sorting. The leading carriage behind 2—4—0 Sharp Stewart No. 43 *Plynlimon* was a five-compartment Parliamentary third followed by a four-compartment second, a similar first class carriage, another third and the brake van. The vague shape behind the flat truck suggests another carriage on the outside line at the dock. The dock-and-cattle road is now separated from the platform by a 3ft high rough stone wall with a rounded coping. Note the early type cattle vans. *E. R. Gyde, cty. Ifor Higgon*

the wharfage rents from the coal merchants, some of whom were four years in arrears.

On 23rd July 1884, a potentially dangerous incident occurred at the station:

> 'As the 9.45 a.m. ex-Whitchurch was running into the Station a 7 year old girl, daughter of Mrs Evenhall, fell out of a 3rd class compartment and dropping between train and platform would no doubt have sustained serious, if not fatal, injuries but for the presence of mind of a gentleman [name unknown] and Foreman Bamford, the former of whom held her head up while the latter jumped between the buffers of the coaches and prevented her legs from coming into contact with the wheels. She received no injuries beyond a severe shaking and a fright.'

It had been realised that the company no longer needed to encourage the presence of bus and cab proprietors by turning a blind eye to their unofficial use of the company's premises, and the Cambrian started quite an uproar by charging them between £2 10s 0d and £5 for the privilege. John Potts, the town porter, was charged £6 per year for his right to ply for trade from the railway station.

On 18th September 1884, while Carter James Fisher was adjusting the load on his dray, the horse bolted, knocking him down and pulling one wheel across his back and side. It was subsequently stated that 'He is progressing satisfactorily towards recovery.'

Arguments between the two railway companies went on, and in 1884 it was discovered that the Manchester & Milford were siphoning off goods traffic via Pencader Junction and the Carmarthen & Cardigan line; a firm protest was duly lodged.

Electric bell communication between the signal box and the booking office was installed for £7 12s 6d during 1885, which allowed the signalman to advise station staff of the approach of trains. Owing to heavy traffic, the company had trouble fitting in the Whitsuntide special in that year for 'The Annual Movable Committee of the Order of Oddfellows.'

In 1886 there was local dissatisfaction about the Manchester & Milford's cartage arrangements for shopkeepers at Llanrhystyd, Llanon, Aberayron and New Quay (connecting with the Bristol steamer), all villages south of Aberystwyth and firmly in the M & M's catchment area. The Cambrian put on a carter and a pair of horses from Aberystwyth to poach the traffic, and perhaps to score a point. By the end of the year, the service showed a profit of £2 0s 8d and it was decided to keep it going, but it was to be 'watched carefully'.

In response to a suggestion from the mayor and the local Board that the railway embankment should be raised by two feet at a cost to the company of £700, the Cambrian replied that the proper way to protect the town was not by banking up the line and holding the flood waters in suspension to the detriment of Llanbadarn, but by properly restoring the Rheidol defensive embankments.

Local farmers were aggrieved by the increases in the tolls at Aberystwyth's Smithfield Market, and were seeking to set up their own rival market. Accordingly,

The great flood of 1886. The Manchester & Milford's trestle bridge across the Rheidol can be seen descending under the water, and of the Cambrian line on the right there is no trace at all. Photographs of disasters of this period are virtually non-existent and an artist's impression is rare indeed.
Cty. Phil Lewis

they asked for a siding to be installed at Llanbadarn, — and that the train carrying the dealers, the 9.45 a.m. into Aberystwyth, should be stopped there on Fair days. This was refused, despite the fact that it had been preferred by 'the inhabitants of Llanbadarn in vestry assembled.'

Because the provision of footwarmers had been so successful at Welshpool, it was decided in 1887 to remove the old timber bookstall from the omnibus arcade at Aberystwyth and to replace it by a large footwarmer apparatus costing £46 3s 8d, and to let the spare space so gained for £4 per annum.

The Manchester & Milford completed the replacement of the old trestle bridge across the Rheidol with a plate girder type in January 1888, a structure that was to last until the closure of the line. The trestle had been damaged by the great flood of 1886, which had also caused the collapse of the Trefechan road bridge; that too had been restored, using 4,500 tons of stone brought from the quarry at Ystrad Meurig.

In May 1888, the committee approved the installation of a tablet instrument, connected to another at Bow Street, and interlocking of signals, all for £183. There was also much correspondence from the mayor because 'the inhabitants wanted the mail train to be run more for their convenience than for that of the Post Office' (who would concede nothing).

By 1888, the station had facilities for loading and offloading horses and carriages, and the Belle Vue Hotel omnibus met all trains; further, the Queens, the Belle Vue and the Gogerddan Arms & Lion Royal hotels all gave highly euphemistic descriptions in the Cambrian public timetables of the comforts available to those gentlefolk who could afford their prices.

On 10th June 1889, Miss Mary Morgan of Upper Borth attempted to get into a carriage while the train was moving, missed her footing, and fell onto the footboard: 'Fortunately Guard Rees Lloyd was close by and at once rescued her from the dangerous position in which she was placed and she escaped with a severe flesh wound to her leg.'

During 1890, the old Manchester & Milford timber workshops were replaced by a larger structure, made of corrugated iron. It was decided that to comply with the Regulation of Railways Act 1889 the number of lines between the station platforms would be reduced from four to three and the 'arrival platform widened'.

In 1891, there was still one wire-locked facing point, for which a signalman had to go down and lean on the lever at ground level when a train was due to pass through it. The signalling at Aberystwyth was not brought fully up to the standard required by the 1889 Act until 1893.

In time for the summer traffic of 1892, the cattle pens against the other edge of the up platform were removed to the back of the goods yard.

In July 1893, the Board agreed to purchase the excise licence of the Three Tuns for transfer to the proposed new refreshment rooms, which were to be let to Spiers & Ponds. Arrangements were also approved for the lengthening of the arrival platform, another item arising from the new interlocked layout. The latter was inspected and passed on 25th November, soon after the completion of the new verandah (on 30th September) which had become necessary as a result of the widening of the platform. At first, it was planned to re-use the old verandah at Llanidloes, but it would not fit. Then it was proposed that it could be remodelled and fitted on the Manchester & Milford side for £600; however it was considered that enough money had already been spent, and sanction was refused.

The Manchester & Milford's contract for the installation of cabins, signals and interlocking required under the Regulation of Railways Act 1889 was let to Saxby and Farmer in 1894, and included the work necessary at the harbour branch junction.

The new refreshment rooms in the former signalman's house on the down platform had been completed by the middle of November 1894.

The erection of six brick-built coal offices along the Lewis Terrace front of the yard was ordered for £500 during 1895, and a verandah was to be erected over the newly-arranged 'omnibus entrance' at a cost to be approved by the chairman. The licence of the refreshment rooms was transferred from Mr Alfred Aslett (the general manager, who had since resigned) to Mr Joshua Ellis (the Spiers & Ponds secretary).

On 4th September 1895 it was reported that:

'The Aberystwyth Roan Horse has died of a rupture of the stomach in the greater curvature with the escapement of ingesta into the peritoneal cavity. I may add that this horse was purchased by the late (and suspect) Mr Trevitt in 1891 for £33 and was then understood to be only seven years of age. Mr Hughes, however, assures me that at the time of its death the age of the horse was from seventeen to twenty years.'

Records indicate that the Manchester & Milford were still working mainly mixed trains into Aberystwyth during 1895.

In March 1896, the Board accepted the Aberystwyth Improvement Company's quotation of £297 12s 0d for installing an electric lighting system. The gas company promptly reduced its charge.

Due to an impending royal visit, new passenger directive notices and a train guide with a double-faced clock above it were erected at the entrance. The royal occasion was the installation of Edward Prince of Wales as Chancellor of the University College of Wales on 26th June 1896, whilst Princess Alexandra opened the new Hall of Residence for women students, and the new pier pavilion. Mr Gladstone came, too.

Special excursion trains had been scheduled as follows: two trains were timed to run from London simultaneously. Both left at 1.30 p.m., one from Euston (via Birmingham New Street at 3.40 p.m.) and the other from Paddington (via Birmingham Snow Hill at 4.28 p.m.). The former left Wolverhampton Queen Street (High Level) at 4.8 p.m. (via Stafford at 4.50 p.m.) while the latter left Wolverhampton (Low Level) at 4.54 p.m. (via Shrewsbury at 6.5 p.m.). Both had then to arrive at about the same time at Welshpool to be coupled together to leave at 7.10 p.m. A third train left Leeds at 1.35 p.m. (via Manchester (London Road) 3.5 p.m., to Crewe 4.20 p.m.) and a fourth left Liverpool (Lime Street) at 3.0 p.m. (via Chester 4.25 p.m.) and these two had to combine at Whitchurch at 5.20 p.m. to go on to join the first two at Welshpool. The entire ensemble was then to leave as one long train arriving at Aberystwyth at 9.30 p.m. We are left wondering just what did happen? At the next Board meeting, the general manager and all the senior officers were treated to pats on the back all round for their part in making the railway side of events run smoothly.

At that time, the hay collected between Llanbadarn and Bow Street was accumulated by the signal box at Llanbadarn. On 6th August, engine No 77, an 0–6–0 'Aston Goods' on a return excursion which had left at 6.45 p.m., shot out sparks while accelerating to tackle the bank. The ensuing fire destroyed all of the 1896 crop (worth £25) and some of the 1895 crop, which had been sold to Edward Edwards, carrier, of Aberystwyth, who had left it there for his own convenience – 'and consequently no loss will fall on the Company for this.'

By the autumn of 1896, the Cambrian and the M & M were trying to come to an agreement over the apportionment of the cost of interlocking at the main station. The total cost had been £7,837 16s 1d, of which the Cambrian claimed that £5,245 1s 4d was apportionable to the M & M. Typically, they claimed to have been fair in apportioning only £500 of the cost relating to the cattle sidings, which had amounted to £774 6s 9d. The final settlement has yet to be found.

At a meeting with the directors of the Great Western, the Manchester & Milford offered to sell its undertaking for £40,000 in GWR 5% debenture stock plus £210,000 in cash. The Great Western Board turned this offer down, and were then offered a leasing arrangement instead; but as the GWR would only offer £2,500 per annum as a rental to begin with, the negotiations failed.

Because of complaints about the darkness in the goods yard at Aberystwyth, three street lamps fitted with Suggs burners were provided early in November 1896 for the sum of £42.

A report in 1897 about the necessity for some piling contained the startling information that 'recent storms have diverted the course of the River Ystwyth (sic) – actually the River Rheidol – at Llanbadarn'; the piling along the Rheidol cost £250 in the following January.

In February 1897, the general manager insisted that a lavatory should be provided in the goods yard for £56 'as Visitors on Plascrug Walk are daily subjected to the most offensive scenes'. Later on, the cost was reduced 'by providing a smaller drain pipe'. It was also agreed that the company should join with the council in advertising Aberystwyth as a summer and winter resort, and that the contribution should be up to £130.

In March 1898, Mr J. T. Morgan was given a permit to kill rabbits on the line near his farm at Llanbadarn, for £1 per annum.

Meanwhile, the company contributed £150 towards the cost of printing and posting five thousand copies of 'a large pictorial poster' which came to £302 2s 7d in total; the balance was paid by the council and the Aberystwyth Improvement Company.

The Cambrian Board was somewhat concerned about the implications of a proposed East & West Wales Railway Bill, because the inhabitants of Aberystwyth had refused to support the Cambrian in opposing it, and many were prepared to give evidence in its favour. The landowners, and Captain Paul of the Van mine, considered that the route might run through mineral-bearing areas of considerable importance. The Bill was not opposed by the Manchester & Milford, but they did oppose the 1899 Bill which included a rival station in Aberystwyth; it was thrown out.

Since 1838 the gas works had been in Morfa Road (now Park Avenue), but had by this time outgrown the site; in April 1898, the committee therefore approved the laying-in of a siding to the new site on the Plascrug Flats at a cost of £190. The traffic expected was one hundred tons a week, and the gas company paid 3d per ton siding toll.

By midsummer 1898 it was evident that 'a Porter with a light hand cart' could no longer cope with the increasing parcel deliveries, and a horse and van were provided to carry out the business.

The year 1899 started badly, with the London & North Western, who were short of passenger stock, sending an agent down to Aberystwyth to see how much the Cambrian were holding back. They subsequently lodged a demurrage claim for over £1,750. Mr Denniss asked for the provision of twenty new Composite carriages.

The report on the 1898 turnover was depressing too, traffic having gone down because of the weather and the South Wales coal strike; even the revenue from the refreshment rooms was well down. On the brighter side, it now seemed unlikely that the East and West Railway scheme would ever be revived. Although the Aberystwyth Improvement Company was failing, 'a New Team had been conveyed to the town in one of the new Family Saloons', so continued expansion seemed assured.

In May 1899 the erection of a store in the yard for Mr T. E. Salmon, wine and spirit merchant, was approved for £60; this building was to be let to him for £5 per annum 'provided that he consigns his Traffic via Cambrian routes.' In June, the ticket platform was extended at a cost of £70, though it had to be kept within the limit of the down facing points. During September, the council laid complaint that 'as the entrance gate is left open after the last train the public make considerable use of the Refreshment Room as a common drinking place between 9 p.m. and 11 p.m. and additional facility is afforded to the Company's employees when off duty.' However, nothing was done to restrict the use of the room.

On 1st March, Saint David's Day, began the 'affair of the station master'. The gentleman in question was extremely popular, competent enough at his work, and good company outside of it. Charles Sherwood Denniss, the Cambrian general manager, was keeping up his 'new broom' image to a considerable degree. After a meeting of principal station agents and traffic inspectors, Denniss stated of the man from Aberystwyth:

> 'He arrived much the worse for drink and was incapable of dealing with the matters under discussion. His explanation had been "I was Chairman of a Saint David's Day banquet and I had just a few glasses of champagne I was not accustomed to."'

Denniss continued:

> 'He had been warned before but all the Council had supported him in a letter from the Town Clerk asking for him not to be removed.'

The Board backed their general manager. The station master was offered an unspecified clerkship (which he refused), and Mr J. A. Thomas, the Oswestry agent, was promoted to take his place. Of him, Denniss wrote:

> 'He has discharged his duties with conspicuous ability and he has shown an aptitude for dealing with the public and for maintaining the discipline of the staff which I have no doubt will bring about the desired improvement at Aberystwyth.'

The editor of the *Aberystwyth Observer* opened his leading article, headed 'IS THIS A SCANDAL?', with:

> 'The Cambrian Railways have never been popular in the district through which they run, nor indeed in any part of the country.'

Staff at Aberystwyth c.1895. *Photographer unknown*

and in a tribute to the staff:

> 'It must be admitted that under the conditions which surround them they have done remarkably well for the public.'

He then added:

> 'Rightly or wrongly Mr Denniss the Manager has to shoulder the blame, although it may be that there are others behind him ready to use him as a cats-paw, and compel him to rake the nuts out of the fire for them.'

A further long diatribe told of other injuries done by the Cambrian management, such as the removal of a well-known cab proprietor and the turning away of the shoeblack, Mr George White, from the station, 'where he was a great acquisition.' Then he wrote on about the removal of the older officers, George Owen (the engineer), Mr Corfield (the solicitor) and Mr Aston (the Locomotive Superintendent) under the observation 'But it is not only at Aberystwyth that changes have been made during the period that Mr Denniss has been Manager.' He ended with:

> 'Indeed it looks very much as if someone at the head of affairs felt unequal to his position, and is trying to set himself right with himself by getting rid of the older and most valued employees of the Company, and by replacing them with men more after his own standard.'

There was a marvellous write-up of the station master's charm, ability and efficiency, which included a comment on the town's reception of his degradation: 'men who in the ordinary course of events would shrink from uttering a hard word involuntarily uttered curses upon the Management of the Cambrian Railways', and added; 'Managers always shield themselves behind Directors and Directors behind managers.' This prompted others to write into the *Observer* about their injustices at the hands of the Cambrian.

Meanwhile, the company's solicitor pronounced the article to have been libellous, and the Board banned the sale of the paper from W. H. Smith & Son's bookstall on the station, because: 'The Editor of the paper indulges very freely in personal abuse from time to time and most respectable people at Aberystwyth decline to have it in their houses.'

Nevertheless, Denniss's last letter to the ex-station master on 12th May ran: 'Indeed I may scarcely say that if I can in any way assist you in the future it will afford me great pleasure to do so, and there are many reasons why I extremely regret that our own Official intercourse is about to cease.'

His salary was paid up to the 17th May. After he had left the station, it was discovered that he had sublet the house to the Manchester & Milford's inspector, while retaining some rooms as a lodger. The inspector's son was also part of the ménage, and in his capacity as a Cambrian office clerk was reported to have been overheard trying to divert a consignment via the Manchester & Milford. The son had already been favoured by a move from Llanfyllin on grounds of ill health, and was offered a transfer to Newtown, where he could do no more harm; however, he chose to resign instead.

The ex-station master was promptly appointed by the Manchester & Milford as their goods agent, and as such he still had the right to enter the station whenever he wished. 'Such an appointment is an unfriendly act on the part of the Management of the Manchester & Milford Company and cannot but lead to strained relations in the future', reported Mr Denniss. They were also bickering about the apportionment of the passenger running costs, then fixed at two-thirds to the Cambrian, who had attained a greater increase in traffic than had the smaller company.

In December 1899 relations were even more strained, as Denniss had forecast, when it was discovered that the Manchester & Milford were once again trying to bring in a Bill for the construction of their own station adjoining the Board School in Smithfield Street.

In February 1900, it was ordered that the refreshment rooms should close at 10.0 p.m. from 1st November to 31st March, whilst in June, it was directed that additional lavatory accommodation was to be installed, with completion required by the end of July; in the event a sense of realism prevailed, and the job was deferred until the following spring (but was not actually completed until Whitsuntide 1901).

During October 1900, W. H. Smith & Son learned that their re-tender of £1,400 per annum for the station bookstall and advertising had been undercut by only £58 by the South Wales Railway Advertising Company. They informed the Cambrian that they would reopen in the town close to the station, and were allowed to stay on!

After receiving complaints from passengers in through carriages, the general manager reported in December 1900 that the carriage cleaning was unsatisfactory throughout with the gang of four men he had available. He was ordered 'to take steps to ensure that the Company's carriages were efficiently cleaned.'

On 22nd January 1901 the Cambrian general manager advised his Board that they should make an offer for the Manchester & Milford Railway Company. The engineer had made a survey, and had found that the permanent way and bridges were in good order, but there were insufficient wagons. This move was leaked to the town council who, according to a letter passed to the Cambrian Board, sent a deputation to meet the Great Western chairman, Earl Cawdor, 'to urge upon the Great Western Company that they should prevent the line getting into the hands of the Cambrian'. By 3rd April, the Cambrian had evolved a list of the terms under which they would be willing to take over the M & MR, which included unvalued (free) handover of all locomotives, rolling stock and stores. They were also (very unwisely) still trying for their pound of flesh in the matter of Llanidloes station, which the Manchester & Milford never would be able to use.

During that year, Cambrian engine No. 86 (a nearly-new 4–4–0 Sharp Stewart) derailed at the Middle Road

Left: At first, trips involved embarking up a narrow gangway onto a sailboat. From a 3¼in square lantern slide c.1900.
Right: The wealthy could afford the comfort and silence of a modern steam launch. c.1900.

Cty. E. W. Hannan and photographer unknown

The seafront c.1903. The double-headed 'train' was taking rubble from Constitution Hill to the southern extension of the promenade.

Cty. E. W. Hannan

The barque *Caradoc*, an Aberystwyth-registered sailing ship, c.1895, captained by a relative of Mrs. Penelope Davies, possibly her uncle. Hans de Mierre writing in *Clipper Ships to Ocean Greyhounds*, mentions *Caradoc* of Aberystwyth in Newcastle, New South Wales, 'a really trim little barque – most of the crew fore and aft were related and there was as much Welsh spoken as English'.

Cty. Mrs. Penelope Davies

trap points because the driver had failed to notice that the signalman had pulled off the signal for Platform Three by mistake.

An enquiry was instigated by the Cambrian in 1901 concerning the provision of a steamer to ply between Aberystwyth and New Quay. On 13th February 1902, Denniss reported on the costs of running such a service:

Hire, including Insurance.	£20 0s 0d
Coals (25 tons at 15s)	£18 15s 0d
Wages – Five Men at £1	£ 5 0s 0d
Pilotage, dues, stores (etc.), say	£10 0s 0d
Cost per week	£53 15s 0d

The forty-mile return trip to New Quay was proposed for Mondays, Wednesdays and Saturdays with local trips from Aberystwyth on the other days. The hope was expressed that 'if we obtain a Steamer with passenger accommodation for not exceeding five hundred pounds there is no reason why we should not obtain an average daily revenue of not less than £10 placing the estimate at a very low figure; this would be only a hundred passengers at 2 shillings'.

Because of the impossibility of berthing in Aberystwyth harbour at low tide, it would have been necessary to moor the steamer off the promenade, and hire boatmen to ferry the passengers and their luggage. One can imagine the risk involved in a choppy sea, and so, as a Cambrian Railways venture, the proposal seems to have foundered.

In July 1902, the council asked for a small space at the edge of the yard for public urinals. The company agreed to the request, and asked for the usual easement of £1 per annum. However the council had expected to pay only 1 shilling, and abandoned the idea in the following October, putting the blame down to 'the extortionate demands of the Cambrian'. Also in July, the Cambrian sent a letter to the promotors of a light railway between Aberystwyth and New Quay, offering to construct and work it for them.

The Cambrian offered to lay asphalt paving along the council's muddy footpath area in front of the station in August 1902. The council considered this proposal for a spell, and then asked for flagstones, as were laid on the platforms; although this increased the cost from £35 to £55, the company agreed.

Although negotiations between the Cambrian and the Manchester & Milford concerning the possible takeover failed at this time, a dialogue about a working agreement continued.

In February 1903, Denniss reported on a proposed siding at Plascrug:

> 'I have had a somewhat voluminous correspondence with a gentleman named Mr H. H. Montague Smith who is the Chairman of the Vale of Rheidol Light Railway Coy. When enquiring about their financial stability in considering the expense of the Exchange Siding Mr Smith remarked "I think I may safely predict that the Vale of Rheidol Light Railway will be in existence and in flourishing and good dividend-earning condition from its earliest days long after the Cambrian Railways Company is dead and buried." '

The Cambrian offered to take a 99 year lease on the Manchester & Milford in August 1903, for which the latter company was to receive 4% per annum of the combined net receipts of the two concerns, and not less than £4,000 per annum. This proposal was leaked to the Great Western, but no better offer was forthcoming. The Great Western officials consulted their Cambrian opposites, who considered that an intervention by the Great Western would be an unfriendly act; but they did offer the Great Western the continuance of the existing facilities at Aberystwyth, or even full running powers (Denniss had been instructed by his Board to sound out the Great Western anyway, and had taken the Cambrian's solicitor along in consultation.) By then, Manchester & Milford finance had landed them once again in Chancery, and so rendered these overtures abortive. The Cambrian then set to work to produce another offer, to be made to the Receiver, and to take their case concerning the outstanding unpaid debt relating to Llanidloes to the Court of Chancery.

During June 1904, the Cambrian committee recorded with regret the death of their oldest railway guard, David Jones of Aberystwyth.

Further negotiations took place with Mr Frederick Scotter, the promotor of the light railway to New Quay. Mr Denniss, with Mr Vaughan Davies MP, had held a meeting in Aberystwyth with the affected landowners, who had been unanimous in their approval of the scheme.

In common with other companies, the Cambrian ran annual competitions to foster a sense of pride in the railway. Aberystwyth did well in the 1904 contest for the 'best-kept horse'; of their seven drivers, W. Tregoning won the third prize of £1 with his brown horse, and J. Atkinson won the fourth of 10 shillings with his bay. None of the Aberystwyth drivers won anything in 1905, but the signalmen took joint first prize with Dovey Junction for the best-kept signal cabin in that year. (The Cambrian referred to these prizes as 'premiums'.) It was usual for the 'best-kept station' award to go to one of the smaller and more picturesque locations, where there were fewer passengers to disrupt the staff's efforts!

In their way, the Great Western were still stirring things up, and this prompted the Manchester & Milford to ask the Cambrian for a guaranteed £5,000 per annum and a complete write-off of the Llanidloes station debt; the Cambrian agreed, and started to promote the necessary Bill for the 1904 Session. However, the Manchester & Milford, who had obtained new information from the Great Western side, revoked their agreement to the Cambrian's terms. So, the Cambrian went on with its suit in Chancery.

The Cambrian had won its suit against the Manchester & Milford by January 1905, and was given judgements for obtaining £55,483 15s 10d in respect of the debt at Aberystwyth, and a reduced amount for Llanidloes. The sum of £5,878 8s 10d was awarded in May, with a Writ of Execution for the Llanidloes debt. Against a virtually bankrupt business, this was purely an exercise to establish rights in future negotiations because, also in May, the Great Western opened negotiations with a view to taking over the working of the M & MR as from 1st July. By 4th July Great Western staff had been seen at Aberystwyth, and soon afterwards three 'Dean Goods' 0–6–0s Nos. 2301, 2351 and 2532 (carrying Great Western cast brass number plates bearing the numerals 8, 9, and 10 respectively) quietly steamed in.

News of this clandestine undermining of the Cambrian's position was discussed by their Board on 8th June, and copies of the Great Western offer were examined. This included for 19% of the line's gross receipts for the proprietors, and the Cambrian resolved to make a counter offer of 25% to the Court of Chancery. This was duly accepted, and caused the cancellation of the Manchester & Milford's agreement with the Great Western. While this was going on, the *Cambrian News* offered the opinion that for the Cambrian to attain full control over Aberystwyth station would be the death of the district.

The Great Western then retired to consider what it could achieve next in the dirty tricks line, and on 7th December the Cambrian learned of the intention of the Manchester & Milford to lease its railway to the Great Western for 999 years. The Cambrian retained Counsel, Mr Balfour Browning, to oppose the impending Bill, and Denniss was instructed to liaise with Sir Frederick Harrison of the London & North Western to secure their cooperation; but this was all useless effort.

Meanwhile, on 27th February 1905 the committee approved the installation of a gas supply system, similar to that at Oswestry, for £115, whilst in April, the dispute over the public urinals at the corner of the yard was settled, and arrangements were to be made for their placement. In August, the expenditure of £210 was approved for new sidings, but by February 1906 this had been overtaken by the engineer's report that the entire yard needed relaying without delay. This time, the approving minute was for the use of 'second hand rails' with an expenditure of £400 on 'crossing timbers'.

An undefined alternative scheme for the New Quay railway was considered in November 1905, and it was decided to promote a General Powers Bill for extending the station yard, increasing the engine shed accommodation, and for powers to acquire the necessary land. On 3rd January 1906, the committee took note that a syndicate with a capital of £2,000 had been formed to proceed with the proposed Aberystwyth & New Quay Light Railway.

The committee agreed to allow the council's engineer to erect a ventilation shaft to the culvert which crossed underneath the yard and the station, and to secure it to the wall of the warehouse for a wayleave of 1/-. In February 1906, they also assented to an exchange of land with the council, so that the latter could plant a row of trees in front of the station.

The final chapter of the Manchester & Milford story began in January 1906, when that company's Board and proprietors approved the Great Western's offer of leasehold; the Parliamentary Bill was then prepared, to be hotly pursued and equally hotly contested.

Aberystwyth Town Council expressed an opinion that, since the Great Western had appeared in the station, there had been a marked improvement in service and relationships. Further, the Manchester & Milford's secretary stated that his company had pre-

Edward Jenkins about to deliver coal to a householder. Behind him are a coal cart and the original Cambrian coal offices. c.1900.
A. J. Lewis

ferred the security of the 19% offered by the Great Western to the 25% proposed by the Cambrian, about which they felt less certain (the Cambrian was having difficulty in keeping up with the payment of dividends to its own shareholders.)

Once the Great Western had overcome opposition from the London & North Western and the Midland Railway Companies, there were only the final details to be agreed with the Cambrian. A clause enabling the Great Western to build their own station at Aberystwyth was dropped, and the Cambrian agreed to give way on the point of the £63,000 debt established in Chancery, and to accept a little over £11,000 instead. The Cambrian was also given the option of owning the derelict Llangurig branch, if they so wished. The Act became law, and the lease became effective from 1st July 1906.

Reflecting back on the Manchester & Milford Railway, it is important to understand why the project diminished from its imagined brilliant future and why it was conceived at all. Its promoters and financial backers were divisible into two factions. The first group were the Welsh Railway Unionists who considered that an alternative port for Lancashire generally was a desirable alternative to the stranglehold exercised by Liverpool. It was also seen as desirable for the development of a trading port in West Wales. The second and more powerful group were the Liverpool consignees who sought an alternative port because the Mersey was in danger of silting up and little or nothing was done about it. As soon as Liverpool realised that it was about to lose its livelihood, dredgers were belatedly provided, and since there was then no need for Milford as an alternative, those with vested interests withdrew their support.

Newspaper reporters rejoiced, and one proclaimed: 'The GWR has come to stay. There is now no fear of a Cambrian monopoly', while the more factual *Cambrian News* noted that there was little change to observe other than the presence of a number of Great Western staff. It also reported the plight of the eight Manchester & Milford employees who were too old to be taken on by the new management, and would be destitute but for the generosity of Mrs Barrow, the Manchester & Milford's principal proprietor; even so, they were being thrown 'helpless into the world'. Particularly hard-hit was the locally-famous old driver Edward Benbow, after whom a gouged-out hollow by the track (where it descended to the Rheidol bridge) was named. Here, at 'Twll Benbow', he had applied the brake on his engine, the Sharp Stewart 2–4–0 *Lady Elizabeth*; unfortunately, rotten sleepers had given up their chairs, and she had rolled over. Mr Benbow had worked on the line since the opening day (and indeed during its construction, too).

The story ended on 1st July 1911 when, under the Manchester & Milford (Vesting) Act, their undertaking became the unencumbered property of the Great Western. The ordinary and preference shareholders lost everything, and the holders of the debenture stock, who were mostly entitled to 5% interest, received £92 of Great Western stock per £100 held; but it bore an interest rate of only $2\frac{1}{2}$%.

The arrival of English-speaking employees after the Great Western had acquired the Manchester & Milford produced a number of witticisms at their expense. For example:

Welsh Passenger (in Welsh) 'Single ticket to Pencader please.'
English Booking Clerk: 'Please speak in English, I don't know Welsh.'
Welsh Passenger: 'Single ticket to Top of the Chair'
English Booking Clerk: 'I don't understand'
Welsh Passenger: 'You don't understand English or Welsh then?'
(From *Humours of the Iron Road* by Thomas Phillips)

And Tom Evans would relate with a twinkle in his eye: 'Oh yes, they sent me a Great Western man to be my porter, and when a train had stopped I would call 'Maesycrugiau', while he shouted 'Same this end' at the other end.

In November 1906, the decision to set up a resident district superintendent for the Coast was implemented by the appointment of Mr W. H. Gough, the traffic manager. Several local authorities in the coastal area had written to the company asking for him to be appointed, and his salary was set at £400 per annum.

However, it was in April 1906 that a row which was to sour the Cambrian's relationship with the council (and which was to continue well into Great Western days) broke out. The council had asked for powers to build a bridge across the line at Plascrug Crossing, to be inserted in the proposed 1906 Act, and for which the council was offering the necessary land at 5 shillings per square yard; this was to be in addition to the provisions for extending the yard and the shed.

The chairman of the council, via the town clerk, had courteously invited the Cambrian officers to attend the meeting of the council on 15th May to present their views. The Board sent Mr C. S. Denniss with Mr W. K. Minshull, the company's solicitor. Two obstructive councillors had, on being told of the invitation, promptly moved and seconded a resolution 'That no resolution of the Council for extending this invitation existed'. The two Cambrian senior officers were then left outside the town hall, pacing up and down, until word was brought to them that the council had resolved that 'the Cambrian General Manager's letter be left on the table'; and they were sent away with the personal apology of the town clerk (as recorded in the Cambrian Board minutes.) Denniss wrote, describing the incident, to the *Welsh Gazette*.

On Thursday, 7th June 1906, the *Welsh Gazette* carried a heading 'ABERYSTWYTH TOWN COUNCIL', under which the following editorial comments made the most of the affair:

'Every ratepayer in Aberystwyth should carefully peruse Mr C. S. Denniss's letter. The complaint contained in that letter is a serious matter for the town; for it affects not only the conduct of the Council but the interests of the Borough.

'If the ignoble minority on the Council pursued an intelligent constructive policy they might have something to say in justification of their conduct ... But to assume an attitude of uncompromising hostility to the majority on each occasion is foolhardy and inexcusable. Criticism is all right in its place but detraction is not criticism; and no good can ever come of inane detraction.

'The blind bouncers on the Council had a perfect right to object to the granting of a piece of land to the Cambrian Railways Company; but they have no right to treat Mr Denniss with such rank discourtesy as they did.

'We do not know whether any members have a personal grievance against the Cambrian Railways; but if they have they have no right to wreak their petty spites in Council and so prejudice the interests of the Council.

'When Mr Denniss says in his letter "I have never before received such discourteous treatment" we can quite believe him; for we do not know of any public body where the members would so completely forget the ordinary rules of civility.

'The electors of Aberystwyth should have no difficulty in saddling the blame for the disgraceful scenes in Council on the right parties; and the sooner the better they weed them out. The process of degradation has gone on long enough. The blind bouncers are hopelessly incorrigible.'

Nobody was weeded out, however, and despite a further apology from the town clerk, the Cambrian Board decided that the provision of newer and better facilities at Aberystwyth must be deferred 'until the Town had a Council with whom satisfactory relations could be more readily established'.

Practical joint working came into effect on 15th March 1908. The Cambrian assumed responsibility for maintenance work on the Great Western's managed areas for 2% of the value of the total maintenance work carried out as from 1st April 1909, and accounts for the partial occupation by the Great Western since 4th July 1905 were rendered to them.

The apportionment of the running costs was:

Rent
Seventy-twentyfourths of $4\frac{1}{2}$% of the capitalized value of the station as a whole, set at about £18,000, plus a full $4\frac{1}{2}$% on the value of additional works carried out entirely for the Great Western section.

Maintenance
Two per cent on the above capital valuations.

Coaching Department
One third of the working expenses of around £800 per half-year.

Goods Department
Loco Coal handled: 1d per ton.
Materials handled: 2d per ton.
Livestock trucks: 1s per truck.
These figures were then deducted from the half-year's costs of about £300 and the residue (sic) was apportioned by reference to the tonnage, e.g. Cambrian 5,500 and Great Western 210.

Water
One third of the Corporation half-yearly account of £15 10s 0d.
One third of the Pumper's wages, coal, oil (etc.) for shed water running at around £200 per half-year.

A typical half-year's account, using 1907 and 1908 as a basis, would be:

Rent	£150
Maintenance	£ 60
Coaching Expenses	£270
Goods Expenses	£ 20
Water – Station	£ 5
– Shed	£ 30
Total	£535

It was approved that the station master should be allowed £50 per annum for rent (etc.) of a house in the town because he had lost space through the movement of the refreshment rooms, though the move was not made at that time.

Following a complaint from the Great Western about the need to bring their cattle and horse traffic into the Cambrian station for shunting (either across to the Cambrian or into their own facilities), a general revision was considered in 1909, as well as a large-scale rebuilding of the locomotive department. It was a marvellous scheme, with much extension of the verandahs (including the covering of the Manchester & Milford bay), and was drawn up after a cost reduction from £27,369 to £21,000. According to reports (and a note on a drawing), the council, by pleading that it proposed to extend Smithfield Street over a bridge across the Rheidol to relieve the traffic through Trefechan, and by delaying its decision over the sale of the land needed, managed to sink the plan. The calculations for this proposal contained two interesting figures. The Manchester & Milford land was to have been valued at £6,000, provided that the council had waived its right of way, and the water supplied to the Great Western locomotives was charged at 6d per thousand gallons. From this point onwards, the joint revenue account was produced half-yearly to the Cambrian Board, but to the Great Western it was a minor matter, being lost in the general revenue accounting.

There was a deposited Capital Joint Station Account amounting to £12,759 15s 11d in Glyn Mills, Currie & Co's Bank; it stood in the names of the Right Honourable Viscount Churchill (for the Great Western), and David Davies (for the Cambrian), the two chairmen. By the end of the Great War it had been patriotically paid over to the Government of the day as approximately £4,500 in 5% war bonds and £10,600 in $5\frac{3}{4}$% exchequer bonds, so, with the £1,600 still on deposit, it had grown to £16,600. But in 1918, the sum of £16,600 was worth far less than it had been before the conflict, such was the savage effect of the wartime collapse in the spending power of money. And how bitterly must the Cambrian have regretted the Great Western's refusal to pay over their share, as they had asked them to do in 1912.

Having been prevented by the council from carrying out a major scheme, the two companies were reduced to making a few improvements to what they had already. The cost of the scheme as put forward in 1910 by the Great Western was reduced by the Cambrian (by £200) to £1,700, and then modified again following suggestions made by the Earl of Powis; so, the precise work that was to be done is hard to define. Then the job was deferred again and again, until such time as the Cambrian itself had ceased to exist. They did, however, join with the council in advertising Aberystwyth as a resort, and paid half of the expenditure of £250.

The arrival side of the station, decorated for the arrival of King Edward and Queen Alexandra to lay foundation stones for the National Library of Wales, Aberystwyth, 15th July 1911.
National Library of Wales

A sad event occurred on 17th June 1911, anticipating those to follow in the age of the motor car. A child of two, sitting on the grass at the side of the road, ran under the horse pulling a Cambrian lorry while trying to join other children on the far side of the road. The heartbroken driver carried the child to its home, where it died a few hours later.

The investiture of the Prince of Wales at Caernarvon brought a royal visit to Aberystwyth on Saturday, 15th July, with all its attendant need for much application and attention to detail on the part of the Cambrian staff and employees. The first moves started on the Wednesday, when detachments of the Welsh Royal Artillery, the 1st and 3rd Field, the Pembroke Garrison, the 6th Battalion of the Welsh Regiment, and the Pembroke Yeomanry arrived at Aberystwyth, continuing through to the small hours of the Thursday morning. Later, there was also a guests' train from South Wales. All of this involved an extremely long list of arrangements and precautions, and notably that:

> all 'Coast' tablet stations had to be open day and night without intermission from Wednesday morning until Saturday night, and Aberystwyth signal box was to be double-manned on the 15th.
>
> Many 'coast' goods trains were discontinued, and Aberystwyth yard was cleared to Ynyslas saw mill siding.
>
> The seven-coach London & North Western royal train was to enter Aberystwyth with the saloons leading and, if the day was a wet one, the leading engine was to be detached before proceeding to Platform No. 3 so as to keep all the saloons against the shelter provided by the verandah.

On the day, fourteen special trains had to be worked in and cleared, starting at 4.10 a.m. with the first of the ten excursions. The other four trains brought more of the army, notably 'Captain Apperley's Special', which brought the horses. Bow Street had been emptied so that some of these trains could be stabled there until required for the return journey.

The royal train arrived in Aberystwyth at 3.05 p.m., and left again at 4.50 p.m., after their Majesties King George V and Queen Mary had laid the foundation stone of the National Library of Wales. The guard of honour at the station was mounted by the 1st Ballalion of the South Wales Borderers.

The returning military trains started at 6.45 p.m. with Captain Apperley's special, consisting of seven horse boxes carrying the officers' chargers, and about twenty cattle trucks carrying one hundred and fourteen troopers' horses and remounts, with their riders. All the army trains were scheduled to depart by 10 p.m.; and what time the weary Aldershot, Chatham and Windsor contingents got back to their barracks can only be a matter of conjecture.

In 1911 the Cambrian made a further attempt to close the refreshment rooms, and this time they proposed to close them entirely during the winter; but the Great Western would not agree.

By 1912, the council were spending £775 per annum on advertising, towards which the Cambrian was prepared to offer £200.

In another accident typical of the period, a cab driver collided with a Cambrian horse lorry and fell off his box. He died shortly afterwards, and the verdict was given as 'death from epileptic fit brought on by alcoholic poisoning'.

Besides the extra traffic already described at Bow Street, the years of the Territorial camps brought additional traffic to Aberystwyth for the Lovesgrove camps in the Vale of Rheidol. The West Riding Division was there in 1913, and there were many special arrangements, notably that cattle wagons and horse boxes were to be marshalled inside the leading brake with carriage trucks inside the rear brake on arrival; and tickets held in bulk by the officer in charge of the train were to be examined at Machynlleth – did they really count heads?

During the weeks of arrival and departure, mineral traffic (other than that for the camps, or loco coal) was cancelled, as was all cattle and perishable traffic. Aberystwyth and Bow Street yards were to be cleared (but to where was not specified), Ynyslas saw mill siding was to be cleared to hold twenty-two empty coaches, and Borth down refuge to accommodate twenty.

In view of the diversity of origins, timetables for the troop trains had to be agreed with the Great Central, the Lancashire & Yorkshire, the London & North Western, the Midland, and the North Eastern Railway Companies. Over both arrival and departure weekends, Cambrian towns and villages echoed the whole night long with the passage of the full trains as they delivered their sleeping loads, and again on the following night as the empty stock was returned to the parent companies; and two weeks later, it all happened again, in reverse.

When considering the introduction of the one penny platform ticket, it was deemed advisable by Mr Samuel Williamson, the new general manager, to 'communicate with Aberystwyth Corporation as the proposal by the London & North Western met with much opposition on the North Wales Coast'. The Board agreed to have the platform tickets.

Yet another attempt to get the refreshment rooms closed for the winter was defeated by the magistrates, who refused to grant a licence for a part of the year only.

W. H. Smith's boy newsvendors waiting to sell to the seated passengers through the drop-light windows in the carriage doors before the train pulls out. c.1920. *A. J. Lewis*

The station master, Mr J. A. Thomas, died on 25th February 1914; under the joint working agreement, his successor had to be appointed by the Great Western.

The National Library of Wales had requested a donation, but this was refused. For the National Eisteddfod of 1916, however, it was deemed to be within the company's powers to offer a £5 prize to be awarded by the Arts and Exhibition Committee for the best advertising poster, which was to become the property of the Cambrian. They could also continue the £200 subvention to the corporation's advertising expenses.

In that year, there was a training camp for the 10,000 men of the South Wales Division of the St. John Ambulance Brigade. The station personnel had been told to form a team to compete in the St John Ambulance Association Cambrian Shield competition, but they do not seem to have had much enthusiasm for the challenge. In 1914, the Aberystwyth team scored joint bottom with Oswestry Works 'B' team with $51\frac{1}{4}$ marks.

The rebuilding of the station within the site already owned was still being considered, and the engineer asked for the appointment of the Oswestry firm of architects, Shaylor and Ridge, 'as I am not an Architect'. Unfortunately, Germany declared war on France and violated Belgian neutrality on 3rd August, and on 4th August, Great Britain honoured her treaty with the Belgians by declaring war on Germany; the rebuilding was therefore deferred once more until the end of hostilities.

The new owners of the Queens Hotel agreed to pay £1 for the right to use a waiting space for their omnibus. This hotel had been a point of discussion by the Board

The Cambrian strike of September 1919, with many passengers crowded onto Platform 4 hoping to travel from Aberystwyth down the GWR's line to Carmarthen. *A. J. Lewis*

during the previous year, but they had declined to purchase it.

As from 1st January 1915, penny-in-the-slot platform ticket machines were installed, with some objections from the council, and a lot from the tradespeople, 'as I had expected' wrote Mr Williamson. At the end of the half-year, he was able to report: 'With all the troops present platform tickets have increased the annual income'.

The station master's house was declared to be in a bad condition with dry rot, and also suffered the added unpleasantness of the smell from adjoining public lavatories. It was therefore agreed with the Great Western to implement the earlier decision to allow him to rent a house in the town, but still at the old rate of £50.

Spiers & Ponds ceased the provision of lunch baskets around this time.

On Sunday, 16 January 1916, a bank manager was run over by the mail train at Plascrug Crossing. The verdict recorded was accidental death, but the company's solicitor observed that it was most likely to have been a suicide, as a bank inspector had found irregularities. The jury still added a rider 'that the Company should make arrangements so that the safety of the public is better guarded'. The pedestrian footway crosses the line on a curve here, with restricted visibility towards the station – hence the plans for a footbridge across the line (though it was never built).

A letter was received from Mr H. W. Thornton, the general manager of the Great Eastern Railway. He had heard, while he was on holiday at Aberystwyth, that the pier pavilion and a block of shops in Pier Street 'can be purchased from the mortgagee on advantageous terms'. As they had done in the case of the Queens Hotel, the Board declined to become involved.

At the end of a letter to the Railway Executive Committee dated 21st October 1916, concerning the possibility of taking up less-used sidings so that the rails could be re-rolled into new to be sent to France, Mr Williamson added: 'It is no business of mine, but there can be no harm in mentioning that there is a derelict railway running up Constitution Hill, Aberystwyth. The railway is the property of a Syndicate.' This was not acted upon, and the cliff railway is still there.

Immediately before the signing of the Armistice on 11th November 1918, the Cambrian intimated to the council that they were considering proposals 'for widening the line' (a commonly-used expression meaning conversion to double track). There was also some talk about making Plascrug Crossing into a cartway, to facilitate the transport of material from the Clayfield.

In March 1919, an offer was received from Sir Thomas Tacon, Bart., to sell the pier pavilion, the pier, the Constitution Hill cliff railway, and the recreation grounds to the Cambrian; this proposal was passed on to Cambrian Coast Hotels Ltd., to which the company

The original caption on this card was 'Attempt to stop the Great Western motor bus at Aberystwyth' but the unconcerned attitude of the gentleman reading his newspaper with his feet on the mudguard makes the affair look much less serious. *A. J. Lewis*

The less-than-happy but totally well-behaved passengers at the road entrance to the station offer an excellent study of their holiday garb and luggage. *A. J. Lewis*

A view of the inside of the Cambrian station during the 1919 strike, looking towards the roadway, with the refreshment room (built into the old signalman's house) on the left. *A. J. Lewis*

Passengers stranded. While the man with the dog talks to the three boys, W. H. Smith's manager (in straw boater) appraises the situation from the 6ft way. The departure/up platform was much longer than the arrival platform (a defect in the layout corrected in the 1924 reconstruction of the station by the GWR). *A. J. Lewis*

Although there were no porters to help these magnificently-hatted ladies, they seem to have been lucky enough to have been directed to a train. *A. J. Lewis*

A Cambrian official photo of 1906 showing the ticket examiners' platform adjacent to the Cambrian shed and offices. Beyond is the Manchester & Milford shed (with a curved roof), coal stage, crane and fitting shop. Beyond is the Field siding in the 'V' of the junction with the Manchester & Milford line. The water tank is shown as built with one row of cast iron tank panels. Note the typically Cambrian weighted one-way point levers, the wire-worked rotating lamp disc signal (No. 39) and the tall signal with three ringed arms.

Cambrian Railways

has subscribed some capital. Later, they were also offered the Waterloo and the Belle Vue hotels.

A conference about widening the line was held on 9th May 1919 at the Queens Hotel, to which all the local authorities affected were invited. No firm decisions were taken.

In October, Aberystwyth Town Council amazed everyone by sending a letter thanking the two companies for the improvement in the services to and from the town. Then they surprised everyone for a second time by asking for the joint station to be rebuilt, to help the unemployed!

On 10th February 1920, the Cambrian Board agreed to approach the Great Western with a view to continuing the deferral of the rebuilding, to which proposal the Great Western concurred. After further consultation with the Great Western, a letter was sent to the council stating that 'no useful purpose would be served by having a meeting as the necessary money is not available'.

This picture features a GWR steam rail motor parked on the Manchester & Milford shed road. The extension of the ticket platform towards the station was authorised in 1899. The line of engines is as abandoned by the strikers. *A. J. Lewis*

The authors of all the passengers' misfortunes. *A. J. Lewis*

General view c.1920 with ex-Metropolitan 4—4—0T No. 34 in Platform No. 2. Platform No. 3/4 on the left had been widened at the expense of eliminating one of the four lines between the platform faces. The verandah above Platform 3 had been extended to match. Compare this view with that on page 197.
L & GRP, cty. David & Charles

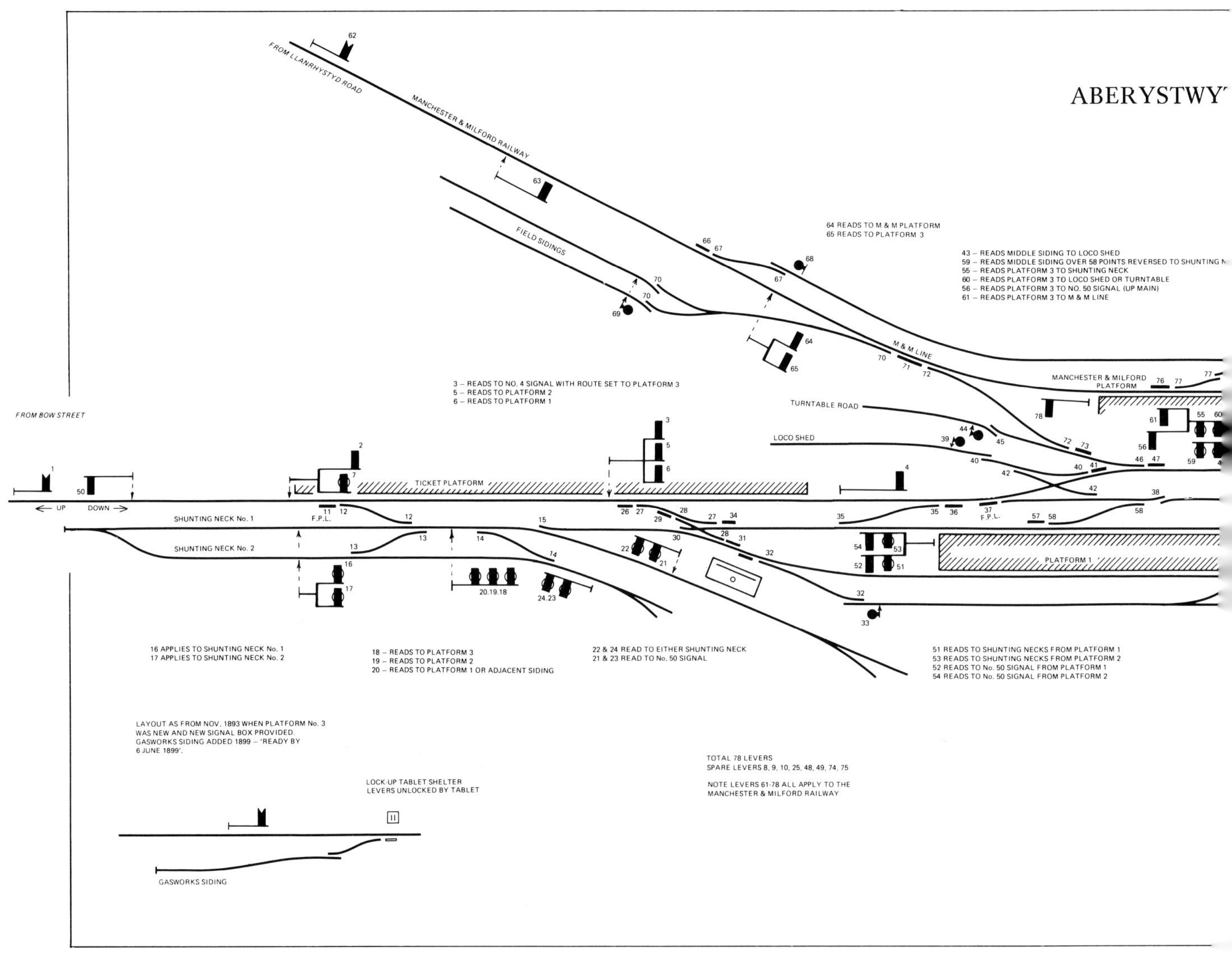

The magnificent collection of signals at the end of Platform 3. See the diagram alongside for an explanation of the lines to which they applied. *L & GRP, cty. David & Charles*

GNALLING DIAGRAM

PLATFORM 3
DDLE SIDING
PLATFORM 2

Another c.1920 view of the station, clearly showing that the awnings were no longer than the buildings on Platform No. 3.
L & GRP, cty David & Charles

Large Sharp Stewart 4–4–0 No. 66 waiting for the departure whistle and guard's green flag at Platform 1 while the station pilot (ex-Metropolitan 4–4–0T No. 34) waits in No. 1 siding ready to shunt when No. 66 has departed. A goods train with a lime-washed cattle van can be seen on Weighbridge Road. c.1920. It was No. 34 with its polished brass dome and big bulgy cylinders which impressed the author so much at the age of four in 1920 that thenceforth there would be no other line half as good as the Cambrian. *A. J. Lewis*

It was recorded on 31st March 1920 that Guard Joseph Williams, a former Mid-Wales employee, and latterly a popular figure on the trains between Oswestry and Aberystwyth, had completed fifty years of service.

With the approaching amalgamation of the Cambrian Railways into the GWR, matters were being tidied up in 1922. The subscription to the town's advertising had been suspended at the outbreak of war, and it had not been possible to reinstate it, but the £3 3s 0d subscribed annually to the Aberystwyth Infirmary had been kept up. A special donation of £10 10s 0d was sent in appreciation of the care given to the Aberystwyth men, Driver Pritchard Jones and Fireman Owen, who had been injured on the footplate of Sharp Stewart 4–4–0 No. 82 on the Aberystwyth to Manchester Express at Abermule, where they had met No. 95 head-on at speed.

For all legal purposes, the Cambrian became part of the enlarged Great Western Railway as from 1st January 1922, along with the 'old' company and four other Welsh railways.

Once the 'new' Great Western had full control of the station, its officers set about drawing up more up-to-date plans for the rebuilding, which had been frustrated

The street front of the old Cambrian station on the occasion of the visit of the Prince of Wales to the University College. Students insisted on towing his car through the streets.
Cty Mrs Margaret Evans

This staff group was taken on Platform 3 c.1920. The sign behind beckoned passengers to the bay lines which started at the end of the station building. The simple, if heavy in appearance ironwork of the roof erected by the Cambrian after the widening of Platform 3 is visible here. *1st row (back):* Unknown; Venables; Joe Williams (guard, Oswestry); Davies (wheeltapper); Tommy Mill; unknown. *2nd row (standing):* 'Darkie' Pryce Jones; unknown; John Lee; Walters; Dai Jones; unknown; Collins. *3rd row (seated):* Roberts (booking clerk); unknown; station master A. J. Thomas; Inspector Bamford; Parry Pryce (guard). *4th row (crosslegged):* Harry Saycell; Billy Anthony; unknown; unknown. The lady attendant on the left is Miss Potts. Aberystwyth was one of the Cambrian's 'top-hat' stations, the others being Oswestry, Pwllheli and Welshpool.
Cty. Inspector Dan Jones

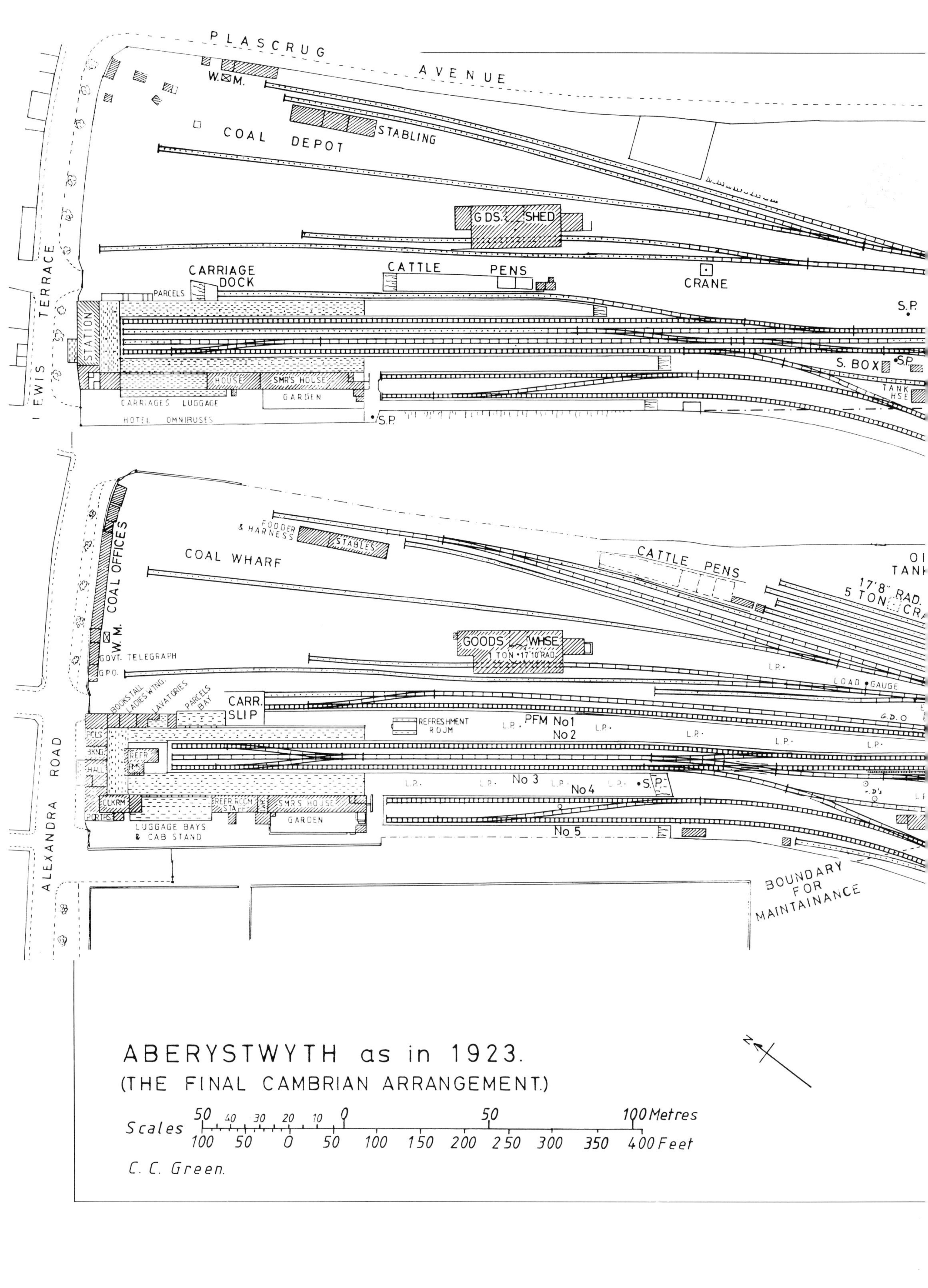

ABERYSTWYTH as in 1923.
(THE FINAL CAMBRIAN ARRANGEMENT.)

C. C. Green.

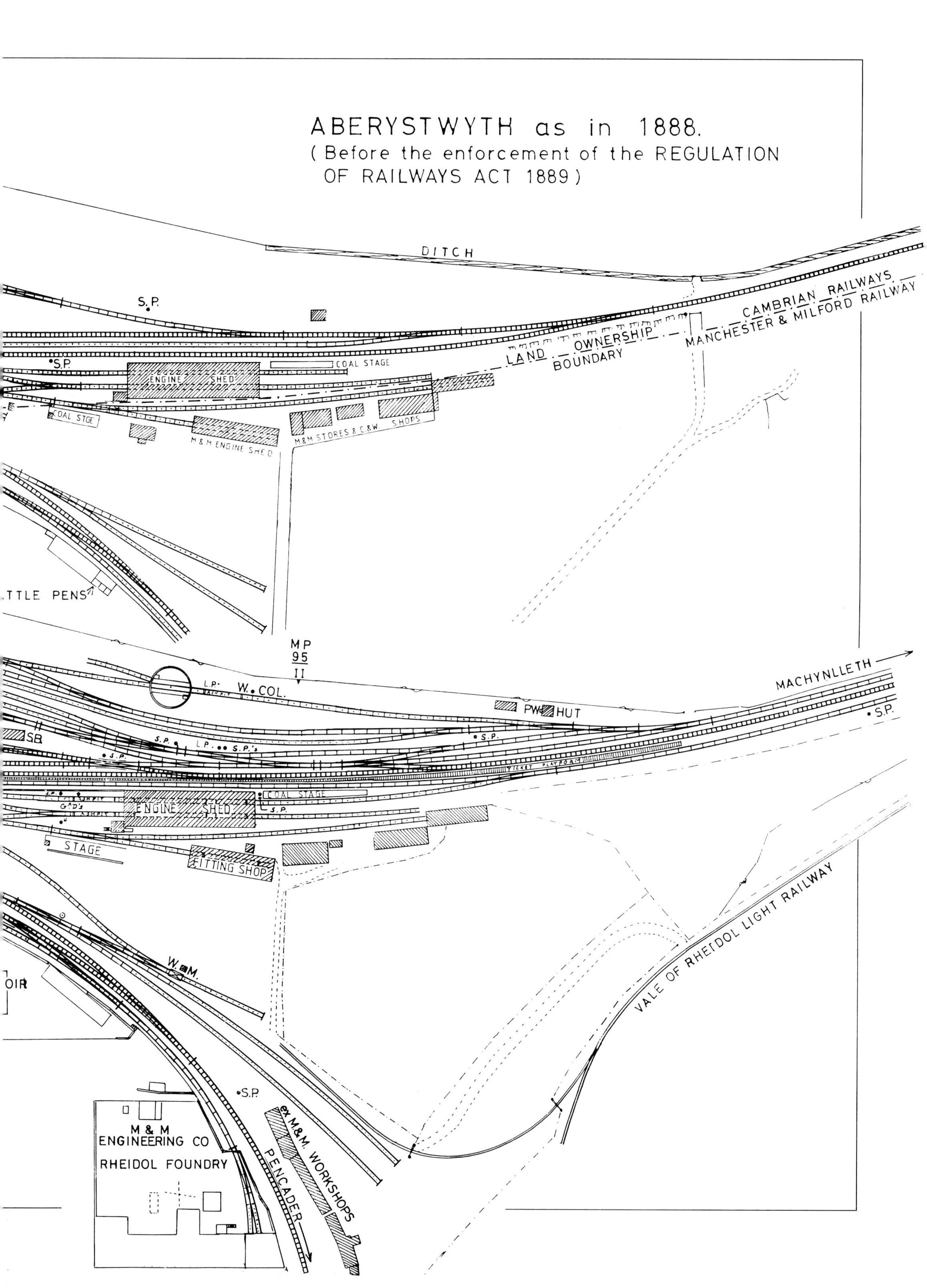
ABERYSTWYTH as in 1888.
(Before the enforcement of the REGULATION OF RAILWAYS ACT 1889)
DITCH
S.P.
CAMBRIAN RAILWAYS
MANCHESTER & MILFORD RAILWAY
LAND OWNERSHIP BOUNDARY
COAL STAGE
ENGINE SHED
COAL STGE
M & M ENGINE SHED
M & M STORES & C.&W. SHOPS
TTLE PENS
MP 95 II
L.P.
W. COL.
PW HUT
MACHYNLLETH
SB
TICKET PLATFORM
COAL STAGE
ENGINE SHED
STAGE
FITTING SHOP
W. M.
OIR
VALE OF RHEIDOL LIGHT RAILWAY
M & M ENGINEERING CO
RHEIDOL FOUNDRY
PENCADER
ex M&M. WORKSHOPS

by the council since 1906. But the first resolution affecting Aberystwyth was passed on 12th January 1922 – to continue the annual subscription of £3 3s 0d to the Infirmary. In September, floods covered part of the main line as well as the yards, and the former was lifted and reballasted early in 1923.

The budget for rebuilding the station, £94,500, was approved in June 1923 but the work was to be spread over three years. The chief civil engineer was most careful to fit everything in onto the land already owned so that nothing could possibly be delayed by having to approach the council. The new station building was carefully planned to be exactly behind the old, to avoid foundation problems and to keep as much of the old building in use for as long as possible, and also to afford a better driveway in front after the final demolition. The architects were Messrs Harris and Sheppherd, and the contract was let to W. T. Nicholls Ltd., the second highest tenderers at £43,994, in December 1923. It seems to have taken around eighteen months of chaos and dust before the first ticket was issued from the handsome new office.

The decision was taken to double the line as far as Llanbadarn Crossing, which would greatly ease the working of Aberystwyth station. A frame for the new signal box was ordered on 29th August 1923 and the doubling of the line was completed the following year.

The Vale of Rheidol line was installed in a new terminus alongside the Carmarthen line bay during 1925. With an overspend of £136, this had cost £1,086.

Beyond the new building, the platforms received long Great Western-style awnings which, at last, covered the old Manchester & Milford platforms as well. The signalling was altered so as to be more effectively positioned, with some on concrete posts. Yard trackage was extended and improved, and the goods warehouse was overhauled for £410.

Once the mess had been cleared up, the old station master's house on Platform 3, the old verandahs on Platforms 1 & 2, and other minor survivors were repainted for a mere £417.

It was now a really splendid station, and the new building was hailed as a fine example of the English Renaissance style which we now term neo-Georgian. Above the station offices was a large assembly room, which served as a restaurant and, having a marvellous sprung dance floor, was the daily venue for what was known as a 'Thé Dansant', for which a three-piece orchestra played every weekday afternoon during the summer.

In 1926, the Great Western general manager, Sir Felix J. C. Pole, paid a visit to see how work had progressed. The secretary had sent a letter to the mayor advising him of the great man's intention and of his time of arrival; but when the door of the gleaming chocolate and cream saloon had been opened for him to step down, there was only the station master there to greet him. Now, one has to consider that he ranked as an industrialist of great power, with only three others of equal standing in Britain (his salary was

This picture of a delivery dray about the town shows the lettering on the horse's tuxedo.
Cty Mrs. Margaret Evans

The neo-Georgian Great Western station building viewed in 1926, from a series of photos all taken by Mr. A. J. Lewis (known as 'Lewis The Mart' after his photographer's and bric-a-brac shop). *A. J. Lewis*

In 1926 few heads were turned when sheep were driven through the streets. The four-faced clock was fitted up by the GWR's signal and telegraph department. *A. J. Lewis*

We should get an expert to identify these motors, but the author thinks he can recall Austin, Morris, Welsh Pony, Unic, Singer and Sunbeam. *A. J. Lewis*

The station bus services were remarkably effective and plentiful. *A. J. Lewis*

Any one of these motor cars would be enough to set heads turning nowadays. Small Welsh boys were often given these large caps. *A. J. Lewis*

£8,000 a year). The story is told that he promptly blew his top and, with some observations which questioned the council's attitude to the Great Western's efforts to improve their town's facilities, he ordered that all work on the station building was to be stopped immediately. Unfortunately (or perhaps fortunately), there was only a small amount of tiling outstanding in the gentlemen's lavatories which could be left as a bare wall, so that his order could be seen to have been obeyed.

On the administrative side, Spiers & Ponds had their lease terminated from 1st January 1926, and railway catering was installed. From 1st February, all private cartage from the station ceased with the purchase for £76 of the 'plant' belonging to the former agents, Jones Brothers.

The company continued to support local events with a donation of £10 10s 0d towards the expenses of the Royal Welsh Agricultural Society's show in 1932.

The station built by the GWR featured a large uncluttered circulating area behind the buffer stops to Platforms 2 and 3, with exits to the road either side of a central booking office. This view is looking towards the northernmost exit to the road.
A. J. Lewis

Holiday season passengers, with their customary heaps of luggage, entrain on a short train standing in Platform 1. The extension of the station awning by the GWR to cover part of this platform is evident here. *A. J. Lewis*

The awning above Platforms 1 and 2, a couple of years after completion. The centre panels were all glazed, giving a light and airy atmosphere. Large 17 gallon milk churns like the one on the left were not easy to handle when empty and a lot heavier when full. However, when balanced at about fifty degrees with one hand revolving the boss pressed into the lid, such cans could be bowled along the platform at considerable speeds. This was a full can as evidenced by the two-man lift. *A. J. Lewis*

Maintenance and repair of the company's buildings and structures was, of course, an essential part of the civil engineer's activities. In 1932, a fault had developed in the new roof over the down platform, and £700 was expended in rectification work. The old goods warehouse was deteriorating badly, and the requisite reroofing cost £150. During the following year, a new goods warehouse was erected at a cost of £400.

The Great Western held a financial interest in many road transport concerns, including the Crosville Motor Services company (in common with the LMS); during 1933, part of the GWR's bus garage was let to the Crosville company. Two years later, the Great Western adapted some premises on Park Street for use as a road motor repair depot, in support of its own transport operations.

In 1935, the carriage sidings adjacent to the Carmarthen line were improved at a cost of £250.

By the mid-thirties, the 'tea dance' was declining in popularity, and catering services had been reduced to

A view towards the buffer stops at the end of Platforms 3 and 2, showing the engine release crossover at the end of the main arrival platform, No. 3. The gas cylinder wagon, used for replenishing the gas cylinders on coaches, was usually parked at the end of the middle road.
A. J. Lewis

GWR 4–4–0 'Dukes' Nos. 3283 and 3262 *Comet* (leading) shortly after arrival at Aberystwyth on 15th August 1935. *H. F. Wheeller*

Looking towards the buffer stops after completion of the rebuilding of the station by the GWR, showing the added length on Platforms 3 and 4 (in the foreground) and the new awnings to all platforms. Compare with the similar view of the station in Cambrian days (page 216).
Cambrian Railways

A down train after arrival in Platform 3, with the M & M bays (Platforms 4 & 5) behind. *Ifor Higgon*

a small café at platform level. In 1933, the assembly rooms had been taken over by the Postmaster General, whose telephone exchange now stood on the sprung dance floor; the Postmaster made a complaint to the Great Western in 1935, as a result of which the company instigated waterproofing treatment to the walls and roof at a cost of £250. The facing stonework on the front of the station was deteriorating, as happened to so many other examples of this form of cladding, and the results were being felt by the occupants of the building.

Goods traffic was still flourishing at this time, and warehouse accommodation was again extended, at a cost of £215.

On 15th July 1937 the royal train arrived at Aberystwyth, carrying their Majesties King George VI and Queen Elizabeth; a motor cortège took them up the hill to open the library with the finest view in the world, the National Library of Wales.

In 1938, goods and parcels were collected and delivered free of charge by lorry service.

The Second World War halted all but essential growth and reconstruction; however, the alterations at Aberystwyth had just been finally completed by the provision of the new engine shed and reversing triangle.

After a last revision of the carriage sidings (for £1,450) in 1947, the remainder of the Aberystwyth story is one of decline, interrupted only on 20th May

A busy scene with up trains ready to depart from three platforms. The 'Duke' on the right is piloting a Cambrian 0–6–0 Jones Goods. The GWR signal with the mechanical route indicator stood at approximately the site of the signal shown on page 215, but did not fulfil the same function. It applied to Platform 4, and was midway down the platform because that was where the points giving access to the M & M line led off (see the plan on page 255). A long train for the M & M line (not that there were many of them!) could thus not use Platform 4, only two-thirds of which was available to M & M line trains. 1926.
A. J. Lewis

1968, when the first Vale of Rheidol train left from yet another new terminal inside the Carmarthen line bay platform faces.

Aberystwyth's last days as a steam station were marked by the presence of three railwaymen of great personality and note. Inspector Dan Jones would never have a 'Region' badge on his cap, and kept his old Great Western 'poached egg' clean and bright with fire-extinguisher fluid right up to his retirement. Because of his way of asking the men about their work, he was nicknamed after a well-known wireless programme of the day; and as he was spotted approaching, someone would mutter 'Here comes Twenty Questions'.

Then there was 'Mr Rheidol', so named for his great regard for the lein fach; the ever-courteous Lewis Hamer, always with a fine rose from his garden in his buttonhole. After him, as station master, came a second 'Mr Rheidol', Harry Rees, the staunch champion of railwaymen's causes. There have been many, many others who contributed, but those were the three who, most of all, made Aberystwyth a memorable station.

A sad event took place on 6th February 1984, when the operator of a demolition crane dropped the heavy cast-steel ball through the roof of the signal box and dragged the entire superstructure onto the ground, where it was smashed up and burnt. The brick undercroft was then pounded to flinders. Ground frames had been installed at each end of the loop, and it became an advantage to have the shunters trained as long-distance runners, as the two frames are a quarter-of-a-mile apart.

The yard was subsequently reduced to a skeleton layout; deliveries of coal by rail ceased after the coal strike of 1983.

The last of the yard sidings had been lifted by 1990 and the whole site was available for letting or redevelopment; since then, there have been many rumours of proposals and postponements. The shed yard beyond the coaling ramp and the site of the Carmarthen line have now been car parks for several years, whilst the great runs of awnings have been cut back to the station building line.

The Aberystwyth of today is a natural centre of a most attractive area, and railway devotees will be well rewarded by a visit to the Ceredigion Museum and the station nearby. This is now a listed building, and houses Mrs Margaret Evans' wonderful 'Aberystwyth Byegones' exhibition. Both displays have many items of travel and railway interest.

With a super-hot fire, safety valves lifting and cylinder draincocks still open, a 'Duke' class 4–4–0 is starting its heavy train away from Platform No. 2. 1926. *A. J. Lewis*

Looking eastwards from Platform No. 3 c.1927, with the signal box on the left and the goods sidings behind. The loco shed in the centre was dominated by the combined water tower and coal stage put up in 1926. Loaded wagons for the coal stage were propelled up a ramp from the far side, and the buffer stops on the coal road can be seen atop the bank. The M & M lines were widely spaced on the sharp curve as it veered off to the right, the line from Platform 4 diverging well before the platform end.
L & GRP, cty. David & Charles

A pair of 'Duke' class 4–4–0s take their train away from Platform No. 1 on the ex-Cambrian side of the station in 1926. On each bracket signal, the higher arm read to the main line, and the lower bracketed arm to the line alongside the shed, the 'engine road'. All the signal posts were in reinforced concrete, part of the GWR's experiment with the material for signal posts in the 1924-26 period. *A. J. Lewis*

A pair of 0–6–0 Dean Goods taking a heavy train onto the Carmarthen line. The bracket signal on the left read to the M & M single line or (lower arm) the Field siding. The other signal read to the single line or the Foundry siding. 1926. *A. J. Lewis*

The Great Western's post-1925 arrangements for the terminal station of the Vale of Rheidol branch. The large shed on the left was the ticket office and the small hut on the right the PW shelter. Another shed, out of sight beyond the hut, was sometimes used as a practice venue for the Aberystwyth Silver Band. These pictures, taken c.1935, show No. 8 shunting a dropside wagon and a spare coach. The wagon and coach were swapped around and left against the buffer stops on the short spur for the waiting PW men. The final picture shows the engine reversed again for the driver to speak with the guard before returning to the loop. *H. B. Tours*

Holidays for all in the 1930s. A. J. Lewis was still producing his clear sharply-focused cards which stand out in comparison with the unsharp arty-crafty products of the larger firms typical of the period. *Cty. Mrs. Margaret Evans*

NOTICE

The more modern scene in 1962. The large hoarding was brought out each summer to attract tourists to ride on the Vale of Rheidol line. *Author*

Alexandra Road in 1962. *Author*

Terrace Road in 1962. *Author*

There was a small car park on the south side of the station, which gave access to the back of the old station master's/signalman's house, latterly used in part as the parcels office. 1962. *Author*

The clock tower and northern end of the station building in 1962. *Author*

Above the circulating concourse, the GWR built an apex roof of glass, allowing natural light to the whole of the concourse area. This view, looking towards Platform 2, reveals that beyond the new roof over the concourse, the earlier Cambrian Railways awning above Platform 2 was retained, even when the awning was extended at the far end by the GWR roofing shown on pages 224 & 225. 1962. *Author*

The interior elevation and booking hall. The original concept of a large circulating space was later diminished by the placement of a large pictorial hoarding depicting places of beauty served by the former Cambrian lines, and two long benches. There were three ticket windows, the right-hand one being reserved for Vale of Rheidol passengers. This picture was taken at 2.10 p.m. with the customary queue of passengers looking for the early afternoon Vale of Rheidol train. The refreshment rooms were moved, in the GWR rebuilding, from the old Cambrian buildings to the room on the right. 1962. *Author*

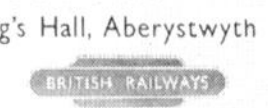

The circulation of passengers in the area behind the buffer-stops on Platforms 2 & 3 was further restricted by the installation of Wymans bookstall (now Lewis's). Behind are the refreshment rooms (left) and the gents lavatories. 1962. *Author*

WYMANS
BOYS!
EAGLE
Girl
argosy
CONSUL
BOOKS
BOOKS
BRITAIN'S
COMPLETE
SPORTING
NEWSPAPER
ON
SALE
HERE
Post

When the GWR extended the awning above Platform 3 towards the engine shed end, it did not replace the existing Cambrian awning which already fronted the full length of the station building. In this view, the join between the old and the new can clearly be seen. Note that the platform numbering had been reversed from the old Cambrian scheme of numbering used throughout this book. The southernmost M & M platform became No. 1 and the northernmost No. 5. Platform 3 was not renumbered.

A view of Platform 3, looking to the buffer stops, again showing how the new GWR awning extension was matched up with the old Cambrian awning. The semi-circular tops to windows and doorways betray the early origins of the former Cambrian station buildings. *Author*

'Wagon' buffers utilised on the buffer stops at the end of Platform 3. 1986. *Author*

The view from near the buffer stops on Platform 5 in the early 1950s. The quantity of stock parked in the Garden sidings suggests a Bank Holiday. *P. J. Garland*

No. 7826 waiting in Platform 5 with a Carmarthen line train. *P. J. Garland*

It would have been 'naughty' to start this Carmarthen-bound passenger train from this position in Platform 4, for the last vehicle is beyond the loco release points, which became 'facing' for this movement – the points were not fitted with a facing point lock. *P. J. Garland*

The down ends of Platforms 1 & 2 (later renumbered 5 & 4). The 'wave' in Platform 2 is clearly visible in this view. 1962. *Author*

Looking towards the loco shed from Platform 2. The short signal in the centre of the platform (lever No. 100 in the box) protected the points between the platform line and the Middle siding. Here the original 'wave' at the up end of Platform 2 is even clearer. *K. G. Draper*

A view towards the buffer stops along Platform 2 (later No. 4), showing the 'wave' in the platform where the platform line merged with the Middle siding. The stock of the evening Mail train stood throughout much of the day in Platform 1 on the right. When the signal on Platform 4 (left) was renewed with a steel post, a second arm was added. Compare with the view on page 228. 1962.
K. G. Draper

Looking across No. 1 siding to Platform 1, showing the full length of the GWR addition to the awning on the up side of the station. *Author*

Original Cambrian verandah to carriage loading dock on Platform 1. *Author*

1962, and over Platform 2 the original Cambrian veranda of the 1870s still survived. Note the ticket collector's barrier, and the gated entrancing in the back wall, which led to an end dock across the rear of the buffer stops at the end of Platform 1 and No. 1 siding. *Author*

At the end the quatrefoil brackets are in timber. *Author*

A view of the goods yard on the up (north) side of the station, taken from beside the clock tower, showing the goods shed for general traffic to the left, and the coal sidings to the far left. Empty carriages were parked in the Garden sidings beyond. Again the GWR extension of the Cambrian platform awnings is evident. As the awning was not carried behind the existing building on Platform 1 (in the centre), it was customary not to use the two carriage lengths nearest the buffer stops (except for vans) unless absolutely essential. 1962. *Author*

A view at 90 degrees (left) to the one above, looking north and showing the end of the coal sidings and the back of the coal offices facing Alexandra Road. 1962. *Author*

As recounted in the text, over the years a number of traders were allowed to put up their own offices and warehouses in the goods yard. This very untidy and overcrowded scene was the result. The former horse stables are in the left background. *Right:* The Great Western 8 ton van used as a store. 1954. *Author*

The coal sidings and merchants' dumps. 1962. *Author*

A view into Platform 4 from the ramp at the end of Platform 5, which shows again that only just over half the length of Platform 4 was available to trains using the M & M line to Carmarthen. The GWR signal with mechanical route indicator applied to the No. 4 platform line, and could read to the M & M line, the engine shed or the main line. *Cyril Mountford*

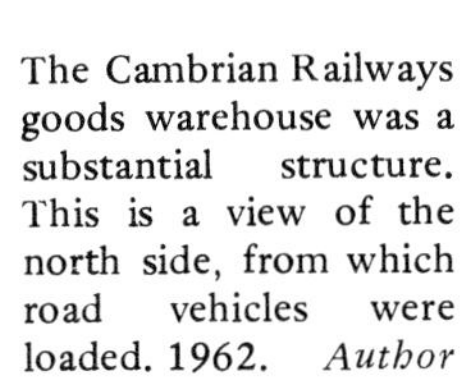

The Cambrian Railways goods warehouse was a substantial structure. This is a view of the north side, from which road vehicles were loaded. 1962. *Author*

The interior of the goods warehouse, showing the original Cambrian crane in 1962. *Author*

Left: The 6 ton general purpose crane, in between the 'short coal road' (behind) and coal roads 2 and 1 (in front), dominates the left-hand part of this scene photographed in 1962. *Author*

The goods warehouse, seen from Platform 1, with the later corrugated iron extension in the foreground. *Author*

The extension (grain) warehouse. 1962. *Author*

A view of the south-east corner of the goods warehouse — an unattractive and untidy corner of the yard. 1962. *Author*

The back of the signal box was, perhaps naturally, less attractive in appearance than the front, with only two windows overlooking the goods yard. The ladder hung on the back wall was provided to allow the signalmen (at quiet times) to clean the outside of the windows. 1962. *Author*

The front (south side) of the substantial signal box, showing the end verandah which sheltered the main doorway from the winds off the sea. The centre pair of windows were often left ajar, and the stain down the front of the box (opposite the stove) bears witness to countless pots of tea emptied through the gap. 1966. *T. J. Edgington*

By 1966 half of the slip connection beside the box had been taken out and it was no longer possible to run from Platforms 1 & 2 (now renumbered 5 and 4) to the loco shed – hence the armless doll on the bracket signal on the left. Plascrug crossing is just around the corner – the footpath runs behind the castellated building in the background. The water column, to the right of centre, served the nearest siding and (in case of necessity) an engine standing on the up main line. 1966. *T. J. Edgington*

The signal cabin seen from beside the loco shed. The deep lower windows allowed light to the room under the operating floor which housed all the mechanical interlocking for the lever frame. 1962.
Author

The yard pilot in 1962. It was said that far heavier repairs were carried out on 7428 at Aberystwyth than should, strictly speaking, have been done 'on shed', just to keep her out of the hands of Swindon where she would have had the splendid lettering painted over. *Author*

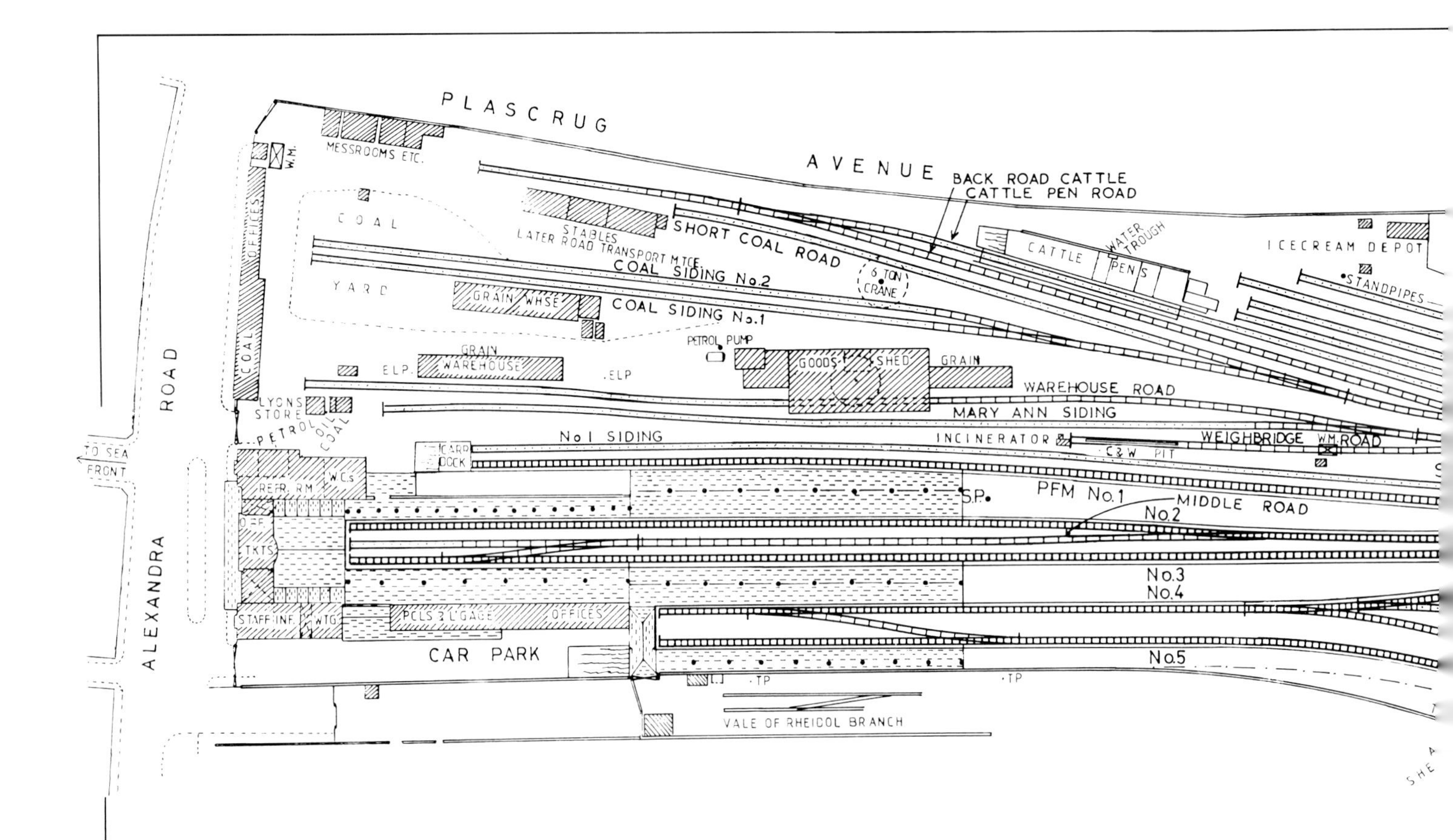

ABERYSTWYTH as in 1947.

(THE FINAL G.W.R. ARRANGEMENT)

Scales: 50 40 30 20 10 0 — 50 — 100 Metres; 100 50 0 50 100 150 200 250 300 350 400 Feet

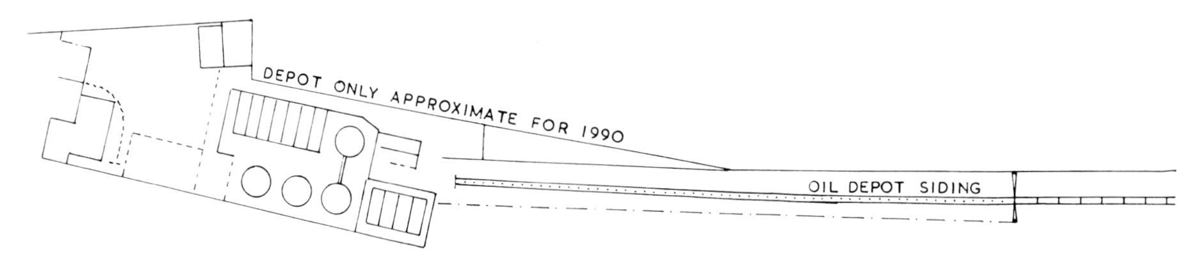

C C Green

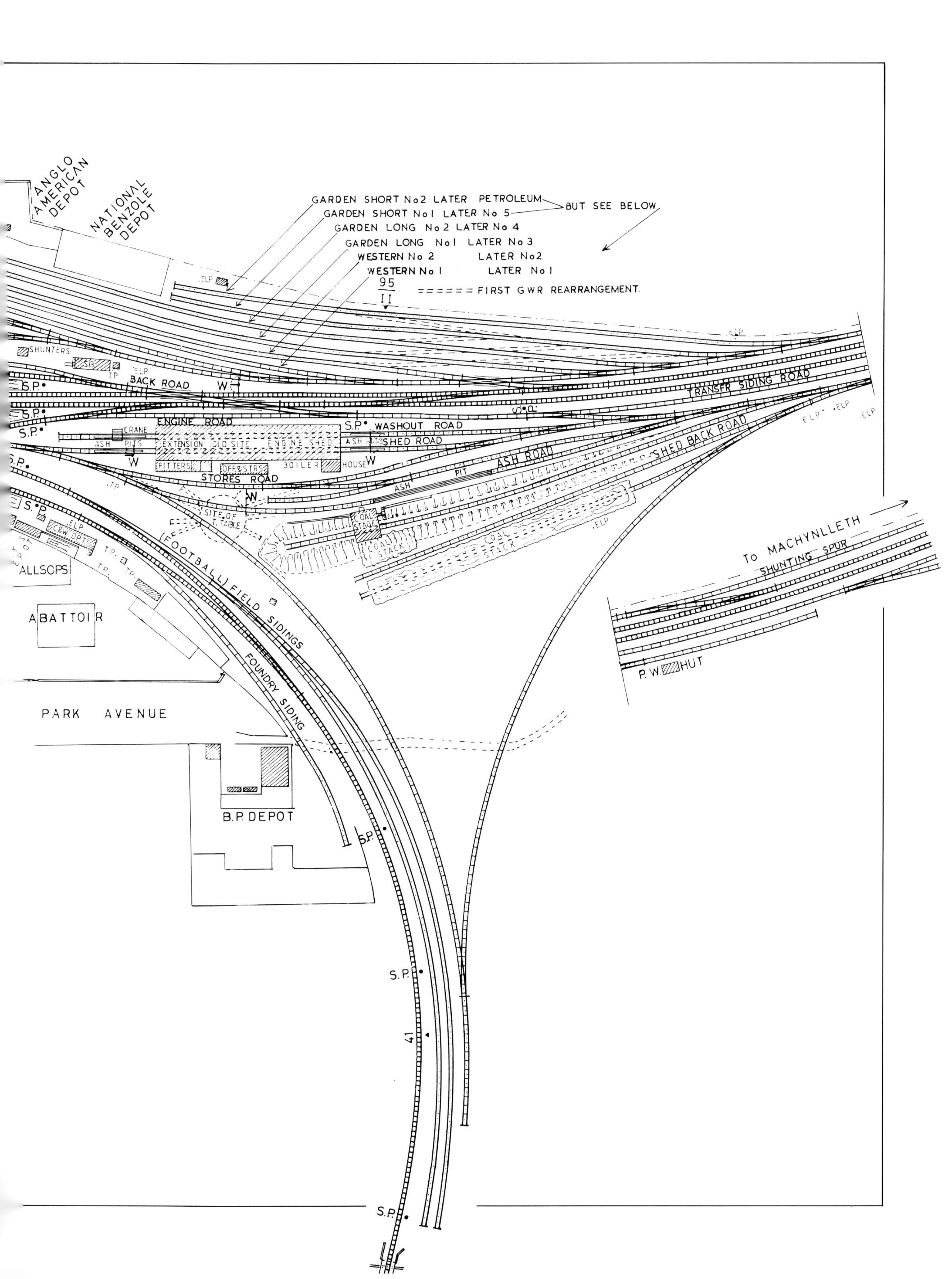

ANGLO AMERICAN DEPOT
NATIONAL BENZOLE DEPOT
GARDEN SHORT No2 LATER PETROLEUM
GARDEN SHORT No1 LATER No 5
BUT SEE BELOW
GARDEN LONG No2 LATER No 4
GARDEN LONG No1 LATER No 3
WESTERN No 2 LATER No2
WESTERN No 1 LATER No 1
95
11
====== FIRST GWR REARRANGEMENT.
ELP
SHUNTERS
SB
TP
BACK ROAD
W
S.P.
TRANSFR SIDING ROAD
ENGINE ROAD
CRANE
ASH PITS
EXTENSION OLD SITE ENGINE SHED
WASHOUT ROAD
SHED ROAD
FITTERS
OFF&STRS
BOILER HOUSE
STORES ROAD
ASH ROAD
SHED BACK ROAD
ASH PIT
SITE OF T.TABLE
COAL STAGE
COAL STACK
ALLSOPS
ABATTOIR
FOOTBALL FIELD SIDINGS
FOUNDRY SIDING
PARK AVENUE
B.P. DEPOT
To MACHYNLLETH
SHUNTING SPUR
P.W. HUT
41

A Cambrian Railways official photo of 1906, showing the two-road loco shed with its substantial stock of coal. The inside dimensions of the shed were 146ft 6in long, 35ft wide, with heights to wall plate and ridge of 18ft and 30ft respectively. Inside, each line had two pits measuring 81ft and 37ft long with 48ft pits outside the entrance. The two-storey office on the end of the building served as an enginemen's cabin. The building in the left background was a 69ft x 17ft carriage shed, whilst the adjacent building to its right was a stores measuring 58ft 6in x 17ft 6in. According to official records, the nearer of the two shed lines was used by the Cambrian and the other was used 'for the Accommodation of GWR Running Engines'.
Cambrian Railways

The water tank tower in October 1906, showing the additional palisade of Cambrian 4ft cast-iron panels extending the capacity of the tank to the point that it burst at one end. There is a tantalising peek down the Manchester & Milford yard, showing just the ends of two of the original collection of shacks which constituted much of that company's repair and storage facilities. The old 40ft 6in turntable was removed in May 1915. The rails, supported on wooden girders, were 43ft 6in long. The two hand winches, just visible, engaged with a circular fixed rack & pinion. *Cambrian Railways*

ABERYSTWYTH SHED

Opened: 23rd June 1864.
Closed: 10th April 1965.
Converted to Narrow Gauge: Winter 1967–68.
First Vale of Rheidol engine steamed for service: 20th May 1968.

The shed (as first built) was a two-road structure, one hundred feet long, and held only four of the original Sharp Stewart locomotives. In 1869, the committee stipulated that it might be extended so as to hold just one more engine (and not two, as the engineer had deemed to be necessary). George Owen patiently explained to his non-technical masters that, with a two-road shed, this could not be done, and he secured authority for a fifty-foot extension costing £371 13s 4d.

Over many years, the practice of chopping up old sleepers in the tank house for lighting of engine fires had resulted in a considerable carpet of splinters in that building; these caught fire in 1886, causing damage in distorted or melted lead pipes to the value of £25. Thereafter, all firewood was to be kept and chopped inside the running shed.

In August 1894, only three engines (Nos 61, 63 and 66, all 'Large' Sharp Stewart 4-4-0s), were actually shedded at Aberystwyth, indicating that most or all of the shunting not performed by the horses was carried out by the visiting train engines.

When the shed doors had to be opened in a gale during 1902, tiles were blown off the roof; reroofing was ordered in May of that year for £150.

The Cambrian attended to all breakdowns, including those on Manchester & Milford territory, and even after the latter had been taken over by the Great Western.

In May 1904, the traffic manager proposed the replacement of the 40ft turntable by a 50ft unit on the same site. The chairman was asked to consult the solicitor, who advised against it because of possible difficulties with the Manchester & Milford, on whose land the existing one was sited. A new table was therefore ordered for a new site on the opposite side of the running lines, near Plascrug Avenue, to cost £276, plus £260 for foundations, £536 in all. In July, the engineer reported that the site chosen was a very bad

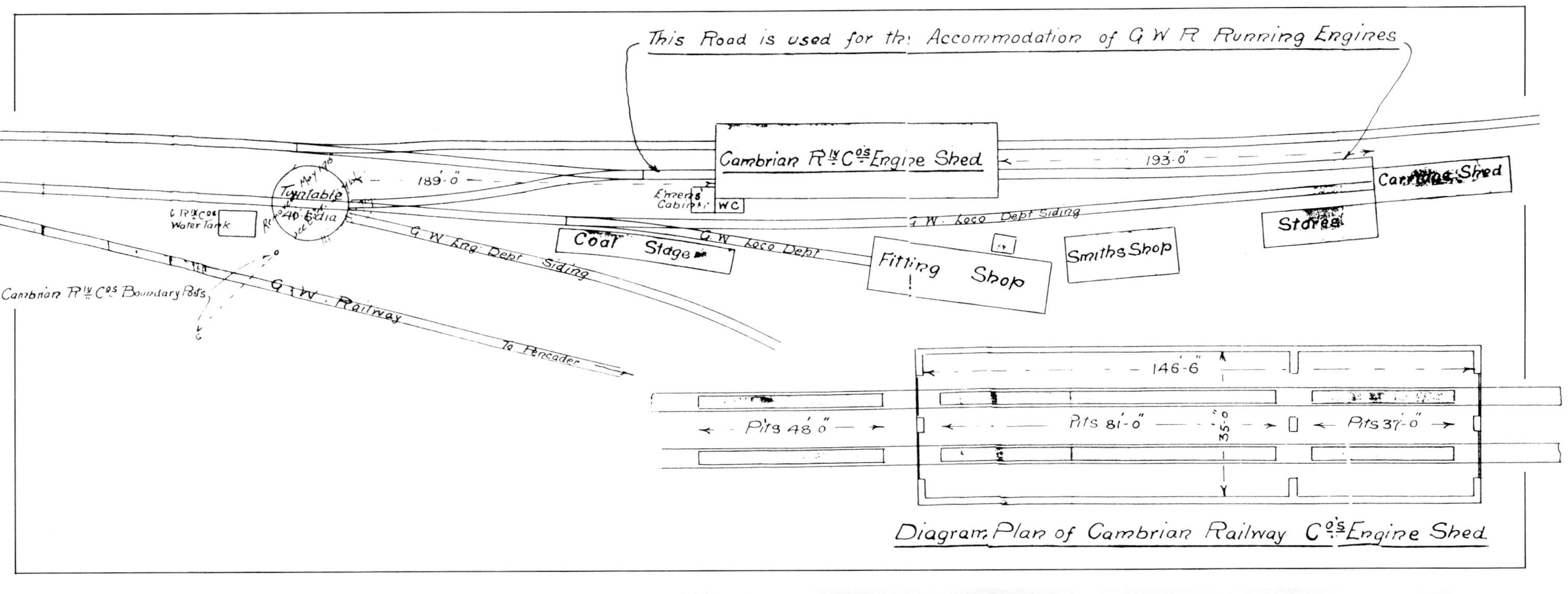

New arrival. Great Western 0–6–0 Dean Goods No. 2532 masquerading as Manchester & Milford No. 10 soon after 4th July 1905.
Cty. Miss Nicol

one, in peat bog (the whole station site is on soft ground, not far above river level) known by then to be at least ten feet in depth. The new turntable was not completed and put into use until 12th December 1904. It was noted that, by then, the Manchester & Milford had enlarged both their engine shed and their fitting shop.

The new engineer, G. C. McDonald, reported that it had required sixty-six piles, each fifteen inches square and forty feet deep, to support the weight of pit, pivot and table. The adjoining engine ash pit was cast into a less-expensive, wide concrete bed, though even that had sunk four inches, and the rails had needed to be raised and re-levelled. McDonald's report commented that: 'The original estimate (which was not made by me) only allowed for the lightest of foundations and the design for the pivot stone was, in my opinion, much too weak and I increased the size accordingly . . . which proves the correctness of my view that the piles were the only safe way of dealing with the situation'. He was, of course, trying to justify his final cost which had risen from the original £536 to £1,494.

The fractured water tank. *Cty. M. E. M. Lloyd*

In November 1905, a proposal for wholesale revision of the station area included much-improved accommodation for the shed and for repairs, with acquisition of land for extension of the shed yard; for reasons similar to those affecting the station, it was not put into effect for another thirty-four years. From 4th July, the first three 'Dean Goods' had been brought in on loan at a cost to the Manchester & Milford; one of the trio was allocated to Aberystwyth, the others to Carmarthen Junction. That company's ancient locomotive stock was subsequently reduced to the two, newer 2–4–2 tank engines, and the 0–6–0 Webb engine bought from the London & North Western. Once the Great Western had full control of the Carmarthen Line, the first 4–4–0 'Dukes' and '3521s' appeared. The first three Dean 0–6–0s lost their '8', '9' and '10' number plates, and were joined by other members of their class.

The water supply was recorded as costing 6d per 1,000 gallons (£280 per annum) in 1906. A forthcoming increase was to raise the price to 10d per 1,000 gallons (i.e. £470 per annum), and this for a supply that had become totally inadequate in the summer months because of the very poor rate of flow – trains were leaving late because the engines had to stand while the water trickled into their tenders once the storage tank was empty. The engineer recommended an increase in storage capacity from the 15,000 gallons then held, and the sinking of a well in railway land 'thus rendering us entirely independent of the Aberystwyth Corporation'.

It was left to the chairman to decide how best to augment the inadequate water storage facility, and he opted for the cheapest way by the addition of a second row of castings above the single tier of the existing tank; this was to save £40 against the cost of a new structure. However, on 9th October, the old plates gave way at one end under the increased pressure, and £60 had to be spent on new castings! The augmented tank measured 29ft × 17ft 6in × 9in, and was rated as holding 28,455 gallons. At the same time, they had been trying to evade the extra cost of the water coming in by seeking permission to use an old council-owned well at Plascrug; but, naturally, the corporation refused.

The well and pumping machinery had been approved in July 1906; after the work had been completed, it was reported: 'The Engine and Pumps are working most satisfactorily, the latter delivering 6,500 gallons per hour equal to 153,600 gallons per day against a maximum consumption of 70,000 gallons per day.' McDonald hoped that, after an analysis had been made, the station could also be supplied from the well and tank; but, fortunately, the station was kept on the corporation supply. The installation was shown to be fully justified on the occasion of the Welsh National Agricultural Show held over August Bank Holiday of 1907 when 62 engines took water, with no delays. This

A view of the former Cambrian shed from beside the end of Platform 5, c.1930, showing the lifting gear installed by the GWR.
Cyril Mountford

was the last Cambrian revision of locomotive facilities, and the last for nineteen years.

At the well, there was a vertical boiler pressed at 80 lbs per square inch supplying a single cylinder J. J. Lane horizontal engine (Cambrian No. 10, and GWR No. 1419), driving a three-cylinder ram pump built at the Oswestry works. These were replaced by an electric motor and a more modern pump, probably during the 1925 revisions, and again since; the latter units are still suppling the water for the Vale of Rheidol engines.

A gale stripped the roof off the old Manchester & Milford fitting shop in December 1914, a building in which the Great Western were storing their steam railmotors during the summer months. The Cambrian engineer considered that its repair was unnecessary, but the Great Western CME, G. J. Churchward, thought otherwise, and the structure was restored at a cost of £91.

After the Great Western had taken over, many improvements were projected, but had to be left until the new traffic arrangements had been finalized. Then, in 1926 (and with clear memories of the disastrous flood of 1922, when engines had stood impotent with drowned fire-grates), the whole shed yard was replanned and raised at a cost of £700. The old (and overloaded) Cambrian water tank was replaced, as it was by then subsiding. The new (and even larger) tank was sited above the replacement coaling stage – the days of hand shovelling into tenders and bunkers were over. Additional external ashpits, less liable to water-

The shed cleaners and firebox boys c.1925. This is how steam drivers started. The next stage was trainee firemen. *Cty. Owen Baul Jenkins*

0–6–0 Jones Goods No. 99 as GW 893 minus rods for re-wheeling c.1926. *Photographer unknown*

A local train approaching Platform 3 behind 'Barnum' class 2–4–0 No. 3252 while another engine waits at the far end of the Engine road, beside the shed, to come 'off shed' and take up its duty. This picture shows the town end of the old Cambrian shed with an 0–6–0 Jones Goods which has been lifted at the rear end. The Cambrian carriages on the left are shown in GWR livery. *R. W. Kidner*

logging, were provided, as well as a hot water washing-out plant, and a re-wheeling hoist with, naturally, a rolling cradle for removing the one-ton cast iron weights from behind the front buffer beams of the Moguls. The 40ft turntable was taken out and a 50ft unit installed in its place; whether it was the old one from 'across the way' is not clear.

Aberystwyth shed was identified by the letters 'ABH', carried by its engines either on the underside of their cab roofs or below the running plates. Old shed men I have spoken to remember that several carried the letters 'ABS' rather than the official version. In the early 1930s, the shed became subordinate to Machynlleth ('MCH'). After nationalization the shed became '89C', the code of its parent shed.

The shed men now operated extremely effectively with the bettered externals, albeit with rather crowded working conditions inside.

4–4–0 'Duke' class No. 3265 *Tre Pol and Pen* and Cambrian 0–6–0 No. 54 as GW 874, at Aberystwyth in 1930, just three years before 874 was shattered on the Friog rocks.
Cyril Mountford

This turntable, on site of the original Cambrian/M & M Joint station turntable, was a GWR replacement. This picture shows 4–4–0 'Duke' No. 3257 (formerly *King Arthur*) being turned ready for an up working. *H. F. Wheeller*

'Duke' class 4—4—0 No. 3273 *Mounts Bay* and Cambrian Nasmyth Wilson 0—4—4T No. 3 as GW No. 10, at Aberystwyth shed on 4th August 1929. *P. J. T. Reed*

'517' class 0—4—2T No. 1478 at Aberystwyth shed on 16th August 1935. *H. F. Wheeller*

An official portrait of the shed from the east end, believed to have been taken in 1935. This photo shows clearly the length of the Cambrian shed and the extension of 1869. 'Duke' class 4–4–0 No. 3291 *Thames* is being fired up for her next turn and the fireman is checking the operation of the blower.

National Railway Museum

The Aberystwyth 'Castles', 4—4—0 'Duke' No. 3290 *Severn* and No. 3265 *Tre Pol and Pen.* 16th August 1935.

H. F. Wbeeller

View southwards across the yard in 1930.
Cyril Mountford

Looking north-east from the coal stage road, with an unidentified 0–6–0 shunting coaches in the Garden sidings.

'Duke' class 4–4–0 No. 3291 *Thames* leaving Aberystwyth on 16th August 1935. The leading coach is a Cambrian 7-compartment third and the second is a Jones corridor composite.
H. F. Wheeller

A view of the east end of the loco shed layout, and entrance curve into the passenger station, seen from the footpath at Plascrug Crossing in 1930. The buffer stop at the end of the turning triangle features behind the gate on the left, whilst leading off the centre foreground is the Transfer siding. This divided into two: the right-hand line ran alongside the VoR siding, for the interchange of traffic, and the left-hand route became mixed gauge with the Vale of Rheidol. *Cyril Mountford*

In the latter 1930s, the Board authorised the replacement of the old shed at a cost of £5,280, with an additional betterment authorisation of £3,800, i.e. £9,080 in all. Work began during 1938, and in their 1939 annual report, the engineering department advised that 'The engine shed has been completely reconstructed at a higher level and lengthened to 210ft'. The new shed was on the same level as the running lines, whilst the yard was also raised a little, making flooded ashpits a thing of the past. At the end of 1940, the chief civil engineer had to go back to the Board the explain why it had overrun the budget by £747.

To save the labour and time involved in shunting over to the turntable and back again, an engine reversing triangle was constructed adjacent to the shed; this facility was in use in 1940. Again, the immediate wartime rise in costs caused the project to exceed its budget.

The advent of the turning triangle allowed the introduction of longer and heavier engines.

The shed turntable and water tank were the responsibility of the locomotive department, and not the engineer. The Great Western tank had a nominal capacity of 50,000 gallons, which would weigh about the same as a pair of Moguls with their tenders. It received a glass-fibre lining in 1986, and was re-rated at 7,500 gallons for the Rheidol line.

For the engine shed, the stores held the usual bales of cotton waste, drums of cleaning oil and rape lubricating oil, matches, firelighters and firewood, and also brick dust for scouring the copper caps and brass safety valve covers. Being a heavy maintainance shed (code 2ABH), there were the running spares such as piston rings, packing and brake blocks, fire bars and arch bricks, various small valves, glands, piping and gauge glasses, and a wide variety of cotters, nuts and bolts. It could take more than two hours to unload the weekly van, and as the stores was next to a through road, the half-unloaded vans often had to be shunted to allow the movement of engines and coal wagons.

There was a shed driver and fireman's duty turn, and these would normally turn the locomotives at the table, and later on the triangle, to have them facing ready for the train crews to take over. The first engine to coal, water and turn in the new Western Region green livery was No. 7827 *Odney Manor* off the 'Cambrian Coast Express', then timed 10.10 a.m. ex-Paddington and 4.05 p.m. into Aberystwyth.

The first DMU called at Aberystwyth on Sunday, 8th September 1957.

On the run from Shrewsbury, the drivers of 'Manors' would take a great delight in putting back the time lost between Paddington and Shrewsbury by the 'Castles' and 'Kings'. Richard Foster has recalled leaving

Shrewsbury 26 minutes late behind No. 7814 *Fringford Manor* and coming to a halt at Platform No. 3 only two minutes late.

For the enthusiast, Aberystwyth had become one of the most exciting sheds to visit, particularly on Bank Holidays, because of the great numbers of locomotives from distant sheds which came there to coal, water and turn. Their variety was limited by weight alone, for the Manchester & Milford route (now known as 'the Carmarthen line') had been rebuilt to 'Blue' category and 60 m.p.h. standard by 1939, while the Welshpool and Shrewsbury route, termed 'the Aber road', was rated 'Dotted Blue' with a 40 m.p.h. speed limit.

The sidings adjacent of the coaling stage had been focal areas for holding vast emergency coal stocks during the war, and there were still 1,200 tons there in 1963. The loco men were ordered to load it away – not their job, as they claimed, and it became a national issue at ASLEF level. In fact it was frozen solid and could not have been moved anyway, as the depot staff representative Mr John Davies proved when he took a pick-axe to it.

From 15th July 1963, when London Midland Region took over, the scene changed. The 'Moguls', which had taken over when the 'Dukes' and other elderly types had been withdrawn, disappeared in their turn along with the 'Panniers', and more use was made of the 'Standard' classes. Nevertheless, the process was fairly gradual; the appointment of an ex-LMS man as superintendent at Oswestry had started the changes during the 1950s, and he had naturally preferred the products of Crewe and Derby.

The end came on 10th April 1965, when Aberystwyth closed as a standard gauge steam shed, leaving just 15 of the previous complement of 85 men to care for superficial adjustments to the incoming diesels, carriages and wagons, and to carry out the full maintenance of the Vale of Rheidol stock under the control of Machynlleth.

All that is left is the shed building, a small area of the yard, the coaling ramp and the water tank, all now under the control of the Brecon Mountain Railway Co Ltd. Deterioration has rendered the water tank too expensive to maintain and the BMR has erected a cylindrical tank on an attractive timber crib constructed of material recovered when the Vale of Rheidol bridge over the Rheidol was rebuilt.

The east end of the loco shed during rebuilding in 1938/39. *Pope/Parkhouse Archives*

The new engine shed, looking in the up direction in 1962. Compare with the old shed on pages 256 and 261.
Author

The 'station' end of the shed with an 0–6–0 pannier under the re-wheeling hoist, and showing the turning triangle line curving away sharply to the right. 7th August 1955.
Cyril Mountford

The down end of the shed, showing detail of the re-wheeling hoist. 1962. *Author*

The highly specialised contraption used to remove the 1 ton cast-iron weights which had to be added as an afterthought to the 43XX class Moguls to keep their front ends down. *Author*

The view into Aberystwyth station from the Carmarthen direction, with the M & M line (flanked by the Foundry and Field sidings) on the left, and the loco shed on the right. The nearest line on the right was part of the turning triangle. June 1962. *Author*

The fitters extension and mess room, on the south side of the reconstructed engine shed. 1962. *Author*

The south side of the shed, showing the office and stores. The combined coaling stage and water tower was behind the photographer. June 1962. *Author*

The 'country' end of the 'Western' shed, showing the external pits. The line on the right ended at the re-wheeling hoist – the primary entrance/exit was at the country end. 1962. *Author*

By the time this picture was taken in 1962, BR standard types had come to be seen in this 'Western' loco shed. *Author*

Aberystwyth shed, seen from the bank leading up to the coal stage with the 'Ash Road' in the foreground. The stationary boiler featured here had been removed by the time the view on the preceding page had been taken. The empty carriages on the right were stabled in the Garden sidings.
Cty. R. S. Carpenter

Looking up the coal wagon ramp with a BR Standard Class 2–6–4T No. 82021 taking coal on the 'Ash Road' and a rake of empty wagons adjacent, with side doors dropped so that the ash could be shovelled up into them – another thankless task. 1962. *Author*

Left: Detail of stairway, tank ladder and coal chute. *Right:* Cleaning out the smokebox ash of No. 7812 *Erlestoke Manor* on the 'Ash Road'. June 1962. *Author*

Left: The water tank tower and coaling chute with Standard Class 2–6–0 No. 78000 taking coal before turning. *Right:* The end of the ramp. Full wagons were pushed through the coal stage and let down by gravity when the preceding wagon had been emptied. 1962. *Author*

The 'Dukedog' locos were for many years the mainstay of Cambrian line passenger services, and this line of locos, withdrawn from service in favour of larger GWR types and 'Standard' engines, was a sad sight for those who appreciated the character which these locomotives had brought to the Cambrian. The sacking tied over the chimneys was the accepted method of ensuring that the locomotives had been rendered unusable for the winter and could be deleted from the boiler insurance documents. They were Nos. 9016, 9022, 9013, 9015 and 9017. 1956. *Ifor Higgon*

Out cold – two 0–6–0 Collett goods with nothing to do. The nearer is 2217 parked out amongst the coal stack. 1962. *Author*

The view from the slopes of Pen Dinas, the hill dominating Aberystwyth from the south side and separating the valleys of the Afon Rheidol (seen here) and the Ystwyth (behind the photographer). This 1958 picture features a solitary 2–6–0 completing its run around the triangle ready for its next turn. *Author*

A view of the loco shed in 1962, with the curve of the M & M branch in the foreground. On the left is the Foundry siding, with its oil discharge pipes for the adjacent BP depot, and a set of oil wagons. The siding – indeed the whole layout here – was bisected by an occupation crossing, which could not be obstructed by parked wagons. *Author*

No. 7823 *Hook Norton Manor* with a goods train from Carmarthen, crossing Afon Rheidol and the Vale of Rheidol line in June 1961. *Author*

Looking from the loco shed towards the station with, on the left, the lower half of the signal controlling the shed exit, with its mechanical route indicator. From here engines could get to any platform line – straight along beside the shed for Nos 4 and 5, and via the compound crossings to Platforms 3, 2, 1 and No. 1 siding. The two oil tanks in the yard were waiting to be shunted across to the Foundry siding beside the M & M branch. 1962. *Author*

A view eastwards over the throat of the loco shed in June 1962 showing, in the middle distance, the buffer stop at the end of the shed line, with Plascrug footpath crossing beyond. The lines converging into the siding were (from the right) the turning triangle, the ash road, the coal stage road (note the hand-held trap point to catch any wagons inadvertently running away down the ramped siding) and four shed roads. The group of wagons next to the buffer stops were parked on the transfer (to VoR) siding, adjacent to which the up and down main lines can be seen, with the shunt necks to the goods yard beyond. The signal featured was the Aberystwyth up starter, with fixed distant for Llanbadarn Crossing beneath. The SW (sound whistle) board for Plascrug Crossing was mounted on a post so tall that it must surely have been the highest on the GWR. Both the signal and the SW board were to the left of the shunt neck, and so had to be visible over any vehicles being shunted in the sidings. *Author*

Appendix 1

SAFETY AND SIGNALLING

In order to understand many of the events in the early operation of railways such as the A & WC and the Cambrian, it is necessary to have an appreciation of operating methods and terms very different from those of the 20th century.

Scotch blocks were one of the first crude methods of controlling trains stabled in sidings. The basic system involved a 9 inch square baulk of timber placed at the exit end of a loop or siding and which lay at right-angles across the rails against a check block. A train could not leave on to a single line until the signalman or pointsman had turned the scotch block to one side. It prevented those early trains with only hand-screw brakes on the tenders and break vans, and often none on some wagons and coaches, from rolling away on their own.

'Loop' is the term for a short section of double track in a single line railway where two trains could pass one another, or goods wagons could be stabled or shunted. 'Loop sidings' were not authorised passing places although they were often so used (in breach of regulations) to get one train past another when the timetable had gone to pieces.

The Cambrian of the 1860s used semaphore arms at right-angles to the line. These fell down to a vertical position inside a sheath (in which position the arm was out of sight) when cleared to show that it was safe for the train to pass. 'Sheath' was the term then used, but by 1890 they were more commonly known as 'slotted posts'.

If there were two stop signals applying to one direction of travel at any station, the first to be reached was termed the 'Home' signal, and the one authorising the driver to proceed into the section ahead was called the 'Starting signal' or 'Starter'. At most places, even those with crossing loops, there was just one signal post (usually near the centre of the station) with one arm on each side, applicable to each direction of travel. Clearance of the appropriate arm on the 'station signal' authorised the driver to enter the station. Permission to proceed on to the next section of single line was given verbally to the driver, usually when he was handed or shown the 'train staff'. When in later years it became common for drivers to pass some stations or sidings without stopping, it became the practice to provide auxiliary or 'distant' signals, which gave the driver advance warning of what the stop signal was showing. At first the arms of these signals were square-ended like the stop signals, and instructions to drivers were that they were to stop at the distant signal and then come on cautiously to the stopping point for the home signal. Later the rules allowed that the distant signal could be passed at reduced speed if at 'danger', and the end of the arm was given a fish-tailed notch to show its different meaning.

No train was permitted to leave the loop unless the driver was carrying the train staff, or he was shown the train staff and given a paper ticket as his authority to proceed. The staff was a large and usually coloured wooden baton of a distinctive colour, bearing the names of the two stations between which possession of the staff authorised the driver to go. He was not permitted to go on any further after he had reached the next staff station without exchanging the staff for the piece of line behind him for the staff for the piece of line in front of him. There was only one staff in existence for each section of line so that strict observance of these rules meant that no train on a single line could meet a train proceeding in the opposite direction. If one train had to follow another, the first driver was shown the staff and was given a paper ticket of authority to proceed on to the single line. The second driver was given the staff and after a suitable interval warned to keep a good look-out and proceed. The system of maintaining a space interval between following trains on a 'time interval' system was replaced as soon as the electric telegraph was available. Thereafter the first train had to be telegraphed as having arrived at the further end of the single line staff section before the second train (carrying the staff) was allowed to proceed into the section. The next train in the opposite direction brought the staff back. The committing of a staff irregularity, i.e. proceeding without the staff, which meant that there was a substantial risk of a collision on the single line, was regarded as so serious that it meant getting the sack.

The other safety device of the early years was the Stevens Point Indicator. This was a 'vertical' arm pivoted at the lower end which swung 30 degrees to the right or to the left to show which way the points had been set. The problem was that this indicator was attached to the stretcher bar of the points, and was not sufficiently sensitive, so that the arm might indicate that the points were fully 'over' when in fact they were open by a material amount. After accidents had occurred from this type of malfunction, the pointsmen were required to lean on the levers as the trains passed through, and 'thumped tummy' became an occupational hazard. Another early signalling device was the 'wire-locked' point, worked locally by a hand lever but locked when the signal authorising a train to proceed through it in a facing direction (i.e. the direction in which the point could divert the train from one line to another) was pulled to clear. Unfortunately, the mechanism was unreliable, the 'Swan's-neck' shaped plunger component being liable to fracture. Again it became necessary to instruct that the pointsman/signalman hold the lever in place while each train passed.

The train staff and ticket system of operating single lines was very restrictive. If, because of a failure of an expected train or plain bad management, a staff was at the opposite end of a section from that where a train was waiting to proceed, it simply could not do so. When Edward Tyer introduced on the market his first electric instruments through which, from a pair of electrically interlocked machines (one at each end of the section) only one metal disc (the tablet) could be withdrawn at any one time, the working of single lines of railway was revolutionised, and the Cambrian (short of money though it always seemed to be) was amongst the first users of the system. No trials on quiet branch lines here – the first section of line to have tablet apparatus installed was that from Machynlleth to Glandovey Junction. The apparatus required careful use and maintenance, and was usually housed in the station master's office since only he (and perhaps the signalman if one was appointed at the station) was authorised to use it. Not until after the Abermule accident of 1921, when use by all and sundry of an instrument in the station office contributed to the confusion which led to a destructive head-on collision on the single line, did it become the normal practice to house the tablet instrument in the signal box and under the signalman's sole control.

Many of the early 'signal boxes' installed by Dutton & Co. were little more than huts covering small frames of 6–14 levers. Since they controlled running signals, however, they were dignified by the title 'signal box'. In many instances points were worked by adjacent hand levers, but sometimes these were grouped into lever frames (usually termed 'ground frames' to distinguish them from signal boxes, though the frame might actually be above ground level, and sometimes had a shelter or building which made it indistinguishable from a signal box). If the points affected the working of the running lines, they were sometimes (but not always prior to 1889) interlocked with the signals.

Following the train disaster at Armagh that year, the Regulation of Railways Act 1889 required companies with primitive signalling installations – and the Cambrian had a lot – to come up to a required minimum standard. The principal requirements relating to signalling were the interlocking of points and signals (wire 'interlocking' not being acceptable) and the introduction of block working. The other principal requirements of the Act related to the working of mixed trains (i.e. freight and passenger vehicles combined into one train), and the adoption of continuous automatic brakes on trains carrying passengers.

Much new signalling work was done on the Cambrian Railways in the period 1889–1892. Many other smaller companies had similar problems, and the signalling contractors had a very profitable time (though some suffered from an overload of work). Most work on the Cambrian was given to the relatively new firm of Dutton & Co. of Worcester, and that firm's equipment was thereafter to be seen all across the system until semaphore signalling and lever frames were replaced by electronic signalling methods in the late 1980s.

Demolition of Aberystwyth signal box on 25th April 1982. *Author*

Appendix 2
ABERYSTWYTH WORKING INSTRUCTIONS

1903:

Two engines coupled together were permitted to run from Aberystwyth to Borth only, and at a speed not exceeding 30 m.p.h. This speed limit had been removed by 1907. In Cambrian times, two engines coupled were not allowed between Borth and Dovey Junction, or vice versa.

Excursion train guards arriving were not to have their rest period disturbed by being given other duties.

Cambrian trains carried one white light over the right-hand buffer, whilst Manchester & Milford trains carried a white light on the buffer plank.

On 1st and 15th of each month, an empty wagon was to be placed in the 10.0 a.m. up goods for the collection of all empty oil cans at all stations for refilling and subsequent return.

Electric Bell Communication between Aberystwyth Station and Junction Box.

Authority given Bow Street to take out Tablet for Down Passenger Train	4 Beats
Ditto for Goods Train	8 "
Allow Up Train to proceed to Bow Street to cross Down Train ...	7 "
Allow Down Train to come to Aberystwyth before Up Train leaves ...	5 "
M. & M. Passenger Train leaving Llanrhystyd Road	6 "
Ditto Goods	9 "
Allow Train standing at Arrival Platform (No. 1) to set back for Engine to run round train	3 Pause 2
Error Signal. Cancel last Signal sent	11 Beats

Red Lamps are fixed at the end of the three buffer stops at Aberystwyth Station, and every caution must be displayed by Enginemen of incoming Passenger or Goods trains, as well as in shunting operations, to ensure their trains being under proper control.

WHISTLE CODE

Main Line to No. 1 Platform	1 Long
Main Line to No. 2 Platform	2 Long
Main Line to No. 3 Platform	3 Long
Main Line to No. 1 Siding	1 Short
Main Line to No. 2 Siding	2 "
Main Line to No. 3 Siding	3 "
No. 3 Platform to M. and M. Line	1 Short 1 Long
No. 3 Platform right away	1 Long 2 Short
No. 3 Platform to Turntable	2 Short 1 Long
No. 3 Platform to Carriage Siding	2 Short 2 Long
Middle Road to Carriage Siding	4 Short
Middle Road to Down Main Line	4 Short 1 Long
Middle Road to No. 2 Platform	5 Short
No. 3 Platform to Neck No. 1	1 Crow
No. 3 Platform to Neck No. 2	2 Crows
No. 2 Platform to Neck No. 1	1 Short 1 Crow
No. 2 Platform to Neck No. 2	1 Short 2 Crows
No. 1 Platform to Neck No. 1	2 Short 1 Crow
No. 2 Platform right away	1 Long 1 Crow
No. 1 Platform Main Line right away ...	2 Short 2 Crows
No. 1 Siding to Main Line	5 Short
No. 2 Siding to Main Line	3 Crows
No. 3 Siding to Main Line	1 Short 3 Crows
From M. and M. Main Line to Bay	2 Long 1 Short
From M. and M. Main Line to No. 1 Cam. Platform...	2 Short 2 Crows
From M. and M. Main Line to Loop ...	2 Long 2 Short
From M. and M. Main Line to Field Siding ...	6 Short
From Loop to Main Line	3 Short 1 Long
From Cambrian No. 3 Platform to M. and M. Main Line right away	1 Long 3 Short
From Engine Shed to Down Main Line	1 Long 2 Crows
From M and M. Engine Shed to Turntable ...	1 Long 3 Crows
No. 1 Neck to Up Main Line	1 Long 4 Short
No. 1 Neck to Down Main Line	1 Long 5 Short
Down Main Line to Turntable	5 Short 1 Long

1912

Ticket collecting arrangements were as follows:

Down Trains: Collect all tickets not collected at Bow Street and nip all those for the Great Western line and beyond.
Up Trains: Examine all tickets and nip Return Tourist tickets for the Great Western line and beyond.

Carriages of all major trains were to be cleaned inside and out.

Those firemen on the 'short trip' trains were not permitted to couple or uncouple trains for running round and/or moving to another platform for departure.

1943

From the Appendix to the Service Timetable:

Down Trains—Double Headed.
Whenever a train is worked by two engines in front and is run on to any of the platform lines, the engines must remain coupled together until the train has been withdrawn either by means of another engine from the rear and the two engines have been shunted clear of the platform line or the two engines have propelled the train from and clear of the platform line.

Should it be necessary for an engine or two engines coupled together to remain at the dead end after the coaches have been removed, the person in charge must advise the Signalman of the circumstances and a clear understanding must be arrived at before any movements are performed.

Working of Assisting Engines—Aberystwyth to Borth.
When a second engine is required to assist a passenger train from Aberystwyth to Llandre or Borth, the assistant engine will be dispensed with as follows:

1. Trains stopping at Llandre.—Assistant engine will be detached at Llandre.
2. Trains running to Borth without a stop.—Assistant engine to be detached at Borth.

If a second engine is attached to a train for the purpose of working to Dovey Junction or beyond, the Traffic Department must be advised by the Locomotive Department of the circumstances.

The Signalman at Aberystwyth to advise Llandre and Borth on the telephone when an assistant engine is going to be detached at those stations.

Electric Bell communication between Signal Box and Station.
"Line Clear" given to Llanbadarn Crossing for Down Passenger Trains—1 ring.
Passenger Train leaving Llanilar—2 rings.

Points leading from No. 3 Platform Line to Middle Road or vice versa.
An Electric Bell is provided in the Signal Box and is operated from a point near the Ticket Barrier on No. 3 platform. Enginemen requiring the Signalman to reverse the points leading from No. 3 platform line to the Middle Road or vice versa, will give one long ring on the Bell.

North End of Sidings.
A klaxon horn is fixed on the Up Advanced Starting Signal for signalling to Drivers of trains and shunting engines in accordance with the standard instructions shewn on page 157 of the General Appendix to the Rule Book, and is worked by Yard Staff with button fixed on a pillar near the Up Starting Signal.

A telephone is fixed on the Down Branch Home Signal for use of the Yard Staff and Trainmen to communicate with the Signalman at the Station Signal Box.

Shunting outside Carmarthen Branch Down Home Signal.
No shunting must be performed outside the Down Branch Home Signal whilst an Up Train is proceeding to Llanilar until a telephonic advice has been received by the Signalman that the train has arrived complete or has passed Llanrhystyd Road or "Train out of Section" signal has been received from Llanilar.

Spare loose screw couplings, four No. 5 and four No. 6 types, were to be kept readily available.

WHISTLE CODE

Down Main to No. 1 Siding and vice versa	1 long, 1 short
Down Main to No. 1 Platform and vice versa	1 short, 1 long
Down Main to No. 2 Platform and vice versa	2 short
Down Main to No. 3 Platform and vice versa	3 short
Down Main to No. 4 Platform and vice versa	4 short
Up Main to Carriage Sidings and vice versa	1 long, 2 short
Up Main to Goods Yard and vice versa	2 long, 1 short
Up Main to No. 1 Siding and vice versa	1 short, 2 long
Up Main to No. 1 Platform and vice versa	1 long
Up Main to No. 2 Platform and vice versa	2 long
Up Main to No. 3 Platform and vice versa	3 long
Up Main to No. 4 Platform and vice versa	4 long
Carriage Siding to No. 1 Siding and vice versa	1 short, 1 crow
Carriage Siding to No. 1 Platform and vice versa	1 crow, 1 short
Carriage Siding to No. 2 Platform and vice versa	1 short, 2 crows
Carriage Siding to Middle Road and vice versa	2 crows
Carriage Siding to No. 3 Platform and vice versa	2 crows, 1 short
Carriage Siding to No. 4 Platform and vice versa	2 short, 2 crows
No. 2 Line to Middle Road and vice versa	3 short, 1 crow
No. 3 Line to Middle Road and vice versa	1 long ring on electric bell
No. 4 Line to Loco. Shed and vice versa	1 crow
No. 4 Line to Field Sidings and vice versa	4 short, 1 crow
No. 4 Line to No. 5 (Crossover) and vice versa	1 crow, 2 short
No. 5 Line to Foundry Siding and vice versa	5 short

In 1943, the following instructions were in force for the gas works siding and the pump house:

GAS WORKS SIDING BETWEEN ABERYSTWYTH AND LLANBADARN CROSSING

The Siding is connected with the Up Main Line by means of Facing Points worked from a Ground Frame, locked by Special Key, which is interlocked with Aberystwyth Up Advanced Starting Signal.

Traffic to and from the Siding will be worked by the Yard Shunting Engine, accompanied by a Shunter or Guard who must obtain the Special Key from the Signalman in the Station Signal Box.

The Shunter or Guard must show the Special Key to the Driver of the Shunting Engine, who must regard the Key as his authority to pass the Up Main Advanced Starting Signal and the Up Main Outer Advanced Starting Signal at Danger when proceeding to the Siding.

Before the Signalman withdraws the Special Key from the Locking Frame, he must set Siding Points No. 13 from the Yard to the Up Main Line, and must keep them in this position until the train has returned from Gas Works Siding.

Whilst the Special Key is out of the Locking Frame no train or engine must be allowed to go forward towards the Up Advanced Starting Signal until the train has returned, and the Signalman has been informed by the Shunter or Guard that the Up Line is clear.

On completion of the work at the Siding, the Shunter or Guard must set and lock the points for the Up Main Line, and after the train has returned into the Yard clear of the Main Line, at once hand the Special Key to the Signalman.

On the forward journey the train will be propelled with Brake Van leading, in which the Shunter or Guard must ride, keep a sharp lookout and be prepared to warn anyone on the line. A White light to be placed on the leading vehicle on the forward journey and a red headlamp to be carried on the engine on the return journey after sunset or during fog or falling snow.

The line is on a rising gradient of 1 in 75 and the greatest care must be exercised in performing the work at the Siding. Before the engine is detached, the Guard or Shunter must apply the Van Brake, also a sufficient number of wagon brakes, and if necessary, make use of sprags on the rear wagons in accordance with Rule 151 to prevent the train or any portion of it moving.

Unloading of Material at Locomotive Department Pump House, situate alongside Down Main Line between Llanbadarn Crossing and Aberystwyth Station.
When it is necessary for the Locomotive Department to unload material at the Pump House, situate as above, a clear understanding must first be arrived at between the Signalmen and Shunter concerned and the wagon or wagons with brake van attached, and a Guard or competent Shunter in charge, must be worked to Llanbadarn Crossing over the right line; from there the train must be propelled over the Down Line to the Pump House for unloading purposes and after the work has been completed and the Guard or Shunter has satisfied himself that the line is clear, the train will be further propelled back to Aberystwyth.

During the time the train is being propelled the Shunter or Guard will ride in the brake van and be prepared to warn anyone on the line of the approach of the train and handsignal the Driver.

The train when propelled on the return journey will be signalled in accordance with Double Line Block Regulation 8 (Clause c).

AFTERWORD

Well! 'There it is then', as a good old friend at Aberystwyth would say. There has been no attempt at presenting each station to a standard format. Each has a different history and has been allowed to prescribe its own way of relating it.

Some items may have been missed and the author would be grateful to be informed of additional items and photographs which will complete the tale both for this volume and for those to come.

And finally — the author would not have believed the half of it if he had not seen it all set down in black copperplate handwriting, purple-ribboned typescript and brown-foxed newsprint.

OL-NODIAD

Wel! 'Dyna ni', fel y byddai hen ffrind da o Aberystwyth yn datgan. 'Does 'na'r un ymgais wedi ei anelu at gyflwyno pob un o'r gorsafoedd i ryw fformat gyffredinol. Mae i bob un ei hanes ei hun a'i ffordd berthnasol ei hun i fynegi hyn.

Efallai fod rhai o'r eitemau perthnasol hyn ddim wedi eu cynnwys ac fe fyddai'r awdur yn ddiolchgar i dderbyn gwybodaeth ychwanegol am eitemau neu ffotograffiau a fyddai'n cwblhau yr hanes i'r gyfrol hon a'r rhai hynny i ddod.

Ac yn olaf — fe ddywed yr awdur y fyddai'n anodd ganddo gredu rhai o'r sefyllfaoedd pe na fyddai wedi eu canfod a'u gweld mewn ysgrifau-llaw cain, mewn teipysgrifau wedi eu lapio a rubanau gwawrgoch, ac mewn hen newyddiaduron digon brau.

The unwanted. During the limbo period when steam and diesel were intermingled, surplus steam locomotives were held at the far 'up' end of the Tank sidings at Machynlleth. 1962. *Author*

BIBLIOGRAPHY

CAMBRIAN

The Story of the Cambrian — C. P. Gasquoine
The Cambrian Railways Vols. I & II — Rex Christiansen and R. W. Miller
The Cambrian Railways — R. W. Kidner
Cambrian Railways Album Vols. I & II — C. C. Green
Mishaps on the Cambrian — Elwyn V. Jones
Railway Through Talerddig — Gwyn Briwnant-Jones

GENERAL

Aberystwyth Yesterday — Howard C. Jones
Atlas of the GWR — R. A. Cooke
Born on a Perilous Rock (Aberystwyth) — W. J. Lewis
Derwenlas — J. H. Evans
Dovey Ferry — Thomas Wynne Thomas
Ferries and Ferrymen — G. Bernard Wood
History of Modern Wales — David Williams
How I Became a Train Driver — John A. Davies
The Manchester & Milford Railway — J. S. Holden
Narrow Gauge Railways in Mid-Wales — J. I. C. Boyd
North and Mid Wales — A Regional History — Peter E. Baughan
North Wales Branchlines Album — C. C. Green
The Town of a Prince (Machynlleth) — David Wyn Davies
Uppingham — The Borth Centenary Magazine — Uppingham School
By God's Grace (Uppingham School) — Bryan Matthews
The Vale of Rheidol Light Railway — C. C. Green
Wales — G. Bowen

ADDITIONAL INFORMATION

Research can react in a similar manner to the dropping of a stone into a still pool. Long after the first rings of ripples have gone away, echoes return deflected off the opposite bank. These belated discoveries are poste-haste extras, some sent by kind friends after the layout of the book had been completed.

Page 2 — On 12th April 1861 the Oswestry & Newtown passed a minute of formal notice of the Aberystwyth & Welsh Coast Railway Bill and eleven days later the Newtown & Machynlleth resolved to seek powers to make an extension to Aberystwyth if the 'Coast' Bill failed.

Page 7 — On 29th October 1863 Savin had offered to construct the line for £15,000 per mile.

Page 8 — At the meeting on 25th February 1864 it was reported that so many petitions had been lodged against 'a Steamboat Bill' that proposals drafted into the 1864 Bill were withdrawn voluntarily.

Page 14 — Initially the backshunt serving the Era and Ratgoed quarries had been directly along the face of the wharf from the Aberllefenni's loading track which must have been rather inconvenient. This had to be cut off when the standard gauge weighing machine was inserted, as shown on the pre-1906 plan.

Page 125 — Another steamer had been sent before the *Elizabeth* but had proved too long to be turned on the Leri.

Page 127 — During the night of 7th October 1896 'Furious gales and high tides washed out the ballast and the track was suspended'.

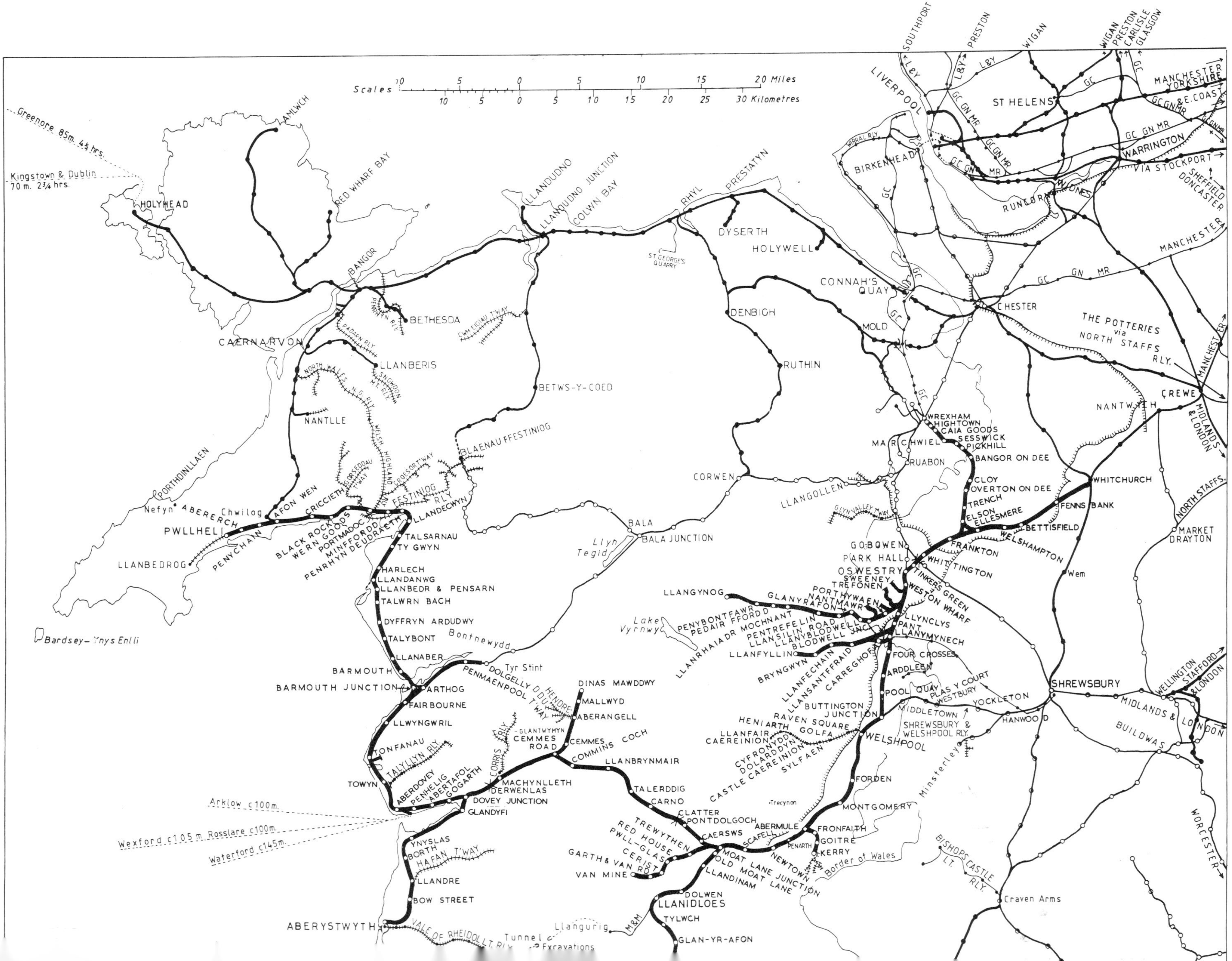

Scales 10 5 0 5 10 15 20 Miles
10 5 0 5 10 15 20 25 30 Kilometres

Greenore 85m. 4½ hrs.
Kingstown & Dublin 70 m. 2¾ hrs.
HOLYHEAD
AMLWCH
RED WHARF BAY
BANGOR
BETHESDA
PENRHYN RLY.
PADARN RLY.
CAERNARVON
LLANBERIS
SNOWDON MT. RLY.
NORTH WALES N.G. RLY.
WELSH HIGHLAND RLY.
NANTLLE
CWM EIGIAU T'WAY
LLANDUDNO
LLANDUDNO JUNCTION
COLWYN BAY
BETWS-Y-COED
BLAENAU FFESTINIOG
CROESOR T'WAY
GORSEDDAU T'WAY
FESTINIOG RLY.
PORTHDINLLAEN
Nefyn
ABERERCH
Chwilog
AFON WEN
CRICCIETH
PWLLHELI
PENYCHAIN
LLANBEDROG
BLACK ROCK
WERN GOODS
PORTMADOC
MINFFORDD
PENRHYN DEUDRAETH
LLANDECWYN
TALSARNAU
TY GWYN
HARLECH
LLANDANWG
LLANBEDR & PENSARN
TALWRN BACH
DYFFRYN ARDUDWY
TALYBONT
LLANABER
Bontnewydd
Bardsey - Ynys Enlli
BARMOUTH
BARMOUTH JUNCTION
ARTHOG
FAIRBOURNE
LLWYNGWRIL
TONFANAU
TALYLLYN RLY.
TOWYN
ABERDOVEY
PENHELIG
ABERTAFOL
GOGARTH
CORRIS RLY.
GLANTWYMYN
CEMMES ROAD
MACHYNLLETH
DERWENLAS
DOVEY JUNCTION
GLANDYFI
Arklow c100m.
Wexford c105 m. Rosslare c100m.
Waterford c145m.
YNYSLAS
BORTH
HAFAN T'WAY
LLANDRE
BOW STREET
ABERYSTWYTH
VALE OF RHEIDOL LT. RLY.
Tunnel & Excavations
Llangurig
M&M
RHYL
PRESTATYN
ST. GEORGE'S QUARRY
DYSERTH
HOLYWELL
DENBIGH
RUTHIN
CORWEN
BALA
BALA JUNCTION
Llyn Tegid
Tyr Stint
DOLGELLY
PENMAENPOOL
DOUDE
HENDRE T'WAY
DINAS MAWDDWY
MALLWYD
ABERANGELL
CEMMES
COMMINS COCH
LLANBRYNMAIR
TALERDDIG
CARNO
CLATTER
PONTDOLGOCH
CAERSWS
TREWYTHEN
RED HOUSE
PWLL-GLAS
CERIST
GARTH & VAN ROAD
VAN MINE
MOAT LANE JUNCTION
OLD MOAT LANE
LLANDINAM
DOLWEN
LLANIDLOES
TYLWCH
GLAN-YR-AFON
SCAFELL
NEWTOWN
ABERMULE
PENARTH
KERRY
FRONFAITH
GOITRE
Border of Wales
MONTGOMERY
FORDEN
Trecynon
Minsterley
CASTLE CAEREINION
SYLFAEN
DOLARDDYN
CYFRONYDD
LLANFAIR CAEREINION
HENIARTH
GOLFA
RAVEN SQUARE
WELSHPOOL
BUTTINGTON JUNCTION
MIDDLETOWN
SHREWSBURY & WELSHPOOL RLY.
POOL QUAY
PLAS Y COURT
WESTBURY
YOCKLETON
HANWOOD
ARDDLEEN
FOUR CROSSES
LLANYMYNECH
PANT
LLYNCLYS
CARREGHOFA
LLANSANTFFRAID
LLANFECHAIN
BRYNGWYN
LLANFYLLIN
LLANRHAIADR MOCHNANT
PEDAIR FFORDD
PENYBONTFAWR
LLANGYNOG
Lake Vyrnwy
LLANSILIN ROAD
PENTREFELIN
LLANYBLODWELL
BLODWELL JNC.
GLANYRAFON
NANTMAWR
PORTHYWAEN
TREFONEN
SWEENEY
OSWESTRY
PARK HALL
GOBOWEN
WESTON WHARF
TINKERS GREEN
WHITTINGTON
FRANKTON
WELSHAMPTON
BETTISFIELD
FENNS BANK
ELLESMERE
ELSON
TRENCH
OVERTON ON DEE
CLOY
BANGOR ON DEE
PICKHILL
SESSWICK
CAIA GOODS
HIGHTOWN
WREXHAM
MARCHWIEL
RUABON
LLANGOLLEN
GLYN VALLEY T'WAY
MOLD
CONNAH'S QUAY
CHESTER
LIVERPOOL
BIRKENHEAD
WIRRAL RLY.
SOUTHPORT
PRESTON
WIGAN
WIGAN PRESTON CARLISLE GLASGOW
ST HELENS
RUNCORN
WIDNES
WARRINGTON
VIA STOCKPORT
SHEFFIELD DONCASTER
MANCHESTER YORKSHIRE & E. COAST
MANCHESTER
L&Y
GC
GN
MR
THE POTTERIES via NORTH STAFFS RLY.
NANTWICH
CREWE
MIDLANDS & LONDON
WHITCHURCH
NORTH STAFFS.
MARKET DRAYTON
Wem
SHREWSBURY
WELLINGTON
STAFFORD LONDON
MIDLANDS & LONDON
BUILDWAS
WORCESTER
BISHOPS CASTLE LT. RLY.
Craven Arms